UNIVERSITY OF EAST LONDON
LIBRARY
MARYLAND HOUSE
MANBEY PARK ROAD
STRATFORD
E15 1EY
0181-590 7722

1 WEEK ONLY

24 MAR 1997
30 OCT 2004
- 4 MAY 2007
10 JAN 1999
17 MAY 2011
30 MAY 1997
- 6 JUN 1997
14 APR 2008
21 DEC 2000
17 JUN 1998
06 DEC 1999
26 MAR 2001
- 5 OCT 2001
16 DEC 1999
12 MAR 2004
14 APR 2008

This book is to be returned on or before
the last date stamped above.

18589/96

NE 9184904 7

Growth and Economic Development

Growth and Economic Development

Siro Lombardini

University of Turin, Italy

Edward Elgar

Cheltenham, UK • Brookfield, US

© Siro Lombardini 1996

All rights reserved. No part of this publication may be reproduced, stored in a retrieval system or transmitted in any form or by any means, electronic, mechanical or photocopying, recording, or otherwise without the prior permission of the publisher.

Published by
Edward Elgar Publishing Limited
8 Lansdown Place
Cheltenham
Glos GL50 2HU
UK

Edward Elgar Publishing Company
Old Post Road
Brookfield
Vermont 05036
US

British Library Cataloguing in Publication Data
Lombardini, Siro
  Growth and economic development
  1. Economic development 2. Development economics
  I. Title
  338.9

Library of Congress Cataloguing in Publication Data
  Growth and economic development / Siro Lombardini.
  Includes bibliographical references and indexes.
  1. Economic development. 2. Economic development—
  Mathematical models. I. Title.
  HD75.L658 1996   95–42285
  338.9—dc20   CIP

ISBN 1 85898 394 0

Printed and bound in Great Britain by
Biddles Limited, Guildford and King's Lynn

Contents

	Foreword	vii
	List of Contributors	ix
1	Theories and Models of Growth	1
2	The Agents	41
3	Models of Endogenous Growth *S. Lombardini and E. Canuto*	76
4	Human-Capital and Technological Accumulation *S. Lombardini and E. Canuto*	96
5	A Schumpeterian Path of Economic Development *S. Lombardini and F. Donati*	133
6	Selection, Innovation and Economic Development. Computational Economics Analysis *S. Lombardini and F. Donati*	154
7	Concluding Remarks	224
	References	232
	Authors Index	239
	Subject Index	242

Foreword

Economists are taking an increasing interest in problems of economic development. One reason for this is that they are trying to reach a satisfactory explanation of the different rates of growth observed for the various countries and of their stability.

I think that our main concern should be a different one. Theoretical reasoning needs to be released from the cage of static analysis. Evolution takes on increasing relevance in framing the issues economists have to face. That has two consequences which we want to stress:

1. The economic system appears to be a very complex one. All models can only deal with some of its synchronic and diachronic properties. There cannot be *the* model of economic growth. The equilibrium paradigm may help us single out some structural features. However, to understand some evolutionary phenomena, we need to turn to disequilibrium or partially equilibrium models.
2. Models built to analyse problems of economic growth and development can offer only tools that our critical reason can use, together with knowledge of social and institutional features of the country involved, to explain concrete processes.

We have oriented our analysis along two lines. The first starts with Solow's model of growth to assess the effects of technological progress assumed to be determined by the optimizing behaviour of both consumers and firms. The second deals with the problem of innovation and social selection. The Schumpeter's theory of economic development is given two formalizations: by a simple model showing how innovation can account for growth (Chapter 5) and by an evolutionary model that allows us to determine the condition in which mere selection may produce growth (Chapter 6).

In some analysis of economic growth, the work of the economist is more akin to that of mathematical exercise rather than to theoretical analysis of the problems involved. To help the reader understand how complex these problems are, I revisited, in Chapter 1, the main theories of growth and development in order to clarify the issues we shall face. In Chapter 2, I dwelt on the theoretical tools usually employed (mostly utility and production functions). References have been made only to those pieces of literature the knowledge of which is required to clarify the issues which are debated and the methods applied.

The final remarks are intended to help us relate the main results of the analysis to the issues concerning growth and development dealt with in Chapters 1 and 2.

My work, mostly in co-operation with Francesco Donati and Enrico Canuto, has been financially supported by Fondazione Eni Enrico Mattei which we wish to thank.

I wish to acknowledge the remarks and suggestion made on the work or parts of it by Andrea Beltratti, Giuseppe Bertola, Ferruccio Bresolin, Onorato Castellino, Terenzio Cozzi, Eliana Candoso, Claudio Franceschi, Edmond Malinvaud, Pier Carlo Nicola, Maurice Fitz-Gerald Scott, Robert M. Solow, K. Velupillai, Geld Weinrich, Stefano Zamagni.

Siro Lombardini

List of Contributors

Enrico Canuto
Centro Studi sui Sistemi
Via Vincenzo Vela, 27
10128 Torino
Italy

Francesco Donati
Dipartimento di Automatica e Informatica
Politecnico di Torino
Corso Duca degli Abruzzi, 24
10129 Torino
Italy

Siro Lombardini
Dipartimento di Economia
Università di Torino
Via Po', 53
10124 Torino
Italy

1. Theories and Models of Growth

1. DEVELOPMENT IN MERCANTILISM AND IN PHYSIOCRACY

Economics was born to deal with development. According to mercantilists, the central economic problem is how to spur development by appropriate economic policies. In fact such a concept of economics is a common feature of both mercantilism and cameralism. The former stresses the role of external commerce that the government can foster; the latter the role of taxation and state regulation of the internal economy.

In both, development is deemed to be the result of state actions. Being conceived at a national level, it is not constrained by the requirement of external equilibrium. In fact, national policies tend to create disequilibria in the balances of trade of different nations. This, in fact, did stimulate lagging countries to adopt growth policies.

The standpoint is changed in physiocracy. Growth is a spontaneous process occurring thanks to the surplus produced by agriculture. By *investing* the surplus, production and employment are expanded: the economy grows. The new standpoint provides one of the fundamental paradigms on which economic science has been built. Processes of production and distribution of commodities are deemed to be governed by natural laws. The *order* that Newton has discovered in nature can be elicited also for society. Economics has to discover the relations between the agents' decisions. Such relations produce growth and lead to a system of natural prices.

Adam Smith has separated the two results. The latter is akin to the notion of order, the former to the other fundamental notion of the Enlightment philosophies: *progress*. Progress is not mere growth; it cannot be generated by the mere mechanism that can produce a coherent set of prices. It is *development*, namely processes that change the structure to which the price system is associated.

2. PROGRESS AND DEVELOPMENT

Let us dwell on the two fundamental concepts of the Enlightenment philosophies that affected the objectives and methods of all sciences: the concepts of *progress* and *order*. The former emerged from an interpretation of history. The latter was suggested by the development of physics.

The concept of progress was linked by Condorcet to the triumph of reason. Smith took up the concept that was to be essentially converted into that of economic development. Economic development can be quantified in terms of increasing consumption. Increasing consumption is the result of accumulation and expanding population. Accumulation enables entrepreneurs to extend the division of labour: therefore the rate of growth of income can exceed that of labour. Growth can be accelerated. The link between accumulation and innovation, which in Smith's time took the form of an intensification of the division of labour, entails that income growth is associated with structural changes.

However, by affirming a correlation between accumulation and division of labour, Smith anticipated certain modern analyses of endogenous growth. In fact, this relation between accumulation and technical progress, of the kind just hinted at, is only an ingredient in Smith's thought. He was well aware of the effects that increases in real wages could have on workers' welfare, of the results of the actions that the State can carry on to improve labour qualification and to keep competition, and of the different prospects of labour division in various sectors. That is the reason why Smith substantially holds a macro-economic view on *development*, which he conceived as *progress*. Structural changes occur with regard both to technologies and to the structure of consumption, since consumption increases not only because of the increase in the number of consumers, but also as a consequence of the increase in per capita income. As Engel discovered in the last century, consumption of the various commodities does not increase at the same rate as consumer's income.

We shall revert to the structural changes associated with economic development. What we now want to emphasize is that economic development, as resulting from the complex interaction between technical progress and accumulation, does not imply a well-defined dynamic of income distribution. Such a remark would seem to be in contradiction with Ricardo's theory of economic development. At a close scrutiny, however, Ricardo's theory is not a theory of economic development; more precisely it is a theory that envisages possible evolutions of the economy, resulting from both the limitation of some factors of production (land) and the increase in population. The method employed is akin to the one that will come to be known as *comparative statics*. It is by using this method and by considering the operation of a factor (population) fostering growth and another (land) curbing it, that Ricardo could envisage a dynamic law for income distribution. The successive equilibria of the economy are characterized by increasing rent and a decreasing rate of profit: the prospect being a stationary state of the economy. By limiting structural changes to those that are brought about by the increase in population and by the limited availability of land we can link the theory of value to the theory of income distribution. If evolution is assumed to be the result of accumulation interacting with technical progress, then we cannot express any definite law about the change in the income distribution variables (rate of profit and wages).

3. PROGRESS AND ORDER

The other fundamental concept brought about by Enlightment philosophy is the notion of order. This notion has been assimilated to that of stable (and thus *normal*) structure. In nature, stable structures enable us to state scientific laws. It has been remarked that the same term - *law* - is used both to indicate natural structures that can be interpreted by scientific laws and individual behaviours that are compatible with a *moral order*.

The notion of order emerges in Smith's theory of natural prices, namely prices that are equal to costs, where costs result from the *ordinary rates both of wages and profits*. The influence of the gravitation theory expressing the order of the universe can be inferred from this Smith passage: 'The natural price ... is, as it were, the central price, to which the prices of all commodities are continually gravitating' (Smith 1904, I, p. 65). However, when he mentions the ordinary rate of wages and profit, he notices that 'This rate is naturally regulated ... partly by the general circumstances of the society, their riches or poverty, their advancing, stationary or declining condition: and partly by the particular nature of each employment' (Smith 1904, I, p. 60). The main issues Smith is dealing with are processes by which *advancing conditions* are produced. Therefore the centre of gravitation for prices reflecting order in the markets is continuously shifted. We cannot state definite laws about the effects of such shifts on income distribution.

The central problem in Smith's treatise is the analysis of the processes producing economic development. For that, the relevant theory of value is the labour theory. Labour is at the origin of every commodity.

'It was not by gold or by silver, but by labour, that all the wealth of the world was originally purchased; and its value, to those who possess it, and who want to exchange it for some new productions, is precisely equal to the quantity of labour which it can enable them to purchase or command' (Smith 1904, I, pp. 34-5).

Labour is thus held to be at the origin of the process of development. Ricardo will put it at the origin of the process of production. From Smith's standpoint, for progressive economies, value is given by the labour that can be commanded, in Ricardo's by the labour embodied.[1]

The two paradigms - progress and order - irreducible to each other, can be worked out also from Marx and Schumpeter theories. Marx adopted Ricardo's theory of embodied labour to explain *relative prices* and the relation between wages and surplus, *the surplus resulting from labour exploitation, given the technology*. However, his main concern, as in the case of Smith, was with economic development causing structural changes which would eventually lead to the overcoming of the capitalistic system. Marxian analysis of economic development, anticipating some modern theory of discontinuous change,[2] cannot be reconciled with the value theory. In fact, while the latter reminds of the Cartesian approach, in the analysis of evolution he was instead influenced both by Hegel, for the philosophical context, and by Darwin, for the concept of competition.

Schumpeter has compared Walras to Kopernik for his theory of general equilibrium. But he did not spend too much time in dealing with the problem of equilibrium conceived as analytical interpretation of economic order, being convinced that economic development continuously disrupts equilibria attained by markets.

4. EQUILIBRIUM AND EVOLUTION IN NEOCLASSICAL THOUGHT

Neoclassical schools have completed the assimilation of economic order to equilibrium. Market is no longer considered as an arena where entrepreneurs can compete and thereby produce the highest rate of growth, being induced to accumulate as much as possible and to accelerate technical progress, but as an allocative mechanism, ensuring that the available resources and technologies are utilized at best to produce those goods that are most wanted by consumers. Ricardo's analysis of the role of land, being available in non-augmentable quantity, was extended to all *initial resources* assumed as given (population being included). Then, the result of the market mechanism is a definite structure of the economy at a certain date, such that the utility of any consumer is maximized, given those of others. The Smithian invisible hand is assumed to be satisfied with static efficiency.

Agents' choices may reflect their expectations: consumers expect to change their consumption in time, entrepreneurs to enlarge their firms' productive capacity. However, the result of the market mechanism is a set of compatible and efficient decisions, all referred to a given date.

Neoclassical economists were well aware that economy grows. Economic dynamics was considered as the result of two set of events: *events occurring outside the economic system*, such as population growth, changes in consumers' tastes, changes in the quantity of initial resources as a consequence, in particular, of consumers' savings and firms' investments; and *adjustment processes* produced by the allocative mechanism represented by the market. The economic system is considered as an *adaptive system* that responds to the external factors for growth by adjusting its structure, so that economic efficiency is assured.

Pareto (1896) distinguishes between two kinds of movements: the *virtual movements* which are required to make the agents' optimal choices consistent with one another, and which do not produce any effect on the economy (the relevant state being thus the equilibrium state) and the *actual movements* which are caused by exogenous changes (as all changes in technology are considered to be). Evolution is determined by actual movements that can be analysed by comparative statics. Exogenous changes can affect agents' choices through expectations. It is because agents' expectations cannot be compared to one another that the state representing equilibrium of the economy at time t, given the initial conditions and expectations, may not appear to be an equilibrium for the same conditions *at time $t+1$*, after expectations are verified.

The way dynamic analysis can be framed is conceived differently by the various economists. Walras has suggested that, in order to 'pass from the static to the *dynamic* point of view ... we need only suppose the data of the problem, viz. the quantity possessed, the utility of want curves, etc., to vary as a function of *time*' (Walras 1926, p. 318). This approach can best be appreciated after P. Samuelson's distinction between four cases: *static and stationary; static and historical; dynamic and causal (non historical); dynamic and historical* (Samuelson 1948, p. 315).

Pareto's approach is different. He is convinced that a truly dynamic paradigm is not yet available in economics. The model of general equilibrium is made up by simultaneous relations only, any variable being functionally related to all others. As we have just noted, the factors accounting for evolution are exogenous to the economic system. What economists can determine is a set of equilibria corresponding to different sets of *initial data*. Such data are not considered as functions of time. External changes can be assimilated to *disturbances*: a succession of disturbances entails a succession of static equilibria.

A different approach is taken by the Vienna and Stockholm school. We shall refer to Hayek's formulation. Hayek acknowledges that evolution can be explained by abandoning the notion of equilibrium. When the notion of dynamics

> is used in contrast to equilibrium analysis in general, it refers to an explanation of economic process as it proceeds in time, an explanation in terms of causation which must necessarily be treated as a chain of historical sequences.... This kind of causal explanation of the process in time is of course the ultimate goal of economic analysis, and equilibrium analysis is significant only in so far as it is preparatory to this main task. (Hayek 1962, p. 16)

In fact, Hayek deems it possible to generalize equilibrium analysis in such a way as to consider the intertemporal relations emerging from the agents' choices, their consideration being essential to solving the problem of capital as has been stated by Böhm Bawerk and Wicksell. Equilibrium does not represent any actual process. We must 'frankly recognize its purely fictitious character' (p. 21). The theory can help us understand how *agents' plans* are changed after changes in the conditions based on which they were formulated. Thus

> the state of equilibrium ... is a state of complete compatibility of *ex ante* plans, where in consequence (unless changes occur in the external data about which economic theory cannot say anything in any case) the *ex post* situation is identical with *ex ante*. (p. 23-4)

Two theoretical developments can be recognized in Hayek's perspective. The first is the von Neumann model of economic development. If accumulation and technical progress are considered as endogenous phenomena, we must shift from the static concept of equilibrium to the dynamic concept of *equilibrium path*. As von Neumann has proved, equilibrium path becomes the relevant concept if inputs and outputs in the production function have different dates, and the essential problem becomes the search for a process of growth entailing the highest rate of growth. Von Neumann's analysis of equilibrium differs from Hayek's, since equilibrium is not defined as compatibility of optimal agents' plans, but as the *optimal path of growth*. The optimality criterion apparently does not refer to individuals' utility but to the economy as a whole, being the maximum rate of growth.

The second is the Stockholm period analysis. The situation at the end of the period is the result of individuals' choices and expectations (*ex ante* variables). Since *ex post* variables will differ from *ex ante*, individuals will change their decisions. A chain of actions and reactions occurs which frames the system dynamics. A mechanical interpretation of the chain leads to *recursive dynamic models*.

Whereas von Neumann has led the way to growth optimizing models, Stockholm period analysis has offered a paradigm whereby to interpret (describe) disequilibria capable of producing fluctuations. The weak point of the latter approach is in the concept of *adaptive expectations* to which we shall revert.

5. ONE POINT EQUILIBRIUM AND EQUILIBRIUM PATH

The von Neumann model determines the most efficient path as it results from the choice of intertemporal techniques. Inputs of consumption goods to obtain one unit of work are assumed to be given. Let us frame the problem by assuming the consumption coefficients as parameters in terms of which to determine both prices and rate of growth. Then let us assume that the rate of growth is equal to the rate of population growth equal to that of workers for the sake of simplicity. We associate to each workers (all being the same) a utility function such as to determine the quotas of income spent on the different commodities. Then we can integrate the two problems and determine both prices and consumption coefficients in such a way as to make their separate solutions congruent with each other.

Thus, the von Neumann path allows us to shape an optimal path of growth, optimality resulting both from the highest rate of growth (and thus the highest rate of expansion of employment assured by the equivalent rate of growth of population) and from a consumption structure that maximizes utility for each worker. We have a kind of *golden rule* that will be clarified later on.

As Lombardini and Nicola have shown (1974, pp. 310-11), the notion of equilibrium by which paths of balanced growth are defined is logically stronger than the Walrasian notion of equilibrium. In fact the former requires not only that the various operators' decisions be consistent in a given period, but also that these decisions prove to have been consistent in all previous periods, so that they will remain consistent in future periods as well.

For equilibrium to exist in a development path, then, it is necessary that goods, taken over from the past, shall, at an arbitrary chosen moment of time, mirror the proportions that characterize the path itself. It can also be said that, in models of steady growth, a system will only be in equilibrium at any given moment if it has always been so. If we assume an origin for time, then what is required is a proper set of initial conditions.

If the equilibrium path results from consumers maximizing their utility over time (as in Solow's and Lucas' models), then only a specific set of initial conditions (of consumption per capita, in particular) is admissible.

In Walrasian and steady growth models, the concept of equilibrium is associated to different concepts of the economic system. In the former, the system is an adaptive system, as has been already remarked. In fact, the Walrasian models postulate circular relations. Circular relations (referred to the same point of time) are also posited between variables with different dates (those with future dates being regarded as expected values or deferred decisions).

Mechanical relations, on the other hand, are the mark of the steady paths equilibrium models. They enable a configuration of laws of movement and the price system is established in such a way as to provide for movement in equilibrium: the rate of growth is the parameter upon which the system hinges. It will come as no surprise, therefore, to discover that the essential features of equilibrium paths of growth (rate of growth and initial 'optimal' conditions) do not depend on the price system. The price system can be determined to link the equilibrium process of growth to agents' optimal choices.

In their turn, Walrasian models do not permit explanation of the relations to be established between growth rate, consumers propensities and the price system for the equilibrium over time to be attained. The optimum structure, as it is interpreted by a Walrasian model, may however characterize the states of an economy growing along an equilibrium path at different moments of time, provided the set of initial conditions is appropriate. This means that not all point-equilibria can be associated with equilibrium paths but only those that have *congruous initial conditions*. If we consider the set of equilibrium paths having the same rate of growth – which in models of the von Neumann-Leontief type, corresponds to the rate of profit – then we can choose a specific set of initial conditions to which a specific value for wages will correspond. Accordingly, we are now in a position to understand

> an essential property for the Walrasian models: their ability to determine income distribution, because they regard the process of growth as of secondary importance with respect to the preservation of a historical accident such as the initial distribution of goods. (Lombardini and Nicola pp. 317-18)

6. RATIONALITY AND EQUILIBRIUM

Equilibrium is usually conceived as the result of simultaneous optimizing behaviours of all agents. However, such behaviours are rational only if the system is in equilibrium. Thus in equilibrium models, the relations cannot be of the causal type. Causal relations exist between exogenous events on the one side and initial conditions and structural parameters of the model representing equilibrium on the other.

Various ways have been suggested to bypass this logical difficulty:

1. The Walrasian auctioneer: either an auctioneer is a central planner (and then the model does not explain a *free* market economy) or it is a service (and then we need a market for *auctioneers*: we are trapped into a *regressus ad infinitum*).
2. The assumption of agents' conjectural functions [3] (Hahn, 1977): then we cannot utilize the equilibrium model for analysis of comparative statics, since the correctness of agents' conjectures at the equilibrium point does not imply correctness with regard to potential situations.
3. The assumption that rationality entails also correct forecasting, as the New Classical Macroeconomics assumes, after the theory of rational expectations.

General equilibrium models have been reformulated in the language of the theory of games. We shall mention the Nash criterion which generalizes Pareto's notion of equilibrium. A set of strategies (each strategy being adopted by a player) is *Nash* if no player can change his strategy by himself and improve his payoff: therefore each player's choice is the best response to the strategy choices of the other players. As Arthur (1989, p. 716) has shown

> there may be many strategy-sets that fulfil the Nash condition. We could bring in further rationality conditions to choose among these, but none are universally plausible, so that modelling 'rational strategic action' in cellular or other games remains to some degree arbitrary and a matter of judgment.

According to Luce and Raiffa (1957, p. 63) the theory of games has only a normative value. If players are informed that α_3, β_2 is a Nash equilibrium,

> then player 1 *should* chose α_3. Possibly, but nothing in game theory says so. If we were player 1 in this case, we certainly would choose α_3, but we should not call another 'irrational' if he did otherwise. Even if we were tempted at first to call an α_3-non-conformist, 'irrational', we would have to admit that player 2 might be 'irrational' in which case it would be 'rational' for player 1 to be 'irrational' - to be an α_3-non-conformist.

The player rationality does not depend only on his information but also on the result of a learning process that concerns not only the strategies available to the other player, but also the mechanisms that can allow us to estimate the consequences of the different actions the rival can carry on. Learning processes are an ingredient of evolution being akin to the process of natural selection (see Chapter 6). Evolution will not leave the players unchanged since the experiments may make it easier to cooperate, rouse feelings of altruism or of revenge.

As to the economic mechanisms that players should know in order to assess the effects of the action of other agents, what can be said ‑ and will be proved throughout our work ‑ is that there exist no unique mechanisms to go by. To prove the validity of Luce and Raiffa's remarks, I shall consider the action that governments have to take when the budget deficit is considered dangerously high. I think that the adjustment must be decided in a long-run perspective, taking into account not only the short-term macroeconomic effects of the level of public expenditures, but also those linked with its structure. The same level of public expenditure has a different impact on inflationary tendencies, according to whether public expenditure is the result of productive polices or of mere welfare interventions. However, the rival player ‑ the big speculators ‑ are convinced that only abrupt and substantial budget deficit reductions can avoid inflation. I believe that this is a wrong belief. However, were I Minister of the Treasury, I would adopt a strategy of sharp reduction of the budget deficit because any other possible alternative is likely to worsen the current situation and to defeat 'rational' policy-making over the near term. I would then try to correct policy orientation so as to avoid being obliged to play the same game in the future.

According to Bernheim (1984), Nash's behaviour is not only deprived of descriptive value; it is not even a necessary condition for rationality. As we shall observe in a moment, economic rationality can be defined only with reference to a more general context than that in which the principle of rationality is applied.

To apply the conceptual scheme of game theory we must assume that all players proceed by making an irrevocable commitment to a strategy before the game begins. As Selten has noted, if players 'can make such a commitment, then this commitment possibility should be formally modelled as a part of a larger game' (Binmore 1987 I, p. 187). Such a remark can be generalized. Each game involving specific rules and justifying sets of expectations, raises two problems. Are they merely rationality rules? Do they imply a specific 'environment', required both to justify the rules and make it possible to abide by them? The two questions are interconnected. Rationality depends on environment, in particular on the social relations. Environment is changed ‑ in particular by laws ‑ to make it more compatible with rational behaviour. Then, a third question arises: every game entails a larger game to make it rational for every player to rely on the commitments of others and to define some fundamental rules that make it possible, together with some technological relations and initial states, to identify the constraints that limit the sets of possible strategies as well as the relations between the various strategies and the results that can be achieved (such knowledge being the eventual outcome of a learning process). To avoid a *regressus to infinitum*, we must assume that at the beginning there was some kind of Hobbesian State. In logical terms, for any *system of games* we can make a remark quite similar to that made by Godel for any logical system.

In the formal logic of the theory of games, it has been suggested that 'meta-games' should be conceived in which a pure strategy is the choice of the machines. That does not solve the problem of the complexity of the choice process and of the costly rationality, since the meta-game, if conceived as a preliminary game, will prove much more complex than the following specific games.

Let us stop for a moment on the relation between rational decisions and environment. If I have reason to believe that my rival is a bad player, I will never play according to any minimax principle (Binmore 1987 I, p. 196). Experience can change the structure of the game. Having detected that certain pairs of strategies (of mine and of my rival's) induce reactions of public opinion or of political forces, we can both decide to play a different game. In the games it plays, the Government will try to learn what are the possible reactions of the various players, not only to choose its strategies, but also to change institutions.

Binmore (1987) has proved that if two players are substituted by universal Turing machines, each player could be

> supplied with the information necessary for an eductive analysis to be possible. ... Within this framework, a perfectly rational machine ought presumably to be able to predict the behaviour of the opposite machine perfectly, since it will be familiar with every detail of the design. And a universal Turing machine *can* do this. What it *cannot* do is to predict his opponents' behaviour *and* simultaneously participate in the action of the game. It is in this sense that the claim that perfect rationality is an unattainable ideal is to be understood.... In summary, the claim is that, if attention is restricted to players who *always* give an answer to problems that make proper sense, then sometimes such players will get the answer *wrong*. It is not claimed that the case for this proposition is watertight: only that those that deny it need to be prepared to explain why they should not be classified along with those who count angels on the end of pins'. (pp. 206, 209)

In a subsequent paper such a possibility is further explained:

> The reason is essentially that the machine would sometimes calculate forever if this were permitted. To avoid this, a 'stopping rule' must be built in. If such a stopping rule guillotines an exact calculation, then the machine

will be forced to employ an alternative 'guessing algorithm'. By its nature, such a guessing algorithm will sometimes guess wrongly'. (Binmore, 1988 II, p. 12)

The concept of rationality inherent in equilibrium analysis is not only disputable in its philosophical foundations, it is hardly relevant for the interpretation of concrete processes.

7. EQUILIBRIUM IN THE SHORT AND IN THE LONG RUN

In spite of the logical difficulties we run into when trying to reach operative concept of substantial rationality, the equilibrium approach is usually justified on two grounds.

1. In the short run equilibrium is unlikely to occur, whereas in the long run, in some way or another, the economy has to settle on an equilibrium position (or along an equilibrium path). In fact, the economy can fluctuate; however, it does not explode, which means that it gravitates towards some equilibrium position, or tends to reach some equilibrium path.
2. Equilibrium means a rational allocation of resources. When applied to dynamics, equilibrium means efficient growth.

Both statements are questionable. As for the first, the Schumpeterian lesson induces to reverse it. In fact, the concept of equilibrium may be of some use in the analysis of short-run phenomena, in order to frame certain problems of economic policy. In the long-run, equilibrium is impossible because of the nature of economic development.[4]

As for the second, we must remember that:

1. The goals of economic development are not uniquely determined. Only if we argue in a static context and accept a specific anthropological view, rationality can be identified with the most efficient use of resources to satisfy consumer wants (Pareto's optimality criterion). If we consider different generations, public goods, interdependences between consumers' preferences and learning processes after consumption experience both of private and public goods, the rationality problem becomes intricate. Such a statement will become clearer after the considerations we shall make in Chapter 2.

2. Any rationality criterion can be defined only in correspondence with some structural conditions of the economy (consumers' tastes, for instance). Evolution of the economy entails continuous changes in these conditions: how can we assess the changes?

Let us dwell a little more on statement **a**. It is true that no economy has ever exploded, even though some (the Russian economy in 1993) have nearly done so. But that must not necessarily be attributed to mechanisms of the economic system. Explosion may eventually be avoided thanks to changes in the political system. Even if we disregard the relations between the economic and the social-political system, to remain within what is usually considered the field of economics, we must remember that all economic models are *partial*.[5] Indeed, we usually classify the models into two classes, *normative* and *descriptive* models. In the former it is usually assumed that changes can be arbitrarily decided by certain agents (the Government, the Central Bank). We may associate a normative model to a descriptive one, so that the former can visualize actions that cause changes in some relations of the latter and the explosion is avoided. Such possibilities have been stressed by Keynesians.

The relations expressing the agents' behaviour may allow for explosions and yet the model may fluctuate along a path of growth, thanks to *ceilings* and *floors*: this is the main lesson of Hicks' *A contribution to the theory of trade cycle* (1950). The main aim of Pasinetti's analysis (1993) is to visualize structural changes that are required, after other changes have occurred, to re-establish general equilibrium.

8. DECREASING RETURN AND COMPETITIVE EQUILIBRIA

Neoclassical economists were convinced that if the main objective of economic analysis is to explain how a competitive equilibrium is reached and can be maintained in time, technologies must be constrained by the assumption of decreasing return. Increasing returns would cause structural changes conducive to non-competitive markets.

Economies of scale can be differently argued. Diseconomies of scale have been assumed to occur in a static framework because of the costs of the specific co-ordination activities required by larger scales (Pareto): they eventually become more relevant than the economies of scale due to the costs of specialization and indivisibilities.

The Marshallian approach presents some peculiarities both in defining processes characterized by increasing returns and in identifying possible constraints to the growth of the firm. The Marshallian distinction between internal and external economies is well known. It is difficult to agree with Knight (1925, p. 333) that the concept of increasing returns, external to the firm, is an 'empty economic box'. Even in a static framework, external economies in the Marshallian sense are particularly relevant if the space dimension is considered in defining the commodities space.[6]

Economies of scale become more relevant if we turn from the static viewpoint to the dynamic one. In fact, Marshall's analysis is substantially carried on in a dynamic context, as it is required by the biologic analogue.

General equilibrium can be conceived also for an economy with certain kinds of increasing returns. In the economy analysed by Chipman (1970) the only input is labour: for every firm of each market the labour input coefficient is constant; for the market as a whole it decreases with the increase in production because of external economies similar to those visualized by Smith, due to the intensification of the labour division made possible by increases in demand. Only if the degrees of homogeneity in the production functions for the various commodities are equal, the competitive equilibrium ‑ which exists and is unique if wages are positive ‑ is Pareto optimum. If such a condition is not satisfied

> *optimal output of the ith product is greater than, equal to, or less than laisser faire the weighted average of degrees of homogeneity of all production functions, where the weights are the proportions of consumers' budget in the respective commodities.* (pp. 365‑66, emphasis in original)

After Marshall and Pigou, we could try to determine tax rates that 'allow the ideal output to be produced and consumed within a competitive market framework'. However, also if such a set of tax rates is found

> we are not entitled to conclude that their mere imposition will automatically bring the desired situation about; for it is conceivable that in this new model of modified competition, equilibrium will no longer be unique. That is, once the optimal excise tax rates ... have been fixed, the possibility cannot be excluded that there might be another labour allocation .... (p. 367)

satisfying the required conditions for equilibrium.

When increasing returns are present, equilibrium is scarcely stable. Let us consider an economy where a commodity is produced by labour only, the labour coefficient being constant. To the fixed price of labour a mark-up is added proportional to the quantity produced: profits are used to enlarge production at the rate of increase of labour (population). Let us start with a given number of firms of the same dimension expecting the same increase in demand equal to the increase in the rate of population growth. We may have an equilibrium path of the economy made up by firms, all equal and all growing at the same rate. Let us assume that the firms remain sufficiently numerous to make it possible to maintain competition in the market. However, it will then be sufficient that one firm should grow at a higher rate – whether due to erroneous expectations or because the entrepreneur has become more aggressive – for the equilibrium path to be disrupted.

9. FEEDBACK EFFECTS AND CUMULATIVE PROCESSES

We can generalize the remarks made on the role of the decreasing-returns assumption by saying that the economic system is, in general, conceived with negative feedback effects. However, positive feedbacks cannot be excluded. Increasing return is only one possibility. Others are cumulative causation, deviation-amplifying mutual causal processes, non-convexity, threshold effects, virtuous and vicious circles. To understand both the reasons and the consequences of such self-reinforcement mechanisms, we sometimes need to enlarge the concept of the system to take account also of some specific social relations. Such are the cumulative causations analysed by Myrdal (1957). Another example is the effect that the mere permanence of equilibrium in the financial market may have on the expectations of agents becoming more optimistic. A higher rate of productivity may allow a country to increase its export. The higher increase of (internal and external) demand for their products may induce acceleration in technical progress by the firms of the country. A deviation amplyfing mutual causal process occurs.

Most phenomena of self sustained growth are 'local'. Such are those I analysed in my contributions of 1953 to the monopoly theory (partially republished in 1994). Firms may grow because of *endogenous factors*. By doing so they create obstacles to entry. Then some structural features of the economy can be maintained if the expected growth rate of the demand for products of the oligopolistic markets is not higher than the potential rate of growth of the firms operating in the markets. However, structural change may occur *from the outside*, for instance, because a potential rival, being more optimistic or more aggressive, decides to enter the market. We may have a kind of Schumpeterian competition, which is not to be necessarily associated with innovation since for economic systems conceived in the usual way it can have only a *historical* explanation.

If space dimension is considered, positive feedback effects may occur both because of external economies (localization of firms employing mostly male workers can create more favourable conditions for the location of firms employing female workers) and because of some favourable effects of spatial association of firms producing certain commodities (industrial districts: see Becattini, 1989). An area may represent a favourable location for certain economic activities, provided proper infrastructure is available. Then, only if public administrations, whose decisions are necessary for such infrastructure to be produced, have correct expectations and are in a position to make their choices accordingly, will the new plants be established in the area. This example suffices to make it clear why, in the presence of a positive feedback, we may have different possible evolutions. It is not difficult to realize why the occurrence of a specific evolution may be due to historical reasons (for examples of oligopolistic markets evolution see Sylos Labini 1956).

At the beginning, a specific evolution may look less efficient than others. However, if for historical reasons it does occur, the resulting process may be irreversible. In my 1953 contribution I illustrated such a possibility by the following example. Let us suppose that there are two possible evolutions: one characterized by homogeneous commodities produced at low costs, the other by differentiated commodities having higher costs. Initially, given individual preferences, the first alternative is the more efficient. However, should all the firms autonomously decide to adopt a policy of product differentiation and this policy proves successful, the second alternative will then turn out to be the less efficient, since individual tastes will have changed. Anyway, the first alternative has no possibility of being implemented because it would be too risky (practically impossible) for a firm to expel the other firms selling differentiated products from the market in order to sell the homogeneous product at a lower cost. A concrete example is offered by Arthur (1989, p. 717). The Sony Betamax video technology, according to industry specialists, is superior to VHS. However VHS had more luck: an irreversible process set in which caused the producer to attain a dominant position in the market.

The beginning of an evolution may be characterized by stocastic processes. Once a certain structure emerges because of this type of evolution and of associated feedback effects, then the dynamics of the system can be mostly explained on the basis of a mechanical model. We are in the context of Prigogine's dissipative models. Quite a few urbanization developments may have this kind of explanation. It is not difficult to understand why these evolutions cannot be efficient. Indeed, if correct expectations about alternative evolutions had been possible from the beginning and institutional conditions realized for their implementation, more efficient evolutions could have come about.

10. INCREASING RETURNS IN DYNAMIC CONTEXTS

As we have already mentioned, in neoclassical theories evolution is induced by external factors (technical progress, changes in consumer preferences and in the available resources, labour in particular) which may cause increases in productivity. Effects similar to economies of scale are then produced. The effects of these factors may be internalized by *agents' expectations* (as is assumed by Knight (1921), according to whom profits are linked to the success of such expectations; they accrue to the efficient management). Expectations of evolution are present also in standard Walrasian theories of general equilibrium. Consumers save because they expect future increases in income which are preferred to reductions in current consumption. Firms accumulate because they expect both increases in final demand and possible implementation of new technologies. Since consumers' and firms' prospects are highly uncertain and expectations are scarcely verified, the equilibrium attained in period t may appear not to be such when looked at in period $t+1$.

In Smith, technical progress can be partly internalized, as we have already mentioned, because of the relation between accumulation and intensification of labour. We shall see how such a line of analysis has been proposed by Solow, Lucas and Romer through their models of endogenous growth (Chapter 3). A limit to the application of the concept of market equilibrium in assessing evolution then appears due to the *external effects* of technical progress which are not necessarily confined to the industry where technical progress has occurred.

Evolution can conduce to economies of scale not with respect to single firms (as it is if the Smithian relation between accumulation and technical progress is considered) but to single industries. That has been pointed out by Young (1928) who was the first to suggest that economic growth can induce specialization of intermediate products, producing a kind of division of labour not within firms but between firms. We can then talk of external (industry) economies that materialize *after growth*: growth can thus be accelerated.

We could apply the concept of external effects to explain the increase in productivity of the Younghian type, as well as to explain the acceleration of growth that, in Smithian analysis, is produced by the effect of accumulation of the division of labour. Specular to what can be considered as the Smithian supply side viewpoint is Schmookler's viewpoint of the demand side: it is the growth rate of demand that fosters innovation.

Not all interrelations between growth and technical progress can be analysed by models of endogenous growth. Only those that can be planned, or are in some way foreseeable, may enter into processes of optimization, after the *production function for technical progress* has been defined (as Lucas' function relating the increase in labour qualification – human capital accumulation – to the quota of labour that consumers allocate to improve their qualification).

Technical progress may be a by-product of growth. Increases in productivity may result from the substitution of old plants, for the purpose of implementing technical progress of the embodied type (Kaldor and Mirlees vintage models, 1962). Since the rate at which substitution occurs depends both on the growth rate of demand and on wages and interest rates, growth has a positive feedback effect. Growth may also have positive effects wich are generated by processes of learning by doing (Arrow, 1962).

11. THE TWO VIEWPOINTS: DESCRIPTION AND OPTIMIZATION

To describe evolution, intertemporal relations have to be considered. The essential one is the relation between growth and investment. In the shaping of this relation two elements contribute: the absolute scarcity of certain factors (land) representing a brake, and the feedback effects of the expansion of demand that enhance growth.

The Harrod-Domar model offers an elementary description of an equilibrium path of growth in which accumulation, interpreted after Keynes' consumption function, occurs at a rate that justifies the firms' investment choices by firms (*warranted rate of growth*). Normal growth materializes when the warranted rate of growth is equal to the sum of the rate of growth of population (assumed to be equal to the rate of growth of the supply of labour) and of the increase due to the productivity of labour induced by technical progress having effects similar to the increase in population (neutral in Harrod's sense).

Harrod was, indeed, more interested in proving the instability of the capitalistic process of accumulation, than offering a possible description of concrete evolutions in the economy. A model similar to Harrod's was already produced (in 1939) by Samuelson. By making consumption dependent on past rather than on present income, the interrelations between accelerator and multiplier was proved to produce, under proper conditions, regular economic cycles. In 1950, John Hicks produced a formalization of the instability of the process induced by the interaction of accelerator and multiplier: business cycle occurs because of a ceiling and a floor preventing explosions and collapses of the economy.

We have already mentioned von Neumann's model. Its aim is to identify an equilibrium path that maximizes the rate of growth by a proper choice of the techniques available. It does not describe processes resulting from market choices of individual agents. It explores the structural properties of an optimal evolution, the main feature being the relation between price structure, rate of interest and rate of growth.[7]

Equilibrium path is not a mere result of the market mechanism that is capable of assuring one-point equilibria, i.e. according to Pareto, those that can represent the states in which an evolving system finds itself at various points of time. The paradigm of the one point equilibrium has been utilized to describe a possible evolution of the system in two different contexts: in that of Hicks' *equilibrium over time* and in that of *multiperiod equilibria*. In the latter, equilibria for many periods ahead can be referred to a point of time in which all agents decide their action for all future periods, their actions being implemented in current and in future markets, all of them brought to equilibrium. In the former, agents decide their action in view of the results attainable in the period and on the basis of their expectations for the following period. An equilibrium over time occurs when expectations are always fulfilled. As we shall see, only for multiperiod equilibria we can state an optimization problem.

Let us remind that the one-point equilibrium (which applies also to multiperiod models) is a different concept from that of equilibrium path of growth. In the former initial conditions are arbitrary, whereas in the latter they must be compatible with the structure of the economy. Walrasian models, if expectations are fulfilled, can describe equilibrium paths of growth that need not be *optimal paths of growth*.

Two different problems arise when models are used to analyse possible evolution of the economy:

1. How a structure of the economy is changed in order to make it compatible with an equilibrium path of growth. The neoclassical solution is opposed to the Keynesian one.
2. How the economy can move from a non-optimal equilibrium path to the optimal one. That problem has been analysed by Cozzi (1966).

As concerns von Neumann's model, which aims at proving only the logical possibility of an optimal path (in the classical sense), the relevant problem appears to consist in visualizing a process that assures the maximum realization of the von Neuman potentiality of growth when initial conditions differ from those appropriate to an optimal growth for a system having the same fundamental structure and specific final conditions to be attained. Such a problem has been solved by the *turnpike theorem* (see McKenzie, 1963; Morishima 1969, chapters X and XII).

Optimal evolution can be analysed in two ways.

The classical-Keynesian way. Optimality is defined in terms of the rate of growth (von Neumann's model) or in terms of the per capita consumption. The second alternative has been clarified by Phelps (1961) by referring to a Keynesian-neoclassical model in which a global propensity to save is assumed together with a production function homogeneous of the first degree. Per capita consumption is maximized when the rate of growth of labour productivity is equal to the rate of growth of population, namely when accumulation is just sufficient to allow the same level of consumption to all generations. The *golden rule* is confirmed if capital is assumed to develop in time in order to maximize some per-capita social-utility integral of the type we shall consider in section 6 of Chapter 2. Such an evolution tends *asymptotically* to a golden-age equilibrium, investment tending to a constant fraction of income. If the discount rate assumed in the process of utility maximization is zero, Phelps' (1961) golden rule is confirmed (Samuelson, 1967, p. 223). We have seen that the von Neumann model can be interpreted in such a way as to produce a *golden rule* in a neoclassical context: what is maximized is both the rate of growth, thanks to the availability of various intertemporal techniques of production, and workers' utility.

The Pareto way. Optimality is attained when some functional of utility is maximized. If we consider a limited number of periods, then we run into a difficulty which has been elicited by Malinvaud's analysis of the problem (1953). This is the problem of how final stocks should be evaluated. A criterion of minimization of monetary cost has to be introduced. In the dynamic models transversality conditions assure that as time tends to infinity, capital tends to zero.

The assumption of perfect competition is usually deemed to be a prerequisite for the problem of optimization to be posed and general equilibrium to be envisaged. In fact as it has been proved ‐ by Negishi (1960), Arrow and Hahn (1971) and Arrow (1971) ‐ we can work out models built on the assumption of monopolistic competition to represent the general equilibrium of the economy. The assumption of monopolistic competition allows Aghion and Howitt to formalize some aspects of the Schumpeterian processes of development (1992 and 1994). I had adopted a similar assumption ‐ in co-operation with Donati ‐ to arrive at the relations characterizing a path of development resulting from both product and technological innovations. Thus a Schumpeterian process of growth: if properly formalized, it does not impede to describe a steady path of growth. What really matters ‐ in describing evolution within the neoclassical framework ‐ is the assumption of flexible versus rigid price, as been shown by Malinvaud (1977).

12. EVOLUTION AND DISEQUILIBRIUM

Joan Robinson (1956) has applied the label of 'golden age' to the optimal equilibrium growth. Such an evolution is indeed unrealistic even if we assume that self-sustainable growth is possible. In fact, self-sustainable growth can occur along different paths, to all of which Joan Robinson has given expressive nicknames.

> A steady state of accumulation of capital may take place below full employment. The stock of plant has the composition appropriate to the desired rate of accumulation, but there is not enough of it to employ the whole labour force. (1963, p. 53)

This growth path has been labelled *limping golden age*. As far as a reduction of wages is possible, the limping golden age may be converted into a golden age. I have suggested another possible remedy: the appearance of *breaking monopolies* which can cause increased accumulation (Lombardini, 1971, p. 242).

> When Malthusian misery checks the rate of growth of population, then, in the absence of technical progress, a situation might be reached in which the rate of accumulation and the rate of growth of the labour force were equal, the ratio of non-employment being great enough to keep the latter down to equality with the former.

This is a *leaden age*.

A 'more cheerful scene' occurs when 'with induced technical progress, it is impossible to maintain as high a rate of growth as firms are willing and anxious to carry out' (p. 54). Two possible outcomes are visualized by Joan Robinson in such a *restrained golden age*. Wages rise or firms, adopting the Smithian strategy in labour market, reduce the increase in productive capacity by adopting an *unconscious parallelism*, to avoid increases in wages. The desired rate of growth may be hampered because of a lack in demand for final products. Then remedies can be provided both by sales promotion activities which, by reducing savings, will change the rate of growth aimed at by firms, or by a rise in wages which will have similar effects on final demand.

Special dynamics occur when the stock of capital is not congruent with the desired rate of growth (*galloping platinum age* and *creeping platinum age*). When because of inflationary pressure (due to the fact that wages cannot be depressed below a particular level), the rate of accumulation is being held in check by the threat of rising money wages due to a rise in prices (as opposed to rising money wages due to a scarcity of labour) may be described as a *bastard golden age*. [italics mine] (p. 58)

In this case disequilibrium is due not so much to the high level of wages, but rather to the low level of demand that may be caused by *pessimistic self-realising expectations*. Various remedies can be thought of: increases in wages, increases in public expenditure, a reduction of the rate of interest. All these remedies may fail to hit the objective if they have a positive feedback on inflation.

Investments can increase relatively to consumption if technical progress reduces labour required to produce the minimum acceptable real wage: here we have a *bastard platinum age*.

Joan Robinson's exploration of different patterns of evolution of the economy is not carried on within a formalized model. In fact, she mentions also mechanisms - as the Malthusian one - which, usually, are not considered in economic model of growth. A formalized scheme for distinguishing different kinds of evolution has been produced by Malinvaud (1977).

His *classical unemployment* may remind us of Joan Robinson's limping golden age (1977). Malinvaud's *repressed inflation* has some resemblance with Joan Robinson's restrained golden age. Malinvaud's *Keynesian unemployment* may be remedied by recipes similar to those proposed by Joan Robinson's for her bastard golden age. In fact, what remains to be shown in Joan Robinson's analysis of different patterns of growth are the possible mechanisms that can make the different kind of growth sustainable. An exploration of different patterns of growth will be made, by means of a Schumpeterial model, in Chapter 6, all interrelations characterizing the structure of the economy being analysed. In facts, I agree with Malinvaud when he personally makes me note that 'with little ingenuity we can imagine hypotheses compatible with steady states and all types of market disequilibria'. What, indeed, has to be done is to explore how certain relevant structural conditions entail non-equilibrium evolution; in what conditions such evolutions can go on indefinitely; how structural changes - possibly induced by economic policy - can modify evolution eventually bringing the system along an equilibrium path.

In the models of endogenous growth equilibrium has been assumed also in the labour market. Therefore several patterns of evolution have been discarded. In fact, disequilibria in the labour market may persist for a long time since excess of demand can induce immigration, whereas excess of supply may be eliminated by emigration.

Models conceived to explain the evolution of 'economic systems' need not be equilibrium model; they may explain explosive and recessive tendencies of the economy. By investigating these tendencies, we can visualize possible structural changes capable of checking such trends. These structural changes can be brought about by means of economic policies or through *historical events*. Should the wage policy preached by Ford - i.e. translating most of the increase in productivity in wages increase - have not materialized, the motor-car would have remained a toy for the rich, and American industries would have experienced an increase in unemployment as expected by Rosa Luxenburg.

The main reason why equilibrium path cannot describe the long run evolution of the economy is the occurrence of Schumpeterian innovations. We shall describe as Schumpeterian such technological innovation as cannot occur according to dynamic laws reflecting fundamental properties of the economy, or result from optimization processes. Its occurrence reflects, to a large extent, entrepreneurs' aggressiveness and expectations and has some stocastic features as well.

In the short run, general equilibrium is continuously threatened by the instability of financial markets. Agents' expectations are formed in such a context; they may foster instability.

13. RATIONAL EXPECTATIONS

We have seen how far expectations have been utilized to link successive one-period equilibria.

Hayek assumes correct expectations as a necessary condition to define non-stationary equilibrium, the analysis of what he assumes to be a preliminary stage in dynamic analysis. The general idea of equilibrium refers to the case where individual plans

> are fully adjusted to one another, so that it is possible for all of them to be carried out because the plans of any one member are based on the expectation of such actions on the part of the other member as are contained in the plans which those others are making at the same time. ... This sort of fictitious state of equilibrium which (irrespective of whether there is any reason to believe that it will actually come about) can be *conceived* to comprise any sort of planned change, is indispensable if we want to apply the technique of equilibrium analysis at all phenomena which are *ex definition* absent in the stationary state. (1941, pp. 18-9)

The perfect forecasting framework is in general essentially unrealistic. In fact, no problem arises as to how expectations are formed, if the economy grows at a constant rate with prices remaining constant. Once the system has settled on an equilibrium path, people will expect prices to remain stable and other variables to grow at the same rates as in the past. If the rate of growth is not constant and uniform, prices change over time: expectations differ for various individuals and affect actual processes. As J. Robinson remarks: 'correct foresight involves highly sophisticated expectations which take account of the influence of the expectations themselves upon the course of events' (Robinson 1956, p. 66).

The possibility of correct expectations has been asserted by the theory of rational expectations for economies working according to the neoclassical theory of market mechanism.[8] However, the assumptions on which rational expectations are based are open to serious criticisms.

1. The unbiasedness property assumes a degree of homogeneity of the agents which makes the theory useless as a model to help understand rational behaviour in uncertain contexts. Even if we should find that the realized value is equal to the one predicted, plus a term that can be considered as a stocastic variable with mean zero, one question would still stand: what is the meaning of the divergence between *ex ante* and *ex post* values of the variable? Expectations do not represent a mere estimation procedure. The set of information is scarcely consistent; it needs to be interpreted. People differ in their capacity to do so. Interpretation does not reduce to a simple logical and statistical exercise; to some extent it is based on intuition, and also depends on the *mood* of the agent. The *error* may reflect stocastic distribution of such possibilities; in which case qualifying the stocastic variables as an error may be justified. However, it might reflect the different formulations of the model explaining the workings of the economy made by the various individuals and also their different computations; in this case the *error* is merely an econometric trick.[9] The *errors* of successive predictions are dealt with as *white noises* not linked in any way by serial correlation. This assumption, contrasting with the experience of business fluctuation, is not compatible with the process of learning that occurs both in interpreting information and in interpreting the way the economy works.
2. Certain activities _ speculation and innovation _ will lose their relevance, should the assumptions on which rational expectations are based be acceptable. The effects of speculation depend not only on correct expectations of the orientation of the price movement, but also on how strong is the reaction of other people to such an expectation. Two cases can be considered. The first has been outlined by Phelps (1987). To begin with, there is an underreaction, which is followed by further reactions. This can be explained in view of the varying ability to work out the information on

the stock exchange market evolution. The second case occurs when all agents operate on the basis of the same information worked out through the same model (stored in computers): here an overreaction is more likely. Let us suppose that a speculator is convinced that the price increase is not justified by fundamentals; he is also convinced that a large number of people expect the price to increase. He is in a condition to envisage a speculative bubble. However, to be rational he must adapt his expectation to the prevailing one, while keeping ready to change it before the *news* of the fall in prices induces other people to change their own. (Recall the remarks about rational players made at pages 11-2). Arthur, having stressed the difference between the particles in physics and the economic agents (the latter act on the basis of *expectations* and of *strategy*) notes that: 'The problem is that if our "particles" form expectations on beliefs that determine structure in the large, there are many such rational sets of beliefs and choosing among them may be arbitrary' (Arthur 1989, p. 715).

3. Revision of expectations cannot be associated to errors. News cannot be assimilated to errors. Even news of *historical facts* − as the oil crisis of 1974 may be considered − can be predicted on the basis of both wider models connecting the workings of the political system to those of the economic one, and of a critical assessment of possible global scenarios. In fact the oil crisis did not come as a surprise for all people. On the other hand, some news − for instance about changes in political regimes − may entail foreseeable changes in the workings of the economy. How is the set of information found to have relevancy changed? How will people change the model on the basis of which they make their predictions, once they have obtained the information? As we have remarked, all economic models are partial models, since a model is *specified* on the basis of a particular concept of the *economic system* in the context of the larger, often implicit, concept of *social system* (see Lombardini 1981). That may justify the co-existence of various models, none of which can be assumed to be the only reliable model, or be discarded as a false theory.[10]

4. As Reichling and Siconolfi (1983) have shown, the model cannot be an exogenous model built by *economists* and in some way imposed on people in order to justify other people's expectations as being rational; it has to be in some sense *endogenized*. A variable which is the result of many agents' behaviour (as the market price in a competitive market) cannot rationally be considered as *exogeneously given*: each agent, if he is to act rationally, has to estimate how his behaviour, together with that of other firms, causes the variable to assume the equilibrium value. That entails a *collusive behaviour* that will lead to a supply different from that equating the marginal costs to the *given* price: both price and profits are higher than the competitive

level. We can add that if rationality is assumed to entail this kind of endogenization of the model, computation becomes impossible:[11] the model may result in being non-computable.
5. As Phelps has noted

> the rational expectations view of the motion of the economy has to come to grips with two problems: one is *learning*, and the other - a logically prior problem - is, *learning what?* In the real world agents have diverse models, so the individual agents must learn not only the parameters that would exist if all shared his beliefs about the model, but also the parameters that enter because other agents have other views. This observation is an obvious corollary of sunspot theory: if everyone else believes, you had better believe too. (Phelps 1992, p. 136-7)

The problem of computability, already hinted at, becomes more relevant.

In exploring a market equilibrium path, specific assumptions have to be made about the way expectations are formed and utilized to optimize choices. One condition for a market equilibrium path to materialize is the fulfilment of expectations. Such an assumption has to be critically assessed, for the purpose of evaluating the empirical relevance of the theory. That we shall do in the model of endogenous growth presented in Chapter 4. If we explore evolutions which are not assumed to occur in equilibrium, specific mechanisms for error corrections have to be assumed as well.

There is an alternative both to adaptive and rational expectations hypotheses that is considered in Lombardini (1992, p. 433 ff.). We must try to understand the links between the models and mechanisms that enable us to define the individual decision process. They are: 1) an optimization model, 2) a formation-of-expectation model, 3) a learning mechanism, 4) a model of error correction. Indeed, to understand individual behaviour, we have to assume learning processes covering not only external factors, but also the mechanism of the economy and the logical procedures whereby to exploit all information and the complex logical-psychological mechanism by which learning processes are carried on, along with procedure for hitting the best options (or, at least, satisfactory ones). However, there are mental activities (referred to under the notion of *intuition*) that cannot be formalized. As Schumpeter has outlined, some expectations cannot be derived by any rational manipulation of data.

The optimization model may be conveniently substituted for by a behaviourist model which cannot be viewed as a *reduced* model of a structural one obtained from an assiomatic system built to *explain* optimal choice, since there are reasons to believe that behaviour is determined mostly by cultural-psychological factors. Then, instead of a model of *substantial* rationality, we can assume an interaction between the other individual decision processes, such as to induce adjustments in the fundamental behaviour. Only if the system is ergodic, can we assume properties of the various processes such as will lead to consistent individuals' optimal choices. In economic *development*, the system cannot be considered ergodic.

When dealing with endogenous growth, the process of adjusting expectations through learning has to be assumed at least for the transition of the economy to a balanced process of growth: in steady growth the problem becomes irrelevant as has been remarked in the quoted passage from J. Robinson. As Goodwin and Pacini (1992) have proved, no process of expectation formation and correction can occur if chaotic movements are possible because of the structure of the model.

14. DISCONNECTED EXPECTATIONS

As specular to the concept of Schumpeterian innovations, we can view the concept of *disconnected expectations*. Both adaptive and rational expectations are *connected*: the former to past evolution; the latter to future potential evolution. Expectations may be disconnected for two reasons:

1. Speculators are not interested in assessing potential future evolution, but rather in anticipating the moods of investors (in stock exchange). Since such anticipations are not related to variables that could enter into the model, we can qualify the expectations entailed as disconnected: they are of a *Keynesian type*.
2. Consumers and firms' confidence depends mostly on their anticipation of a certain political evolution. Reagan succeeded in reversing the business trend not by his economic policy (in fact the economic policy he implemented was, to a large extent, opposite to the one announced), but rather by his ability to tide the American people over the Vietnam depression.

The two types of disconnected expectations are often interrelated, in that they may materialize in non-congruent reactions to anticipated events.

15. EFFICIENCY OVER TIME

Neoclassical equilibrium is an efficient economic structure. It can be proved that, under certain assumptions, a competitive equilibrium corresponds to a

Pareto optimum, it being impossible to increase the utility of any agents without decreasing that of at least one other agent. Malinvaud (1953) has extended the Pareto efficiency criterion to chronics of production and consumption.

The Pareto efficiency criterion concerns the first of the two roles that are played by the market according to Smith (structuring production according to consumers' preferences). The second role consists in assuring the highest rate of growth. If we assume technology as given and consumption increasing only as a result of the increase in population (with individual consumption coefficients remaining constant over time), we could define, after von Neumann, the most efficient evolution as the one that maximizes the rate of growth.

If Schumpeterian innovation and speculation are assumed, then Pareto's efficiency criterion is neither a necessary nor a sufficient condition for dynamic efficiency. The difficulties that have to be faced when we assess efficiency referring to a process of evolution are those concerning the standard to be used. In the static approach, the standard is represented by individual tastes. In evolution individual tastes are irrelevant or at best insufficient for the assessment of efficiency, inasmuch as innovations entail the creation of new products that consumers are induced to ask for through sales promotion activities. The efficiency assessment must also cover some features of evolution (how does social darwinism have to be evaluated? While stimulating individual creativity, it may cause long run unemployment and poverty that lead to inefficient increases in public expenditures).

As for speculative activities, they may hamper, as well as foster, economic development, depending on the kind of interrelations existing between these activities and firms' and consumers' strategies. Therefore we cannot share Pasinetti's view that steady growth is a prerequisite for optimality in the long run both in a market and in a planned economy. (Pasinetti 1974, p. 95). It is certainly true that a system that causes persistent unemployment is not efficient. However, to become more efficient, a system may require that not all resources be utilized. Innovations change the equilibrium path appropriate to the system. No steady growth can represent a model to which economic policy can be addressed in order to keep the economy efficient.

If speculation is of the Keynesian type, evolution may not be efficient even if a unique golden-age equilibrium path is conceived. Let us assume that the system is not moving along the equilibrium path. If speculators have reason to believe that disequilibria are likely to go on for a while, they will take advantage conducive to larger disequilibria. They will eventually realize that the economy is moving too far away from an equilibrium path; their action may facilitate the movement of the economy towards an evolution close to equilibrium. Still, the equilibrium path is likely to be different from the one that initially could be potentially conceived. One way or another, reference to equilibrium path does not prove sufficient to assess the efficiency of the overall evolution.

16. INSTABILITY OF MERE ADAPTIVE SYSTEMS

By assuming different kinds of reaction to disequilibria, it can be demonstrated that the Harrodian process of warranted growth may prove to be stable. That is the case if firms' investment depends not only on the rate of growth of income (demand) but also on the difference between required and available capital. Other temporal relations (lags between increase in income and increase in demand) may lead to business cycle patterns of development. Stability is possible either because of some kind of inertia, or because of certain capacities in forecasting the future which are reflected in some investment functions. Evolution of a mere adaptive system is intrinsically unstable.

This is due to the fact that a mere adaptive system has no internal direction of movement. We can only define, on the basis of its structure, adjustment to external changes. However, adjustments change continuously because the external events requiring adjustments do not occur according to laws that make expectations possible and because, as a consequence, the normal structure to which adjustments ought to *adapt* the system changes. In the following section, by considering many-sectors systems, we shall further clarify what we have just stated. Let us by now recall the observation we made on pages 11-12 about the impossibility that in a game a player will forecast correctly the rival's strategy and *at the same time* act in such a way as to arrive at a Nash solution of the game.

The Harrod-Domar model has been restated in neoclassical terms. An essential feature of neoclassical theories is the assumption that a firm can choose among different techniques of production. If the production function, establishing a relation between output and the quantities of the two factors (capital and labour), is homogeneous of the first degree (as is the well known Cobb-Douglas function), then the capital input can be so adjusted as to be equal to that value of the *output-capital ratio* that, given *the propensity to save*, entails a rate of growth of income equal to the natural rate of growth. (Because of the linear homogeneity assumption, all income is divided into wages and profits.)

As Hahn and Matthews (1965) have observed, the standpoint of the model is reversed, as compared with Harrod's. Harrod is faithful to Keynes in maintaining that the driving force of the economy is demand. Should the spontaneous increase be insufficient, proper monetary and fiscal policies are required. Neoclassical theory makes demand depend on supply: the increase in labour supply causes changes that result in increased supply. If two economies differ because of a different propensity to save, the production function and the population rate of growth being the same, income will expand at the same rate, the difference being a higher capital per man and a higher output per man in the economy having a higher propensity to save.

Investments depend on capital rentability, savings on the rate of interest which in equilibrium should be equal to capital rentability. How can this equality be established? We must distinguish between the rate of interest on capital from the monetary rate of interest in terms of the commodity produced. As Tobin (1955) has remarked, savings can be channelled into a store of value, alternative to real capital, represented by treasury bonds. By adapting the state deficit, changes in the monetary rate of interest are produced, eventually also through changes in the price level, so that equality with the rentability of capital is obtained, savings being equal to investments.

Changes in technology and in savings and investments are unlikely to occur at the right time and at such a level as to assure that the economy will be brought to a full employment equilibrium. Changes in productive structures are gradual as has been shown by vintage models. Investments are more sensitive to changes in expectations. Because of the increased complexity of the financial system, the relation between rate of interest and investments is not so simple as is assumed in neoclassical models. The most relevant theoretical problem is not finding out a structural adjustment that can bring the economy to a point equilibrium, but analysing the stability of a growth path.

The problem of stability for neoclassical models has been faced by Solow, who has shown that any equilibrium path will approach a steady state asymptotically. In fact, what has been proved is the existence of a steady growth path. Since labour increases at a given rate, the production function being linear, capital and product must also increase at the same rate. Cozzi (1966) has faced the problem in dynamic terms (as was done for general equilibrium models by Samuelson in 1948): namely he has analysed processes of adjustment by which from a disturbed steady state we can pass on to another steady state.

17. THE DYNAMICS OF MANY-SECTORS ECONOMIES

In most of the models exploring possible evolution, a unique commodity is considered, being used both as consumption and capital goods. When this assumption is dropped and a many-sectors economy is considered, certain difficulties arise. We shall only mention those that are relevant for our analysis in the following chapters.

In a fundamental contribution, Hahn (1966) has proved that in a two-sector economy the momentary equilibrium is not unique. The problem has been re-examined by P. Samuelson (1967) who has proved that, if the assumption of a unique commodity is dropped, the unique savings rate assumption for both wages and profits being maintained, the golden-age equilibrium is unique and globally stable provided the consumption industry is relatively capital intensive;

> when the consumption-good industry is relatively labour intensive (and particularly when both industries have very low elasticities of substitution...), there may exist two or even an infinity of equilibria, none being globally stable and some being locally unstable. (p. 221)

Hahn's contribution has clarified two important shortcomings in the equilibrium dynamics models. 1) If we assume heterogeneous capital goods, the problem of non uniqueness of the momentary equilibrium is more serious. Such a conclusion

> is largely ascribable to the fact that neoclassical growth models do not incorporate any explicit investment functions. The conditions that the holding of all asset should be equally profitable ... does not determine how much of each assets should be produced. It is thus possible that a given volume of savings may find a widely different allocation between the different kinds of investment at different price constellations, which are compatible with equilibrium. When there is only one capital good and we are concerned with full employment equilibrium path, an investment function is not only unnecessary but may actually prevent the system having a solution.

2) Even in the two-capital case, when 'a single equilibrium path is found, there is a wide class of initial conditions and value of the parameters for which such equilibrium path does not approach the balanced growth path'. The second shortcoming is linked to the necessary role of expectations of future prices of capital goods.

> But, not surprisingly, there is only a restricted set of expectations for every given situation which are consistent with an evolution of the system towards the balanced growth path. Once again the supposition that expectations are not only correct but consequently that they are identical for all economic agents is a hard postulate to swallow, and undoubtedly makes equilibrium dynamics less attractive once we admit that there are hoes as well as shovels. (pp. 644-6)

We have already mentioned the problem of expectations. As for the investment function, Hahn is right in doubting that an investment function can be defined *by* the neoclassical paradigm of the competitive market. That is implied in our remark that a mere adaptive system is intrinsically unstable because there are no internal forces that can push the system along an evolutionary path. The investment function required cannot be conceived in the context of the neoclassical competitive paradigm. We must make some specific assumption, such as the one we shall make in the Schumpeterian model presented in Chapter 6.

18. SCHUMPETERIAN INNOVATIONS AND DEVELOPMENT

It is impossible to conceive equilibrium as a point of gravitation to which the system is attracted in the long run, because innovations continuously tend to change potential structures of the economy. They do not alter productive processes only: product innovations, which are scarcely detachable from process innovations, entail potential changes in the consumers' preference fields. These changes are exploited by firms through their sales promotion activities.

Schumpeter takes up the classical view of the pre-eminent role of entrepreneurs. Their strategies, rather than consumers' needs, orient the evolution of the economy. Competition is no longer conceived as a control mechanism conducing firms to utilize in the most efficient way available resources to satisfy given consumers' needs, but rather as the result of a darwinistically oriented process. Market economies reveal their superiority more in the *arena* offered to potential entrepreneurs, than in the adjustment process that market mechanisms induce, leading to a static efficiency.

In fact, the Schumpterian process of development has peculiar features:

1. The role of entrepreneurs is different from the neoclassical. Both in static models and in models of endogenous growth, entrepreneurs are assumed to strive to reduce costs and to increase revenue, by choosing either the most efficient technique of production among those available or a time strategy to foster economic progress along lines that can be assessed. In the Schumpeterian analysis of development, entrepreneurs strive for power. Profits are both a by-product of the search for power through technology and product innovations and an objective, inasmuch as they help implement the development strategy. The decision to innovate is not an option among well-defined alternatives. It is the result of the entrepreneur's propensity to change the context in which he makes his choices. The result is not

independent from a set of information the entrepreneur will obtain, nor from his past experiences. Moreover, it involves a set of consequences that can be fully visualized only after their occurrence. Even imitation does not result merely from objective data; it reflects agents' propensities and past experiences.
2. Economic development requires a different role of credit. Banks are not mere intermediaries between savers and investors; they can *promote* development by making funds available to entrepreneurs wanting them to implement development plans, in the absence of personal resources obtained through accumulation. Wicksell has already outlined the positive role of credit in spurring expansion; that was possible because of the role of wholesalers. Wicksell's theory has been utilized to develop the monetary theory of trade cycle (Hayek). In Schumpeter's view, the role of credit allows us to regard savings not as the prerequisite for growth, but as the result of growth that is produced by innovations causing profits to increase and making it possible for entrepreneurs to repay their bank debts. Such a position shows some similarities with that of Keynes. For Keynes too, savings stem from growth. In fact growth ⁻ which in Keynes' vocabulary is equivalent to expansion of demand in order to arrive at the full employment of labour ⁻ is induced by investments, savings being the by-product of the increase in income. In the Schumpeter theory, credit has a direct impact on development because it is an essential ingredient of the innovation processes. However, credit is by itself a multi-faced phenomenon. It is linked with macroeconomic policy. This is the most familiar facet. It is a disequilibrating factor, too, since it affects speculation activities through its feedback effects, and enables expectations to be realized regardless of their objective foundations. It is an equilibrating mechanism: such a property connects credit policy with macroeconomic policy.
3. The economic development of a particular country has to be considered as historical process: even the adjustment processes associated with economic development can be inferred only from concrete historical experience. However, the relationship between finance, innovation and development can be clarified by exploring what economic growth paths are possible.
4. The neoclassical paradigm hinges on the notion of equilibrium. As it has been reminded in section 7, most economists are convinced that in the short run equilibrium is unlikely to occur, whereas in the long run, in some way or another, the economy has to settle in an equilibrium position (or along an equilibrium path). The Schumpeterian lesson leads us to reverse such a view. The concept of equilibrium may be of some use in the analysis of short-run phenomena, for the purpose of framing certain economic policy problems. In the long-run, equilibrium is impossible because of the nature of economic development (Iwai 1984a).

5. If the Schumpeterian process of development is taken into account, it is difficult to assess the efficiency of the economy. We can lessen our claim by trying to envisage positive and negative effects in order to arrive at some kind of assessment of oligopolistic competition produced by innovations that it contributes to foster. In fact, certain wastes ineherent in the competitive mechanism producing innovations have been pointed out: duplication of R&D expenditures, excess of expenditures in sales promotion (expenses for advertising are in most countries larger than expenses for education). Moreover we can determine how far, by changing the mechanism through appropriate devices, external economies can be increased and R&D strategy made more efficient. However it is not possible to make an overall assessment of research activity with respect to the efficiency of the economy. Duplication of expenditure, for instance, may be the cost to be paid for the competitive context, the lack of which would sharply decrease the innovation potential. What we can do is to try to compare different possible scenarios which correspond to different structural institutional and economic policies. Attempts have been made to assess the efficiency of innovations, after the usual criteria.[12] Unfortunately, when Schumpeterian processes are considered, we cannot apply Paretian or similar criteria, since innovations affect not only the structure of the economy but also its growth prospects. It is not easy to assess to what extent structural inefficiencies can be more than offset by the positive effects on growth. In fact, evolution also changes the attitude of the agents. Moreover, we must remember that assessment of structural efficiency is made by referring to individual tastes (or, in welfare economics, to a social welfare function). Unfortunately, in the Schumpeterian process of development tastes cannot be considered exogenous.
6. Innovations have spillover effects which represent external economies, difficult to single out. The representation of such external effects, made in models of endogenous growth (see Chapters 3 and 4), is inadequate. Let us confine ourselves to noting the problem of time distribution and localisation of such externalities. Schumpeter has raised the problem by his concept of cluster of innovations. In fact innovations will cause discontinuities in the process of growth.[13]

In Schumpeter's analysis of evolution, all ideas of progress fade away. His position is akin to that of Hayek, with one difference. In Hayek's concept, evolution cannot be controlled through global plans: market mechanism is capable of maintaining an *order*, being the most efficient. In Schumpeter's there is no potential permanent order that can be maintained. Interactions between social and economic phenomena can cause capitalistic market economy to collapse. The problem with efficiency of the social and economic system is that the productive role of entrepreneurs, which in certain conditions can better be assured by a socialist system, must be maintained.

19. GROWTH AND MARKET FORMS

Most of the growth models assume that competition is a prerequisite for optimal growth. As we have just seen, in the Schumpeterian viewpoint, we cannot associate efficiency with competition, at least with competition of the neoclassical type. In fact, even in the traditional contexts the statement that competition entails maximum efficiency has been challenged. Smith himself has recognized that in some cases expectations of monopoly power may encourage innovations.

In Schumpter's thought, innovation is largely associated with large firms. In fact, for Schumpeter, the most favourable context for innovation is oligopolistic competition, or to use his term, *industry monopolistically competitive* (Schumpeter 1934b, p. 312). Innovation is an essential ingredient of this type of competition. As he has remarked (Schumpeter 1942, pp. 84-5) 'in capitalist reality as distinguished from its textbook picture, it is not [price] competition which counts but the competition from the new commodities, the new technology, the new source of supply'.

Several industries have been characterized at the beginning by a kind of competition resembling the textbook concept (Schumpeter has recalled the cases of the car and rayon industries): the result of competition was not to maintain the text-book competition, nor to convert it into a market of monopolistic competition, but to create conditions for competitive oligopoly. In fact, large firms may be capable of realizing more efficient organization. It is mostly for these reasons that 'mergers must ... be listed among the innovations...' (Schumpeter 1934b p. 251).

Schumpeter was well aware that concentration of production in few firms may have some drawbacks. 'Once formed', Schumpeter (1934b, p. 251) remarks, 'the giants in some cases threatened the life of outsiders - both new and old - also in other ways than by their technological commercial superiority'. He recognizes also that small firms may, in some cases, have a technological commercial superiority. Moreover, small firms may enjoy a market power thanks to the protection of laws or trade associations.

On the contrary, large firms do not always enjoy a monopoly position. As the theory of contestable markets asserts, big firms may be constrained to operate according to the rule of competition. Indeed, the notion of monopoly loses its sharpness in Schumpeterian analysis. We can think of two opposite kinds of monopolies. The first enjoys a market power because of the obstacles to entry that cannot be nullified by innovation that is in fact discouraged. The second keeps its market power because of innovation: that happens because (and when) success breeds success. However, it need not always be so. Innovation may allow new firms to overcome old firms having a great market power. The process is better interpreted by giving the term competition a meaning different from the neoclassical one. Then, the notion of competition becomes associated with that of selection and evolution, as we shall see in Chapter 6.

Having said so much, we can note that Schumpeter was convinced that if we refer to all possible innovations large firms appear to be superior.

Indeed we can say, after Schumpeter, that the inefficiencies that monopolistic markets entail in the allocation of given resources, may be more than offset by the higher rate of growth induced by larger innovation activities. In fact, if innovations are considered, we cannot refer to competition as the necessary context to assess the efficiency of the economy. As Schumpeter (1942, p. 106) has pointed out '... in this respect, perfect competition is not only impossible but inferior, and has no little to be set up as a model of ideal efficiency'.

Let us list the possible reason why large firms show superiority in implementing innovations:

1. Large firms, to the extent that they enjoy larger profits, may be in condition to finance a high level of R&D. Research activity may show increasing returns due to specialization. Large firms may then be able to implement a relatively larger number of innovations.
2. Most research activity is risky. We could better say that it is highly uncertain. Uncertainty may be reduced if the activity is carried on on a larger scale and can thus be more diversified. The possible failure of some research programmes may be offset by the success of others. Moreover, risky strategies are unlikely to be implemented with capital borrowed by banks. Only if corporate savings are sufficiently large will such strategies be considered.
3. Some research activities may produce results possibly affecting a variety of commodities and of processes of production. A large firm that covers all the sectors that could benefit from R&D will be able to exploit all its results: a small firm would instead not be able to carry out all possible applications of R&D; nor would it be able to sell any results that it cannot exploit on the market. In fact, this kind of market is lacking, or, when it does exist, transaction costs are such as to reduce benefits for the firm buying the yield of the small firm's research activity.
4. The result of research activity may be new products. For these to be profitably sold, an extensive promotion activity is needed. Only large firms can engage in such an activity, being characterized by large economies of scale.

5. The large firm is in a better position to attract 'superior brains' and to develop a learning-by-doing process.[14]

So far we have considered the innovation potential of large firms. Will large firms be interested in fully exploiting such potentiality? There is a problem, which we shall only briefly mention, that arises when the same potential innovations are open to different oligopolistic firms, namely which potential innovations will be implemented and when depends on the strategy adopted (and therefore on the game played by the firms). The strategies do not reflect mere evaluation of prospective costs and revenues; they reflect also the aggressiveness of the entrepreneur and the optimism or pessimism affecting his expectations. Some interesting remarks can be made even if we disregard the complications of oligopolistic interdependences. We shall dwell on three problems concerning the big firms' behaviour.

1. As Arrow (1962) has shown, profits to be expected due to a change in costs may be smaller if the firm enjoys a monopoly power before the innovation. As has been pointed out in Lombardini (1971) monopolies may have opposite attitudes towards innovation. The state policy may offer large firms a less risky alternative than looking for and implementing innovations, whereas international competition may encourage attitudes favourable to innovation. Innovations are more likely to occur in market situations characterized by entry barriers neither too high nor too low.
2. When we think of large firms it is not easy to associate any well-identified persons with the Schumpeterian term of *entrepreneur*. Entrepreneurial functions are carried on by the management. In some cases, in the managerial structure, a person plays the role of the Schumpeterian entrepreneur, in some others the staff of researchers contribute substantially to the orientation and implementation of research activity. The most favourable conditions occur when a Schumpeterian entrepreneur, say the President or the General Manager, supports a cooperative staff of well organized researchers and is in turn supported by them. Neil Kay (1988 pp. 287-90) has analysed the implications of Williamson's organizational scheme comparing the U-form (unique firm) with the M-form (multi-divisional firm) on research activity.
3. One usually thinks that firms enjoying the most favourable market conditions are those most engaged in seeking and implementing innovations. In many cases this is true: success breeds success. But it is not always so. Sometimes the firms that, because of their market power, make higher profits are less motivated to engage in a substantial R&D activity. On the contrary, those that run the risk of being thrown out by some powerful rivals, may consider research activities as the only means of holding on successfully.

Though large firms have a specific potential for innovations, small firms may contribute to certain kinds of innovations more substantially than large firms can. We must distinguish between innovations requiring large investments, the orientation of which can be established in advance, and those benefiting from the experience and creative capacity that people possess in different degrees. In a competitive market with a large number of entrepreneurs - namely in markets close to the neoclassical model of competition, where firms are small firms - the probability that innovations of the latter kind be implemented will be higher than in oligopolistic markets. In fact, in some industries innovations (in products: think of product design) may be the only way small firms are able to face the power of larger firms.

The large firms may also eventually benefit from the small firms' innovations. Some small firms are born out of innovations carried out by single individuals. However they are not equipped to pursue the R&D activity that is required to assure a possibly continuous flow of innovations. The large firm may be able to take over the small firms and thus enlarge the scope of their research activity.

20. GROWTH AND INCOME DISTRIBUTION

Income distribution is not neutral with respect to growth. In Ricardo's view, evolution is characterized by increases in population associated with rent increases curbing growth. As we have already noted, if technical progress occurs, there is nothing can we say *ex ante* on the relation between growth and income distribution. That emerges from both Smith's and Schumpeter's analysis. Acceleration of growth is likely to be accompanied by increases in profits.

In von Neumann's and Sraffa models - where a unique technology is assumed to exist or a set of intertemporal technologies are assumed from which the most efficient (yielding the highest rate of growth) is chosen - a negative correlation can be established between wages and rate of growth.

Income distribution affects the equilibrium path of growth: it is relevant also in the transitory phase. In fact the process of adjustment bringing the economy along an equilibrium path of growth is linked to changes in income distribution. If there is unemployment, wages decrease. Two are the relevant consequences that are alternatively considered. According to Keynesians, it is a change in the propensity to save (workers have a lower propensity to save) that makes possible, through a higher accumulation, an increase in the rate of growth. In neoclassical analysis, adjustment is induced by the decrease in wages because it makes the more labour intensive techniques more convenient.

As we shall see (Chapters 3 and 4), in models of endogenous growth the shares of income accruing to workers and capitalists are relevant in assessing the effect of human capital accumulation and technological accumulation.

21. IS THERE A TRUE THEORY OF ECONOMIC EVOLUTION?

We have recalled various theories offering different explanation of the processes of economic growth and development. Can we sort the true theory out of them? The answer is no. A theory is characterized both by the specific definition of the economic system and the choice of tools and methods by which to analyse it. All definitions of the system are partial and every tool (or method) is efficient in bringing to light certain specific synchronic and diachronic properties of the system.

In natural sciences current theories appear to have replaced the old theories. That, in fact, is not always true.[15] However, in physics attempts to integrate the results of various research into more general and coherent theories are mostly successful. If we look at the history of natural sciences, we note that theories have been rebuilt on different elementary concepts (think of the evolution of the notion of energy and mass; of the discovery of new elementary units in physics of particles; of the new relevance of the notion of *information* that may replace other elementary notions).[16] In economics, what is considered exceptional in the natural sciences seems to be the norm.[17] Thus it is not surprising to note that we can have different theories and different formulations of the same *general* theory. It is for this reason that theories in economics are only *tools* - as Joan Robinson has remarked - to be used in order to understand real processes and to solve specific problems, and that the use of facts (and preliminarily the *invention* of facts) is not so simple as Popper assumes.

In science all theories refer to an ideal system. That raises specific problems for economics. We have reflected on logical and practical difficulties to be faced when defining rationality and building equilibrium models. However, equilibrium models may help us in the analysis of real processes by clarifying certain structural relations. In Chapter 4 we shall study evolution by means of a model of endogenous growth; in Chapters 5 and 6 we shall deal with the same topic by means of Schumpeterian models. The different approaches will enable us to understand some fundamental properties of economic development. If the equilibrium approach raises the problems we have hinted at in this Chapter, the disequilibrium approach has some disadvantages: the most relevant of these being the arbitrary nature of some of the assumptions on which the disequilibrium model has to be based.

NOTES

1. The theory of value being determined by the labour required to produce commodities has been proposed by Smith, though only for non progressive economies.
2. Suffice it to recall Goodwin (1990).
3. That has been done by Frish (1933) to make the Cournot duopoly model more reasonable.
4. As we shall see in Chapter 6 (section 29), a Schumpeterian process may eventually lead the economy to move along a partial-equilibrium steady path.
5. In the sense that a more complex system can be conceived which allows us to consider endogenous some variables that are assumed as exogenous and/or because some phenomena that are analysed by sociologists can have effects on the structural relations of the model.
6. Suffice it to recall the external economies that are created by the localization of certain infrastructure and of certain activities (services in particular) in an area.
7. In a different framework, the same relations have been explored by Sraffa (1960).
8. Rational expectations have been opposed to adaptive expectations.
9. On the basis of direct experiments, the unbiasedness property has been refuted.
10. Ricardian theory of rent was certainly more useful in explaining the effect of the oil crisis than the Schumpeterian theory of development, which is instead more useful for an understanding of what wnt on in the United States during the 1920s.
11. As asserted by Arthur in Waldrop's quotation:
    '... if it is an off-situation that's never going to happen again, or if the situation is very complicated, so that your agents have to do an awful lot of computing, then you're asking for a hell of a lot. Because you are asking them to have knowledge of their own expectations, of the dynamics of the market, of other people's expectations, of other people's expectations *about* other people's expectations, et cetera. And pretty soon, economics is loading almost impossible conditions onto these hapless agents' (Waldrop 1992, p. 271).
12. See, for instance, Loury (1979) and P. Dasgupta and J. Stiglitz (1986).
13. According to Scott (1989), on a macroeconomic level the process of innovation, closely associated with accumulation, can be considered continuous. However, if we want to understand the *historical evolution* of economies, discontinuities have to be taken into account.
14. See Lombardini (1953, p. 192-194).
15. Darwin's theory of evolution appeared to have replaced Lamark's theory. However, some modern theories of evolution have partially resumed certain Lamarkian theses.
16. See G. Bachelard (1983).
17. The reasons are various: peculiar interactions between scientist and the field investigated; the greater complexity of the system to be analysed; historical evolution that changes the relevance of the elements and relations by which the system can be defined.

2. The Agents

1. THE AGENTS

The agents in the process of growth are: consumers-workers, firms (entrepreneurs) and the state. State action is always relevant, even in those countries that are considered 'models' of the free market economy. In the United States, the demand for major commodities comes to a large extent from public administrations. In all countries, the state plays important roles both in education and research. However, in the models we shall be considering, attention will be concentrated on two agents: consumers-workers and firms. When necessary, we shall mention the relations between their actions and state policies.

Utility functions are considered essential tools to explain consumers' behaviour. They are certainly useful in models aiming at both describing growth along equilibrium paths and envisaging optimal growth. However, in the analysis of some processes of development - for instance, of the Schumpeterian type - utility functions can scarcely be employed. Even in cases when utility functions are useful tools, we must be aware of their specific formalization and of the specific problems that can be grasped by that means.

Firm's choices are conditioned by resources available and by technologies. In neoclassical models a set of technologies, among which the firm can choose the most convenient given the prices of production factors is assumed to be available. The set can be expressed by a production function. There are reasons to believe that technological knowledge is not homogeneous: that technologies that have not yet been implemented cannot be considered alternative to those that have been already applied. Choices of techniques are conditioned by past decisions (vintage models) and by learning processes. Learning processes intertwine with innovations: that makes the concept of production function useless. However, in models of endogenous growth, production functions can be applied to assess the effect of investments in human and in technological capitals.

2. PREFERENCES AND UTILITY

As we have noted in the previous chapter, economic models can be used to describe economic evolution as well as to identify optimal paths of growth. By introducing proper concepts of *utility to be maximized*, the two objectives are pursued at the same time.

The concept of utility has been introduced to determine the change in consumers' demand for various commodities induced by changes in their price and/or in consumers' income. The underlying assumption is that the market behaviour of all consumers is uniquely determined by their preferences which entail an ordered field of all possible combinations for the various commodities. A utility function can be associated with such an ordered field of preferences.[1] We can say that consumers' choices depend on their *tastes* right at the moment their choices are made. Pareto was well aware that *ophelimity* changes in time.

Paretian utility does not reflect only *current tastes*: thus, it can differ from ophelimity. To some extent tastes can be assumed to be inherited from the past and/or to depend on past experiences. Such a dependence may reflect *consolidation of consumption habits* (Duesenberry 1949) or *learning by consuming* (Lombardini, 1957, pp. 125-30). In the latter case the consumer's field of preference may be *structurally unstable*; in the former some *inertia* may make the utility function less precarious.

There is another reason that can explain *inertia* in consumers' behaviour. In most applications of the utility function approach, one assumes that adjustment to external changes (mostly changes in prices and income), can occur instantaneously and continuously. However, if we accept the Weber-Fechner theory of the minimum threshold, only discrete changes in prices of certain amounts can produce changes in consumption patterns.

Tastes reflect also consumers' expectations. They are to a large extent subjective; however they are constrained also by objective factors. Expectations of young people are different from those of the old. The Modigliani consumption function (Modigliani and Brumberg, 1954) has been formalized by considering both initial conditions and the normal pattern of expectations for people having the same life horizon.

The concept of utility (and the logically prior one of ordered field of preferences) is a theoretical concept that enables us to build an axiomatic system from which to derive *meaningful theorems* in Samuelson's sense (Samuelson, 1948, pp. 3-5). Utility has been given an empirical flavour, in the last century, by an Italian mathematician (Antonelli, 1886) and, more recently, by Samuelson (1938): they have proposed to build the utility function on observable individual choices occurring with different sets of prices. Two conditions must be satisfied: 1) needs (or consumer tastes) must remain unchanged during the experiment (which can be conceived merely as a logical experiment just designed to offer an empirical flavour to the notion of utility); 2) the results of the choices which express the gradient of the function must satisfy integration conditions.

A few remarks on the empirical relevance of theoretical concepts may help us to better understand the method we shall apply in our research; in particular the role of certain concepts as that of utility which has been just mentioned. I think that any association of empirical concepts to theoretical ones is not so simple an operation as is usually thought. Bridgman's opinion that concepts have to be defined in terms of measuring operations (physical operations if it is a physical concept, mental operations if it is mental) is not acceptable not only for the reason which has been already pointed out by Einstein,[2] but also because there are theoretical concepts that can be given different interpretations and yet are utilized to explain the same sets of facts.

In economics we must distinguish abstract theories aimed at interpreting rather than explaining real phenomena. With regard to them operationism is disputable. The neo-classical theory of consumption may be conceived as an axiomatic system by which we can *interpret* consumers' demand for the various commodities, which changes when income and relative prices change. In fact, the concept of utility plays the role of the *primitive terms* in axiomatic theories aimed at envisaging not stylized reproduction of concrete processes, but ideal interpretation. If the marginalistic theory of consumption is conceived as *describing* a process through which consumers arrive at their decisions, then the problem of *computability*, which is reminiscent of operationism, becomes relevant. Then, as Velupillai (1994) has shown,

(α) There is *no effective procedure* (in the strict sense of classical recursion theory) to generate preference orderings; (β) Given the class of decision rules (choice function) that do generate preference orderings for any agent, there is *no effective procedure to decide* whether an arbitrary decision rule is a member of that class or not.

3. UTILITY: VARIABILITY AND INTERDEPENDENCES

Let us list the more relevant reasons accounting for variability of the utility function:

1. *learning by consuming,*
2. *changes in other individuals choices* (which become relevant as soon as we drop the assumption of independence of utility functions),
3. *government choices concerning social services.* In fact there are substitutions as well as complementary relations between private consumption and social consumption,

4. *changes in individuals' level of aspiration* (Lombardini 1957, pp. 120-21). The level of aspiration changes as income changes,
5. *product innovations*,
6. *sales promotion activity by firms*,
7. *education and information*.

The neoclassical utility function is based on the assumption that the utility of any individual is independent from those of others. Such an assumption has been disputed. It disregards certain social phenomena such as imitation, keeping-up-with-the-Joneses, snobbish attitudes, envy, philanthropy.

Interdependence between individual welfares may occur also because of consumption externalities pointed out by Baumol

> a consumer may in the process of consumption do a service or disservice to other consumers for which he receives no compensation. Hence he may be led to adjust his consumption, i.e. to allocate the resources at his command, in some manner other than that calculated to result in maximum efficiency in satisfaction of the desires of the body of consumers as a whole. (Baumol 1952, p. 88)

There is a difference between externalities in production and externalities in consumption. Externalities in production can be easily assessed: if a firm producing flowers, by increasing its activity, causes an increase in the productivity of another firm next to it that produces honey, the external effect is positive; in fact we can evaluate it in money terms. If a large number of consumers, by increasing their demand for cars, make cars more useful for other consumers, it is not easy to say whether the external effect is positive or negative.

Individual tastes depend on decisions about public goods and social services, for two reasons: a) changes in the social cultural system occur because of both the interdependence between individuals' preferences and the feedback that decisions about social services may have on individuals' tastes; b) if resources are used for social services, less of them will be available for private consumption.

If we consider such interrelations, identification of rational behaviour with maximization of individual utility functions is questionable: in fact it implies a specific anthropological concept that allows for a simple paradigm akin to that of celestial mechanics.

As we have already mentioned in Chapter 1, two activities are meant to produce changes in individuals' tastes: product innovations and differentiation, and sales promotion activities. The concept of consumer utility needs to be thought out over again.

According to Pareto, by assuming an instantaneous utility function (in his terminology an *ophelimity function*), we compact all relevant inputs that the economic system receives from the social-cultural one by the notion of *consumers' tastes*. However, if we consider the factors accounting for the variability of tastes over time, we can easily note two-ways relations between economic and social-cultural systems. Because of the interdependence between consumers' tastes and the feedback effects of social choices concerning public goods, changes in income distribution cause changes in the *relevant tastes*. Certain social services (education and information) have conspicuous effects on individuals' preferences. Economic growth causes changes in tastes because of changes in the level of aspiration.

4. SHORT-RUN AND LONG-RUN UTILITY FUNCTION

Pareto has opposed the notion of utility to that of ophelimity. Ophelimity reflects individuals' tastes resulting from their *objective* choices on the market: therefore it is a non-questionable fact. We can speak of utility: to do so we must assume 'as a distinctive criterion the material welfare and the scientific and moral progress on which a sufficiently general agreement is achieved by men of civil nations' (Pareto 1896, 1, p. 13). We can distinguish between economic utility and moral utility. Utility can be referred to an individual or a community; it may be direct or indirect utility (indirect inasmuch as individuals and communities are part of larger organizations). In talking about utility, we cannot disregard relations between various individuals (Pareto, 1964, vol II, p. 571). That is why, according to Pareto, ophelimity can be considered a kind of subjective utility. Economics is concerned with ophelimity inasmuch as 'the science of ophelimity is the only one which has reached results with a degree of precision and of certainty similar to that of natural sciences ...' (Pareto 1896, 1, p. 14).

Individual utility, according to Pareto's concept, may have two different interpretations: 1) It may concern the actual advantage for him of certain choices; then the question of who can assess such an advantage arises; 2) It may mean the individual's *ophelimity* in conditions of sufficient information, the individual being sufficiently qualified through education to evaluate the various alternatives. The second interpretation avoids the terrible question of who has the right and the duty to assess individual tastes, but raises the one of how to deal with the relations between social choices (concerning, for instance, education) and evolution of individual tastes.

An alternative approach can be based on the assumption of a short-run and a long-run utility function. The short run reflects individuals' moods and current wants,[3] the long run individuals' basic opinions and stable needs. The short-run utility function is both precarious and variable, whereas the long-run one is more structurally stable in time. We could be tempted to infer the long-run utility function by analysing individuals' behaviour over an adequate period of time. However, because of the variability of individuals' tastes, what we would obtain is not a *utility function at a specific date*.

5. MEASURABLE UTILITY

Various arguments have been put forth to support the view that utility is measurable, in the sense that temperature is ⁻ namely, that the consumer is capable of comparing changes in utility at different periods of time so as to assess whether the *increase* in utility at time t_2 is larger or smaller than the associated change at time t_1. If the notion of utility is extended to analyse choices in uncertain environment, the Morgenstern–von Neumann assumptions restated by Marschack (1950), lead to a measurable utility function.

In the neoclassical utility function, the independent variables represent certain quantities of well-defined commodities. Let us now consider *uncertain prospects*, namely sets of various outcomes having different probabilities, the sum of the probability of the outcome of the same set being 1. Can we associate to an uncertain prospect o_i ($i = 1, ..., n$) a certain one having the same utility? The answer to the question has been given by Bernoulli who has suggested that the *moral expectation* should be considered as the certain equivalent alternative:

$$U(o) = \sum_{i}^{n} p_i o_i \qquad (2.1)$$

where p_i is the probability of outcome o_i.

The events entering into the uncertain prospect are the outcomes of a set of actions. Let us relate *actions* to *outcomes*: $A ¤ \to o_j$ being the association of event A with outcome o_j (this is counterfactual since the statement is true both if o_j is a necessary condition of a and if o_j holds regardless of whether a does). In terms of actions we can provide two concepts of expected utility. The first:

$$U_1(A) = \sum_{j}^{n} p(A ¤ \to o_j) \cdot U(o_j) \qquad (2.2)$$

The second, akin to the traditional moral expectation:

$$U_2(A) = \sum_{j}^{n} p(o_j/A) \cdot U(o_j) \qquad (2.3)$$

The first expresses the assessment of the efficiency of an action capable of producing useful results (outcomes): the expected value of the outcomes of a given action A. The second measures the welcomeness of the news that one is about to perform A.[4]

The reason why utility becomes measurable when we turn from choices between different outcomes represented by certain quantities of well-defined commodities to choices between uncertain prospects is due to the fact that in the latter case what is involved is not only the preferences of the individual for the various commodities but also his probability assessment and, eventually, his attitude towards risk.

6. UTILITY OVER TIME

The neoclassical notion of utility is supposed to explain the individual's actions at a given moment of time. These actions can be correlated to actions the individual expects to perform in the future and to expectations of future events. Therefore in the utility functions the arguments can be bundles of commodities available in future periods. Among the constraints of optimization expectations can come in too.

From the solution of the optimization problem we cannot derive the *evolution* of consumption but a *consumption plan* aimed at maximizing consumer's utility *at a given moment of time*. As Hayek has pointed out, the utility attached to a bundle of goods available in the future is not the utility that an observer is likely to expect the consumer will attach to such a bundle at the time it will be available, but the utility the consumer himself attaches *now* to the prospect of obtaining the bundle at the predetermined time. If there are future markets in which the agents' decision of buying commodities in future periods can be confronted with other agents' decision of selling the same commodities in the same periods, then the agents' plans can be made compatible with one another. Temporary equilibrium in the Hayek sense can thus be defined.

Such an equilibrium can envisage the future evolution provided no change occurs in technology and consumers' tastes and the horizon of the plan coincides with the end of the world. Since the latter assumption is unacceptable, final stocks of the various commodities need to be considered in assessing the utility of the evolution of the economy for the consumer. Then optimization depends on the final stocks, which are justified because the individual expects to consume in future periods beyond the horizon of the plan. For optimization to be complete we must shift the horizon to infinity.

Ramsey was well aware of that difficulty when he made the assumption that:

our community goes on for ever without changing either in numbers or in its capacity for enjoyment or in its aversion to labour; that enjoyments and sacrifices at different times can be calculated independently and added; and that no new inventions or improvements in organization are introduced save such as can be regarded as conditioned solely by the accumulation of wealth. (1928, p. 543)

Moreover, as we shall see, Ramsey assumes that there is a *maximum conceivable rate of enjoyment*. Growth can be induced by consumers aiming at reaching high levels of enjoyment, that being possible because of the effects of accumulation.

Alternatively we can assume that there is no *maximum conceivable rate of enjoyment*; that consumers maximize an intertemporal utility function over an infinite time interval. The utility function must have the usual properties of positive first derivative (marginal utility) and negative second derivative.

In these formalizations, utility of different periods (points of time) are independent from one another and can be added. That entails the assumption that utilities referred to different points (periods) of time are measurable.

We shall dwell a little on a formalization that is largely adopted in the models for endogenous growth. Let $U[c(t)]$ be the utility of c units of the only consumer good that is considered, available at time t. That is not the utility the individual expects for time t, but the utility that he now attaches to the prospect of having c units of commodity at his disposal at time t. The function is such that $U'>0$ and $U''<0$. The consumer will consider the function:

$$U_\tau[c(t)] = \int_0^\tau U[c(t)]dt \qquad (2.4)$$

τ being the consumer's time-horizon. Since at that date consumers do not expect the end of the world, final stocks should enter into the function. We can avoid the problem linked with the final condition by assuming that the function is defined for an infinite horizon.

An alternative is suggested by Montesano (1987, pp. 139-40). We can assume that the terminal time τ is random. Then we can suppose that τ represents the consumer's expected end of life. To make this alternative reasonable we must suppose that the consumer does not care about the conditions of his heirs after his death.

A possible generalization is to consider the utility prospect function depending on time. The consumer can attach different utilities to consumption prospects at different points of time by anticipating changing needs during his life. Then the function to be maximized will be:

$$U_\tau[c(t)] = \int_0^\tau U[c(t),t]dt \qquad (2.5)$$

The Agents

In the models of endogenous growth we shall analyse in Chapters 3 and 4, we shall stick to Solow's approach. We shall assume that there are N consumers all alike and lasting for ever. Think of a population of families having the same structure in terms of number of people, of their age, and of their tastes. When a family disappears a new family appears with the same features. The total number increases at the rate λ.

We shall specifically consider the following *perceived* utility function:

$$U[c(t)] = \frac{1}{1-\sigma}[c(t)^{1-\sigma} - 1] \tag{2.6}$$

σ is generally considered a coefficient of risk aversion. In our deterministic model no risk can arise. Since the perceived utility function (6) has the property that the elasticity of substitution between consumption in time t_1 and t_2 is equal to σ^{-1}, as it can easily be seen [5], we shall consider σ^{-1} as the *intertemporal elasticity of substitution*. It is an index of the easiness for the consumer to substitute consumption at different points of time.

Utility is zero when $c(t)^{1-\sigma} = 1$.

Two values of σ deserve specific attention:

$$\text{for} \quad \sigma = 0 \quad U[c(t)] = c(t) - 1$$

$$\text{for} \quad \sigma = 1 \quad U[c(t)] = \ln c(t) \tag{2.7}$$

$\sigma = 1$ is a watershed: the elasticity of substitution is bigger than 1 when $0 < \sigma < 1$: in this case it is easy for the consumer to substitute future for current consumption; the elasticity is less than 1 when $\sigma > 1$: in this case the consumer's plan is more rigid. As we shall see in Chapters 4 and 5, σ plays an important role in determining the evolution of the economy.

When $\sigma = 0$, the marginal utility is constant; $u = 0$ when $c(t) = 1$. The function is represented by the line l_0: for any value of $c(t)$ utility is higher than for the corresponding value in case of $\sigma \neq 0$. If $\sigma = 1$, the function can be expressed by $\ln c(t)$. u tends to 0, as $c(t)$ tends to $1/1 - \sigma$ (line l_1). If $\sigma > 1$, utility has an upper limit (line l_2). If $\sigma < 1$, the function is represented by the line l_3.

According to Ramsey utility over time cannot increase forever:

> the rate of enjoyment [utility] may never stop increasing as capital increases. There are then two logical possibilities: either the rate of enjoyment will increase to infinity, or it will approach asymptotically to a certain finite limit. The first of these we shall dismiss on the ground that economic causes alone could never give us more than a certain finite rate of enjoyment ... There remains the second case, in which the rate of enjoyment approaches a finite limit, which may or may not be equal to the maximum conceivable rate. (Ramsey 1928–1969, pp. 620–21)

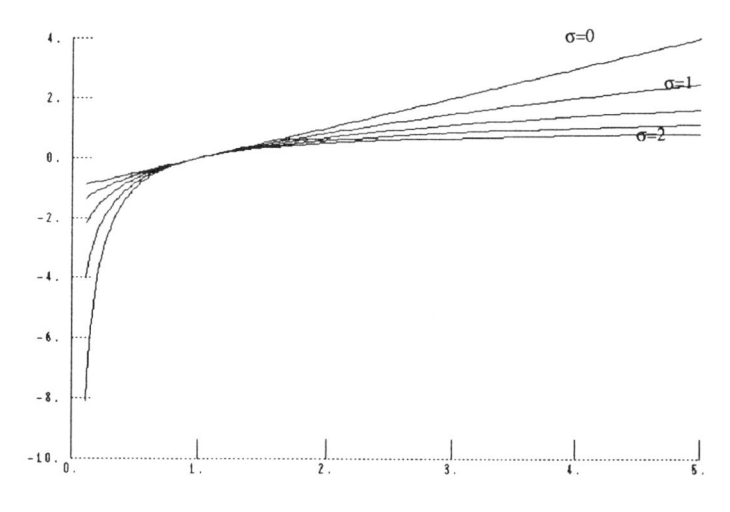

Figure 2.1

In most models of consumers' choices, utility of consumptions at different times are discounted before being added. If the discount rate is ρ, we have the following equation in place of equation (2.4):

$$U = \int_0^\infty e^{-\rho t} c(t) dt \tag{2.8}$$

7. HEREDITY AND UTILITY FUNCTION

In the utility function (8), to be maximized, the time location is relevant only because consumptions in successive points of time are discounted according to the rate ρ. If we assume heredity, we can express the utility function to be maximized:

$$U(c) = \int_0^\infty e^{\phi(t)} dt \tag{2.9}$$

being:

$$\dot{\phi} = u(c) \tag{2.10}$$

That entails:

$$\phi(t) = \phi_0 + \int_0^t u[c(\tau)] d\tau \tag{2.11}$$

Equation (2.8) can alternatively be represented by:

$$U(c) = \int_0^t e^{-\rho t + \ln u(c)} dt \tag{2.11}$$

In the utility function represented by equation 2.8, consumption at time t is independent from consumption in previous periods. The utilities of consumptions in the various periods are added after being discounted: it is with reference to the discounting process that time matters. In the utility function represented by equations 2.9–2.11, in the exponent enters the integral of the utility of consumption up to time t plus a constant term expressing the value of the exponent at time 0.

The reasons why there is some inertia in consumers' behaviour may establish intertemporal links between consumptions at different dates. If an individual having enjoyed an increasing income had been able to increase consumption and acquire certain social habits, his utility would shift upwards.

We can express this assumption by the two relations:

$$U = \int_0^\infty e^{-\rho t} A(t) c(t) dt \tag{2.12.a}$$

$$A(t) = \gamma_u \left\{ \frac{\dot{c}(t)}{c(t)} \right\}^{\sigma_u} \tag{2.12.b}$$

This assumption is in line with Duesenberry's assumption concerning the macroeconomic consumption function.

8. TIME PREFERENCE AND RATE OF INTEREST

The discount rate entering into the utility function covering the consumer's horizon ρ is assumed to express the consumer's intertemporal preferences. Such an approach entails specific assumptions that have been debated. As is well known, the reasons – pointed out by Böhm-Bawerk – that can justify the introduction of a discount coefficient in the summation of utility of consumptions at various points of time are the consumer's greed for current consumption. In Harrod's words, the assumption amounts to assuming that:

> We do not see the future so vividly as the present and underrate the advantage of having money at a future time compared with that of having it now. Professor Pigou has referred to our defective 'telescopic faculty'. Also we may be dead at the future date and not rate the welfare of our heirs as highly as our own. The desire to use the money now is reinforced by animal appetite. Greed may be thought to be as appropriate a name for this

attitude as time preference, though less dignified. Time preference in this sense is a human infirmity, probably stronger in primitive than in civilized man. (Harrod, 1948, pp. 36-7)

Smith took a different view of the subject. According to him, for development to occur, the virtue of *frugality* is required. Such a virtue is considered to be a typical trait of human nature. Weber and Marx added specific reasons for the frugality of those who act as entrepreneurs (cultural factors for Weber, market mechanisms requiring and fostering cultural attitudes for Marx).

We must not confuse the time preference issue with the issue concerning the reasons for a positive rate of interest. These reasons may relate to some properties of the production processes. To use a Samuelson example with reference to Crusue economy:

> If goods kept imperfectly, like ice or radium, Crusue must have to face a negative real interest rate ... If goods were like rabbits or yeast, reproducing without supervision at compound interest, he would have a positive rate of interest. This last case is usually considered to be technologically the most realistic one: that is, machines and roundabout processes (rather than rabbit) are considered to have a 'net productivity', and this is taken to be brute fact. (1958, p. 483)

It may be preferable to think of the process of accumulation as being characterized by innovations and, thus, yielding positive profits. Since - as Schumpeter assumes and we show in Chapter 5 - banks credit plays an essential role in allowing innovation plans to be implemented, interest must be paid by firms to banks and savers.

We must distinguish between monetary and real interest rates. Because of certain motives for savings and of certain unexpected inflationary processes, real interest rates can be negative, as has occurred in some periods. We can summarize these considerations by saying that interest rates are determined by the interplay of many factors (those mentioned by the authors we have just quoted being only some of them): most factors being affected by economic policy decisions.

If the real rate of interest is positive, nobody, no matter what his time preference may be, will be willing to trade a certain sum of money now against a promise to receive the very same amount after one year. In fact, he would always have the possibility of earning an interest by lending his money. The rates at which loans in commodities are made are related to the money rate of interest.

9. COMMUNITY'S UTILITY AND WELFARE FUNCTION

In most applications of the utility function analysed in previous sections, either a representative consumer is assumed or the number of consumers is assumed to change according to a general law, with all consumers held to be alike. Production must be oriented to the satisfaction of their needs, income distribution being determined by production functions and accumulation. When the number of consumers increases at a given rate, all consumers being alike, conditions must be created (entailing specific relations between the rate of interest and the rate of population increase) in order that any new consumer may start with the same capital as the old ones.

After Marshall and Pigou, a social welfare function has been introduced to express goals that are not the result of the choice individuals can make on the markets. They may concern income distribution (progressive tax system), public goods, social services.[6] Bergson has reformulated the function to make it compatible with Pareto's approach involving non-measurability of utility functions.

Different problems have been raised which need only to be mentioned:

1. How can a social welfare function represent goals pursued by economic policy?
2. Can the social preferences expressed by such a function be derived from individual values? That is the problem tackled by Arrow in his famous contribution. In more general terms, we can ask: What kind of relations occur between social choices and individual ones?

Arrow's contribution has shown the logical inconsistencies that social values obtained through a democratic aggregation of individual values may present. Even if we can conceive of a logical process by which social preferences can be derived from individual values, the *social welfare function* we are able to obtain is of no use to analyse choice of economic policy, for two reasons: 1) individual preferences are rather precarious; they reflect different ideologies that are linked more or less consciously to interests having different economic and political power; 2) the relations between individual preferences and social decisions are of a cybernetic type. The State cannot ignore citizens' opinions; however, it has an active role mostly in mediating between social groups. The role can be justified with reference to the community's utility (in the Pareto sense): education can help people to make their ophelimities coincide with their utility so that a more stable social choice may result.

Two reasons need to be stressed justifying the cybernetic process between the society taking its decision and individuals taking their own decisions on the basis of their preferences and of their assessment of benefits obtained from public goods:

1. A large number of individuals have no experience about the usefulness of certain public goods. Once social choices are implemented, individuals' assessment after public goods have been created will differ from their *ex ante* evalutation.
2. Even if individuals' ex ante assessment coincides with their ex post one, no individual decision can be visualized which may lead to an efficient social choice. The dichotomy between decisions concerning taxation and those concerning public expenditure is one of the causes of expanding state budget deficits.

Pareto has asserted that utility (not ophelimity) can be referred to a community (nation). He was convinced that only individual ophelimity is relevant for economic analysis, since it can be elicited from the choices individuals make on markets. We think that also community utility matters, since the community too makes choices that, at least in principle, can reveal its preferences. It is true that - as Morgenstern has remarked - community choices are often precarious and inconsistent, but that can be said of individual choices as well.

A discount rate, expressing time preferences, is usually introduced in the community's utility function. The reasons are different from those we have stated in talking about individuals' utilities. The main reason lies in the different weights assigned to welfare of different generations. When it is positive, welfare of the present generation is increased at the expense of the future generation.

How shall we assess the interest of future generations? The answer is not easy, because we cannot use our own standards to evaluate the welfare of our sons. Only if future consumers will have preferences similar to ours, techniques and products being essentially the same, can we then assume that welfares of different generations are roughly comparable. However, such assumptions are rather heroic. In the motor car civilization, consumers need a large income to buy a car and other durable goods; in this era following the revolution provoked by information technology, (active) leisure is more important than income if the new commodities (services in particular) which are much less costly than cars are to be enjoyed.

A mild positive discount rate may be justified on two grounds:

1. Technical progress will occur enabling future generations to derive a greater measure of welfare from the same quantity of resources.
2. Consumption standards can change in favour of consumption requiring smaller amounts of resources. The computer age may in fact enable people to reach the same utility with a smaller quantity of resources, as long as more time is available for the new consumption activities.

A contrary argument needs to be mentioned. Present consumption may engender future consumption (through pollution): then a negative rate of discount may be admissible.

10. OVERLAPPING GENERATIONS

An optimal path over an infinite horizon can be determined by assuming a representative consumer, whose tastes and composition (the consumer being a family) do not change in time, maximising his utility function. Alternatively we can assume overlapping generations. In his pioneer work Samuelson (1958) has assumed three generations: the young and middle-aged people working one unit and the elderly who do not work. Then a positive interest rate is justified by the need of middle-aged people to bargain with young people trying to bribe them - so to speak - in order to secure resources for consumption during the last period.

If we consider two periods, population being divided into young and old people, then the above-mentioned bargain cannot occur. Then the process is not Pareto optimum. However, if we assume that savings can be kept in money assets, in case of stationary population and prices constant, then young people can save part of their income; they will 'invest their lump savings in currency; in their old age they disinvest their currency, turning it over to the productive workers in return for subsistence' (Samuelson 1958, p. 482). If we assume that the process starts at a certain point of time, we must assume that the old are provided with the money required to bargain with the young. Let us now turn to the case of population growing at the rate m (in each period), money being fixed. Then prices have to fall at the same rate. This is equivalent to saying that a *real* rate of interest is earned on savings at the rate m. Money will cause savings sufficient for the *biological social-optimality configuration*. Samuelson is right in asserting that

> the function of money, if it is to serve as an optimal store of wealth, is so to change in its value to create that optimal pattern of lifetime saving which could otherwise be established only by alternative social contrivances. (Samuelson 1958, p. 482)

Similar conditions must be established when considering a representative consumer in a growing population, as we shall see in Chapter 4. As we have already mentioned, for steady growth to be possible, consumers must save a portion of their income such as to create initial conditions for new generations which are similar to their own.

In both approaches the time horizon is unlimited. Should the time horizon be finite, then in the end money will have no more value. Under the assumption of rational expectations, also in previous periods money will be considered valueless. The process could not start. This aporia reminds us of the one, already mentioned and in a certain sense specular, outlined by Malinvaud in his many-period model of capital accumulation (1953).

Money is an essential ingredient when we consider population growth. As we shall better see later on, that is true whenever we consider changes in initial conditions, be they population, resources, techniques.

In case the economy grows at the same rate of population and consumers have the same utility function, all production will increase at the same rate. We can consider a one-commodity economy, the commodity being a composite one. If per capita income increases because the economy grows at a rate higher than the population's, then changes in the structure of consumption occur.

11. COMMODITIES OR ACTIONS IN UTILITY FUNCTIONS?

In the neoclassical concept, the individual's utility depends on the quantity of various commodities he can obtain as a result of his actions. Two assumptions are required to justify this approach:

1. Individuals' actions are autonomous, each action having negligible effects on the results of the process; therefore the individuals must know how the system reacts and have definite expectations about other agents' actions and any exogenous events capable of affecting the workings of the system. Only under these assumptions made by the New Classical Macroeconomics School does maximization of individual utilities lead to rational individual choices.
2. Individuals care only about the quantities of goods they can obtain through their actions, leisure being included among the goods.

The assumptions made by the New Classical Macroeconomics School do not solve the problem of rational choice; they simply nullify it. Even if we leave learning processes aside, we have to face the problem of how expectations and knowledge of the workings of the system change after the results of individuals' choices. Some remarks on the problem have been made in the previous chapter. Procedural rationality is required if we want to envisage the conditions under which substantial rationality is justified. As we have noted, only if the system is ergodic can the context in which actions are decided remain unchanged, all learning processes having been completed: then substantial rationality is the final 'product' of procedural rationality.

There are some individuals (the Schumpeterian entrepreneurs) who derive enjoyment from their actions. Action is relevant also in framing consumption decisions. In fact, consumption cannot be reduced to mere availability of certain commodities. For consumption to take place, individuals must have sufficient time available. If I buy a picture for the pleasure of possessing it, I do not need to gaze at it. I can keep it in a safe-box: I derive utility only from the availability of the commodity. However, if I buy a computer in order to play some games, to enjoy it I must possess it *and* have time to spend in using it. In fact, leisure is not an alternative to consumption. In fact, it is often complementary to consumption, as some public goods are. Taking a walk in the mountains may be considered leisure: still since it requires shoes (a consumer commodity) and environment (one among the public goods), it may be labelled as consumption.

We can consider individual utility as dependent on both actions and commodities available. Some actions are linked with the individual's economic activity: entrepreneurial activity or labour. Labour reduces the time available for consumption (leisure being a specific kind of consumption) and entails a use of time that may reduce utility or increase it. In the former case we can speak of *labour alienation*, in the latter of *labour gratification*. Let $\mu(l_t)$ be the utility or disutility that is produced by allocating time to labour. Most labour entails alienation with regard to certain activities and gratification with regard to others. Let activities be measured in units of time. Some activities (entrepreneurial activity, meditation) do not require the availability of specific goods; however they do enter into the utility function. Let a_i^b be the action i that does not require the use of any commodity. Other actions require specific commodities: let a_{jh} be the action j requiring commodity h. Some consumption h requires actions j. Then a relation can be established between the action a_{jh} and the quantity x_h of commodity h:

$$\phi(a_{jh}, x_h) = c_{jh} \qquad (2.13)$$

Let us indicate by x_p the *pure* consumption (of the picture for instance), namely of the type that does not require any actions.

We can then write a utility function

$$u = u(a_i^p, a_{jh}, x_{hj}, x_k^p) \qquad (2.14)$$

In the static case the utility function has to be maximized under three constraints:

1. the constraint represented by equation (2.13),
2. the one resulting from the quantity of time available: T. The time required to act and to consume cannot be greater than T:

$$l_t + \sum_i a_i^p + \sum_j a_{jh} = T \qquad (2.15)$$

3. the budget constraint:
$$\sum_h p_h x_h + \sum_k p_k x_k = w l_t \qquad (2.16)$$

When the utility function is applied to determine the choice of the optimum evolution of consumption, the time available for labour may be differently constrained in the various phases of the individual's life. It may be higher in the second phase, when the individual has to raise a family, and decreases practically to zero after retirement. Time for consumption may increase. The elderly have more time for consumption. Consumption may not require time (meditation) or may be implemented only if time is available. In the latter case a reduction in work hours may be appreciated more than an increase in income.

12. UTILITY FUNCTION AND PRODUCT CHANGES

Two fundamental assumptions are required in order to define a utility function: the assumption of a consistent set of preferences (reflected in consistent choices) and that of a given set of consumer goods that remains unchanged in consumers' assessment, the process of learning by consuming having come to an end. To allow for new product and product differentiation, we must move from a commodity space to a space of those properties of consumer goods that are relevant for the consumer. A particular good is then defined as a specific combination of these properties to which specific weights are assigned. A new commodity is a new combination of relevant properties. Thus, we can distinguish product differentiation from product innovation inasmuch as the latter entails changes in the properties combined, whereas the former implies only changes in the weights.

Product differentiation can be induced by sales promotion activities. In fact, advertising may induce the consumer to change his overall assessment of the commodity, namely the weights he assigns to the properties entering into the combinations defining the commodity.

We could define the utility function in terms of relevant properties of consumer goods. Such a function would undergo frequent changes over time, since promotion activities and product innovations change the weight of the various properties in the consumer's assessment. There is another more relevant shortcoming in this approach. In the traditional utility function the quantities of the various commodities purchased correspond, at least in an equilibrium path, to consumptions; consumptions are the actions by which the consumer attains his goal that can be interpreted as utility maximization. If we consider relevant properties, consumers' actions are not independent from other agents' choices.

In fact, the concept of utility loses most of its interest when product innovations and sales promotion, along with product differentiation, are considered. Then we had better assume at the start a demand function that can be affected by the firms' activities just mentioned.

13. PRODUCTION FUNCTION AND UTILITY FUNCTION

Utility and available resources are the initial conditions for framing the consumer's problem; production function and available capital goods are the initial conditions that make it possible to frame the firm's problems as optimization problems akin to the consumer's. In fact, in neoclassical analysis, production is dealt with by a paradigm similar to the one used for analysing consumers' choices. Production is assimilated to exchange. Inputs are exchanged (in a broader sense) with outputs. However, at a closer scrutiny, there are differences between consumers' and firms' behaviours which become particularly relevant when we deal with development.

Changes in consumers' tastes are not the result of consumers rational choices, but are due to feedback effects of external factors or events (changes in income distribution, firms' sales promotion activities). On the contrary, changes in techniques are, to a large extent, the effect of firms' choices: those producing innovations. The number of consumers increases by virtue of mechanisms that are not of an economic nature (unless it is assumed – as we shall do in the models presented in Chapters 5 and 6 – that supply of labour adjusts to demand through emigration and immigration). The change in the number (and in the size) of firms is the result of economic mechanisms. Firms affect the context for consumers' choices by creating new products or differentiating old ones. When production is considered, we can no longer assume a given set of commodities.

The borderline between differentiated products and different products (different *goods*) is largely arbitrary. However, we shall assume that it can be drawn. At a certain moment of time, we have sets of products: the products belonging to the same set can be regarded as differentiated products representing one and the same commodity; the set includes both those products that are actually offered in the market and those that are virtually existent, being planned by old and new firms. Let us turn now to the production function, the tool by which efficient techniques are described.

Neoclassical economists assume that a firm has a set of techniques (blueprints) from which it can choose, the choice depending on the prices of inputs and outputs. However, we shall distinguish between two kinds of knowledge: the *operative* knowledge that a firm has of techniques that it has already tested and familiarized itself with; the merely *technical* knowledge that it has acquired of other techniques not yet implemented. We shall consider as *learning process* an *activity associated with production,* whereby the firm converts a technical into an operative knowledge. We can speak of a production function as a basis for the firm's choices only when all knowledge has been converted into operative knowledge.[7]

14. LEARNING PROCESSES AND PRODUCTION FUNCTION

For the sake of simplicity let us consider one input and one output. We can assume a production function, represented by a continuous line, for levels of production from 0 to y^* requiring inputs ⁻ from 0 to x^* ⁻.which have been implemented. For productions larger than y^*, uncertainty may be such that technical possibilities can only be represented by a *set* (the shadowed area) of possible input-output combinations. If a permanent increase in demand occurs the firm may deem it convenient to change the plant and thereby experiment with ways of producing quantities larger than y^*: the set will then shrink, the production function enlarged.

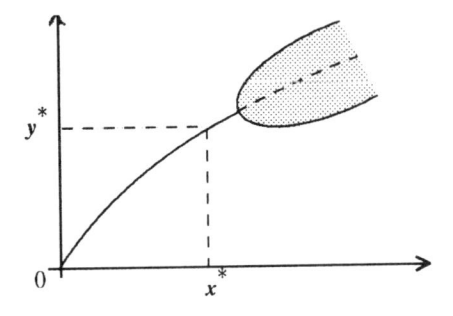

Figure 2.2

In fact, in evolution, making investments, learning and innovating represent the various facets of the firm's economic strategy. However, it may be useful to separate the various moments of the strategy, provided the relations between them are taken into account; such relations depending on the different emphasis laid on the various facets.

Arrow, in his fundamental contribution (1962), has rightly observed that acquisition of knowledge (in our language *operative* knowledge) is possible only in a dynamic context, dynamics being produced by investments that consist in using new capital goods capable of generating fresh experiences. In line with Schmookler (1966), we will consider as *dynamic condition* the increase in demand that induces the firm to experiment with new plants. New plants may coexist with old ones.

If evolution is induced mostly by demand expansion, the learning process may be considered the decisive factor for economic change and we may feel justified in isolating it from innovations. Those innovations that are inevitably associated with learning processes can then be deemed irrelevant. Thus, the learning process may be interpreted in the neoclassical framework as an enlargement of the space interval within which the production function is defined (in the example of Figure 1 from x^* to x^+).

15. PRODUCTION FUNCTIONS

The *commodity space* can be used to interpret processes of production, exchange and consumption as well as learning processes, most of the Chamberlinian product differentiations and soft innovations. If innovations ‑ being of the *hard* type (see p. 65) ‑ engender new goods or products (previously unknown), a change occurs in the commodity space. We shall not consider hard innovations, for the main reason that they are more akin to *historical accidents* than to a result of economic agents' choices, as are those analysed in theoretical formalized models.

We can then visualize three subsets of the commodity space:

1. subspace P of the outputs‑inputs combinations that have been already implemented and are well known;
2. subspace R of possible techniques (each represented by a fuzzy set of combinations) that are known in their essential features but have not been sufficiently tested;
3. subspace V of all new combinations envisaged through innovations that cannot be viewed as possible enlargements of old production functions, but rather as ingredients for new production functions.

The production function in the neoclassical sense can be defined only in subspace P; for the combinations of subspace R a learning process occurs; the points of subspace V are potential combinations that become effective only after innovations ‑ of the *soft* type ‑ have been carried out. The commodity space may not be compact. We could divide subspace V into areas each of which is made to correspond with a set of research activities. While neoclassical production functions are assumed to be known with certainty, uncertainty is an essential feature of research activities as has been shown by Dosi and Orsenigo (1988, pp. 17-9).

In the Schumpeterian approach to evolution, a commodity space should be defined for each firm. Divergencies between the firms' commodity spaces are a prerequisite for innovation; most divergencies are due to the different learning processes. In the models presented in Chapters 5 and 6, we shall further restrict our perception of the Schumpeterian thought by assuming that commodity space is equal for all firms.

Even with such a drastic assumption, our commodity space is different from the neoclassical. In fact, neoclassical theory is valid only under two assumptions: a) research activity has come to an end and therefore subspace R has been enlarged to absorb subspace V; b) the learning processes have been completed so that subspace P has been enlarged to include subspace R. Then evolution is reduced to a mere growth process (the system being ergodic). In fact, innovations, imitations and learning processes are interrelated processes. The topology of the commodity space is continuously changed: we shall never arrive at *one* homogeneous neoclassical space that is the same for all firms.

16. PRODUCTION FUNCTION AND TECHNICAL PROGRESS

Because of technical changes, capital goods change over time. Is it still possible to express a production function? The answer given by many economists is positive: it is sufficient to define capital in appropriate ways.

To simplify the problem, let us assume that capital can be measured in physical units that do not change as a result of technical progress. The only effect of technical progress is an increase in the efficiency of units of capital. Then we do not have any problem concerning the commodity space. As a change in consumers' tastes may increase the utility of a commodity that remains unchanged in its physical properties, in reference to which the various coordinates are defined, the commodity defining the capital good remains the same after innovation as it was before: its productivity has increased. Such a procedure may be justified for *disembodied technical progress*.

In this case, as time goes on, the productivity of all units of capital, no matter when they were produced, increases in time. We can separate the magnitude that expresses the physical units of capital from the one that expresses increased efficiency due to technical progress. The former (K_t) increases because of accumulation (investments): the latter (g_t) because of innovation: the factor entering into the production function being $g_t K_t$. If we assume that the effect of wear and tear and retirement can be assimilated to a reduction in physical quantities, then at time t (under the two assumptions of continuous and discontinuous time) capital is given by:

$$K(t) = \sum_{0}^{t}(1-\delta)^{t-\tau}I(\tau) \qquad (2.17)$$

$$K(t) = \int_{0}^{t} I(\tau)^{1-\delta}d\tau \qquad (2.18)$$

As we shall see, labour productivity can increase over time, too, because of labour qualification (which is engendered by factors some of which are also responsible for technical progress). We shall use a similar notation for the labour factor entering into the production function. An alternative way to deal with disembodied technical progress is to assume that the whole production function is shifted upwards in time.

Let us now turn to *embodied technical progress*. In this case innovations change the productivity of new capital goods, while the old ones remain unaffected. Let us indicate by ϕ the parameter expressing the increased efficiency of investments made at time t (of machines produced at time t). Then at time t we can define *capital in terms of efficiency units*, in the two formulations for continuous and discontinuous time respectively:

$$J(t) = \sum_{\tau=0}^{\tau=t} \phi(\tau)I(\tau) \qquad (2.19)$$

$$J(t) = \int_{0}^{t} \phi(\tau)I(\tau)d\tau \qquad (2.20)$$

this formula being easily adjustable when wear and tear is taken into account.

We can define an *average embodied technical efficiency* ψ:

$$\psi(t) = \frac{I(t)}{K(t)}\phi(t) + \frac{I(t-1)}{K(t-1)}\phi(t-1) + \frac{I(t-2)}{K(t-2)}\phi(t-2) + \ldots + \frac{I(0)}{K(0)}\phi(0) \qquad (2.21)$$

$$\psi(t) = \int_{0}^{t} \frac{I(\tau)}{K(\tau)}\phi(\tau)d\tau \qquad (2.22)$$

We can then write a production function in which the two factors are labour and capital where capital is the result of successive investments of different efficiency engendering an *average embodied technical efficiency* ψ:

$$Y(t) = F[L(t), \psi(t)K(t)] \qquad (2.23)$$

Technical progress involves production of completely different capital goods which change the production function in both its independent and dependent variables, since the product has changed too.

In fact capital accumulation is essentially linked with technical change, not only because of innovations, but also because of the mere process of learning by doing. We cannot but agree with Scott when he points out that R&D and investment activities are interwoven. In fact, the distinction between normal activities (those analysed in the usual equilibrium models) and activities producing technical progress is to some extent arbitrary. New investments always entail some technical progress. Investments in research are linked with investment in capital to be used for production. Scott has thus suggested a definition of investment that covers all uses of resources but consumption. Investment is then defined as the cost, in terms of consumption foregone, of changing (hopefully of improving) economic arrangements (Scott, 1989, pp. 13-9).

17. EXOGENOUS AND ENDOGENOUS TECHNICAL CHANGE

Both disembodied and embodied technical changes can be considered as exogenously given. In case of the latter, an expansion of demand or change in the distributive variables (wages as compared with rates of interest) may cause an increase in productivity. In case of demand expansion, this occurs because new investments, which are more productive, tend to increase as compared with past investments; in case of a change in wages (or rate of interest), because it becomes convenient to accelerate the replacement of machinery (the retirement process).

To assume that technical progress is produced outside firms is to ignore a fundamental feature of modern economies. Entrepreneurs are continuously striving to change the context in which they operate through innovations, thus producing technical progress. The entrepreneurial activity interacts with other activities, among which we shall consider scientific research.

Innovations which for the reasons already pointed out must be distinguished from learning processes, involve both techniques of production and products. The latter changes may be confined to product differentiation. We can speak of innovation, rather than not merely of product differentiation (of the Chamberlian type) whenever the product was not an element of the set of actual and virtual products defining a commodity, represented in the *products space*.

If we leave aside differentiation of the Chamberlian type, two kinds of innovation have to be considered:

1. *soft innovation*, namely of the type that makes it possible to produce goods that were already known in their relevant features, having been planned (for instance, a drug having effects substantially different from those already known, though such as may be expected on the basis of scientific knowledge) and/or to improve production techniques along technological trajectories;[8]
2. *hard innovation*, namely of the type that produces new commodities or radically new techniques of production that generally require the input of new products.

A finer classification is proposed by Freeman and Perez (1988, p. 45-6) who distinguish between:

1. *incremental innovations*: types of innovations occurring 'more or less continuously in any industry or service activity although at different rates in different industries and in different countries, depending on combination of demand pressures, socio-cultural factors, technological opportunities and trajectories'.
2. *radical innovations*: 'these are discontinuous events and in recent time are usually the result of a deliberate research and development activity in enterprise and/or in university and government laboratories' (Nylon, nuclear power etc).
3. *changes in the 'technology system'*: 'These are far-reaching changes in technology, affecting several branches of the economy, as well as given rise to entirely new sectors. They are based on a combination of radical and incremental innovations, together with *organizational* and *managerial* innovations affecting more than one or a few firms'.
4. *changes in the techno-economic paradigm (technological revolutions)*: 'Some changes in technology systems are so far reaching in their effects that they have a major influence on the behaviour of the entire economy. A change of this kind carries with it many clusters of radical and incremental innovations, and may eventually embody a number of new technological systems'.

This distinction between *hard* and *soft* innovations reminds us of the Schmookler distinction between *inventions* and *subinventions*. The soft innovations can be visualized in the commodity space: they activate co-ordinates where virtual commodities are represented. Hard innovations entail changes in the commodity space.

Imitations are attempts to implement some innovations in somewhat different contexts where difference becomes necessity in view of patent-system restrictions or of dissimilar business organization.

Imitation is regarded by some authors (Iwai 1984a, p. 163) as a process of adjustment of technologies to the best ones produced by innovations.[9] Innovation stands as a disequilibrating process, whereas imitation is viewed as an equilibrating process. Should an innovation occur once for ever and the process of imitation be completed, a neoclassical production function would be attained. But innovation is a continuous process [10] and therefore, even if we assume that imitations result in adjusting processes, we shall never be able to express the conditions of production by neoclassical production functions. Should it be possible for the economy to settle down in equilibrium, innovation activity would be impeded since innovating firms would be enable to find the workers they require. Fortunately enough innovation creates the conditions for its further development carrying on, by continuously disrupting any process aiming at bringing the system to equilibrium.

Imitations generally involve two activities, interwoven with each other: a process of learning by doing and a process of minor innovation. Any innovation increases the set of information that can be acquired through various channels. For the firm that made the innovation, the learning process has, to a large extent, occurred in parallel with the implementation of innovation. The imitating firm, instead, has to start a learning process of its own. If the innovation is not patented, the learning process could prove sufficient to bring about the adjustment process we have mentioned above. However, even in this case, the learning process, being realized by a different firm in different conditions, is likely to produce minor innovations. Minor innovations must be sought and implemented when the innovation to be imitated is patented. In fact, the patent is rarely an obstacle to the diffusion of an innovation. Quite often it is possible to discover a new process of production or a new product, different from the patented one, that can achieve the same economic success and, possibly, a larger one.

With regard to imitation, a problem which has been rather extensively analysed is how to determine what chance there is that an innovation may be imitated; which firms are more likely to undertake imitation and which of them will be more successful. Some have stated that firms which have methods of production or products closest to the new one brought about by innovation, will be the first to imitate it. Such a statement may be valid in some but not all cases. There may be entrepreneurs that, because of their experience, inclination and objectives, are more willing to imitate than other entrepreneurs applying methods of production and offering products close to the new ones. (The closeness being often difficult to assess.)

18. THEORETICAL CONCEPT AND ACTUAL REALITIES

Learning processes, innovations and imitations are theoretical concepts. As we have seen, in the real world all learning processes involve some innovation or imitation activity: even what we usually consider investment are associated with learning processes and innovations. The neoclassical production function is supposed to represent a set of techniques available at a given moment of time. When the interval wherein the function is defined is enlarged by a learning process, the new techniques that are implemented are to some extent different from the old ones that were *technically* known, not only because the operative knowledge is more specific than the mere technical knowledge, but also because acquisition of the former is obtained by certain activities that entail some innovation or imitation of other techniques that have been implemented after the old technical knowledge was obtained.

Therefore, imitation is never a mere adaptation of a new technique to a different firm's conditions. In making *new* implementations out of innovations devised by other firms, a firm may discover changes that make the final result substantially different from that obtained by the previous innovating activity. Basalla (1988) has shown to what extent some famous inventions - the steam engine, the cotton gin, the electric motor, electric lighting systems, the transistor - imitated significant predecessors. *Nihil sub sole novi.* The borderlines between product differentiation and product innovation is always, to some extent, arbitrary: the same may be said about the distinction between innovations and imitations. Nevertheless, a distinction is useful in order to isolate innovations that can be considered as abrupt products of Schumpeterian entrepreneurs aiming at upsetting markets, from such technical changes as are produced in order to exploit present market conditions or to adjust the business structure to external changes. The concept of Schumpeterian entrepreneur does not define a *class* of entrepreneurs; it rather supplies a means of isolating some essential activities constituting entrepreneurship. The real-life entrepreneur is always a mixture of the Schumpeterian entrepreneur and the neoclassical.

Parallel to the remark that it is not always easy to distinguish innovation from imitation, we can make another observation: an entrepreneur may find it more convenient to adopt an imitation strategy rather than an innovative one. In fact the same possible innovation prospects may be perceived by different firms. It will then be up to each firm to choose whether it wants to come in first or second in the innovators' race. The advantage of being first is the acquisition of market power which can improve the position in the oligopolistic struggle. The advantage of being second is a reduction in costs and the use of information that, through various channels, can be acquired on what the rival is doing. In the pharmaceutical industry, the discovery of a new drug (a new molecule) may open towards the development of better products with greater efficiency and with less collateral negative effects. That was the case with Glaxo's discover of ranytidin after Smith Kline and French's discover of the cementydin: two drugs that have revolutionized ulcer therapy.

Even the distinction between normal activities (those analysed in the usual equilibrium models) and activities producing technical progress is to some extent arbitrary. New investments entail some technical progress. Investments in research are linked with investment in capital to be used for production.

However, we think that in order to understand how technical progress can take place, it is convenient to distinguish resources used with a view to exploring new production techniques and new products and their feasibility, as opposed to resources utilized for the simple purpose of reacting to market signals, *given resources and technologies*. For the former we will use the term *Research and Development* (R&D), for the latter we will use the general terms of *productive inputs* or, when new production factors are employed to enlarge and improve productive capacity (possibly by implementing new techniques or by turning out new products), the term *investments*.

19. ECONOMIC SYSTEM AND SOCIAL-POLITICAL SYSTEM IN INNOVATION

So far we have considered the role of innovations and imitations as carried on by private individuals (firms) in the process of economic development. However, economic development largely depends on the institutional and social-cultural systems. We have associated innovations with *entrepreneur*. However, as we have noted, this term covers a wider concept than the usual one. The entrepreneur may be an individual who can be supported by different organizations or a managerial structure which, in turn, may be organized in different ways and may react differently with respect to other organizations, in particular the state organization. For Schumpeter, the entrepreneur, being necessarily an innovator (or imitator), stands as a hero with specific features on which the success of his innovative or imitative efforts depends.[11]

American institutions concerned with the economic system have proved to be more favourable to innovations than the planning mechanisms adopted by the Eastern economies (see Nelson 1988). As Freeman (1982, p. 330) has noted, the fact that Japan is striding ahead in some important new technologies 'is related not simply or even mainly to the scale of R&D, but to other social and institutional changes'. In fact, the Japanese socio-cultural system is more favourably inclined to innovate because of the peculiar coexistence of cooperative attitudes with competition. This is true inside individual firms as well within the system of the national economy. The role of the Schumpeterian hero is, to a large extent, played by the nation. Cooperation between Miti and large firms has made a long run strategy in R&D possible, and more efficient technological-economic paradigms as a result. This is particularly relevant with regard to the new outlets opened by the computer age revolution.[12] So far, the American university system has proved to be more favourable to basic research. Such an advantage is likely to be reduced and eventually reversed in the future.

In general we can list some of the reasons why the political system can affect innovation processes:

1. *the antitrust policy.* As has been pointed out by Schumpeter, the most favourable context for innovation is represented by competitive oligopolistic markets. The essential objective of the antitrust policy should be to maintain this kind of market.
2. *the policy helping entrepreneurial activities, small businesses in particular.* Let us recall that some kinds of innovations are more likely to occur where there are a large number of potential innovators operating in the same sector.
3. *the educational policy.* The level and type of education provided by the state are of paramount importance for several reasons. Some basic research (in the universities) relates to education: the basic research activity has a direct impact on the efficiency of the firms' research activities to the extent that these depend also on the university training of the researchers. Certain kinds of education may not have a direct effect on the productivity of technological research. However, they may make consumers more capable of enjoying new products (think of those already mentioned, which are the offspring of this revolutionary computer age) and increase people's capacity of benefiting from further technical education.

Economic studies of innovations usually fail to consider the interrelations between cultural and political systems on the one side and economic system on the other. The education system is assumed as given: its effects on private activity are assumed to be reflected in the parameters of the model (constant in time).

20. THE SCHUMPETERIAN PROCESS OF DEVELOPMENT

Innovation is not an abrupt, isolated event. As we have already noted, all innovations have roots in previous technical and scientific progress. Innovations may offer the clue for further innovations; they stimulate imitations and foster learning by doing. What is scarcely noticed are the adjustment processes to which innovations open the way. A new machine may substantially increase the productivity of all equipment if other elements are changed and overall organization adapted. Especially if innovations in machines are conceived and implemented by their producers, problems of adjusting the entire equipment may arise.

The dynamic of an innovation may make it difficult to assess both its costs and its positive effects on the economy, since these are distributed over time. The problem appears more intricate if we consider the interrelations between the dynamics of innovations and the overall dynamic of the economy. In depression firms may become more competitive and try to better organize production activity; adjustment processes are spurred whereas innovation activity is curbed by lack of finance and deterioration of perspectives.

Because of changes in real capital goods caused by innovations, problems arise with regard to the aggregation processes required for the purpose of writing a macroeconomic production function. In fact innovations, as we have noted, entail changes in the commodity space where micro-production functions are defined. Relative prices change: therefore, in the process of aggregation required in order to define the macroeconomic variable labelled *capital*, changes will occur both in its real components and in the weights represented by prices.

The role of innovations in the process of growth has been analysed by Schumpeter. Schumpeter's theory has been looked upon by neoclassical economists more as fruitless provocation than as a constructive theory. Some of them do concede that Schumpeterian theory may be helpful in understanding economic history. However - as they feel it - the kind of evolution that is proposed cannot be interpreted by such formalized models as would be necessary to convert statements, that might be supported by historical evidence, into scientific laws. Such a conception is untenable. In fact, recently formalized models have been produced to analyse the implications of some parts of the Schumpeterian theory. These researches indeed present some peculiarities with respect to the neoclassical theory. Different sets of simplifying assumptions are possible. That is not surprising since the goal of arriving at *the* (formalized) *theory of the mechanism of economic growth* is not even conceivable.

One reason why it is so hard to formalize Schumpeterian theory is easy to understand. It is much more simple to analyse the structure of an ergodic system than to study evolution. As we shall see in Chapter 6, Schumpeterian innovation entails processes akin to Darwinian evolution. For an ergodic system, we can assume that the process of learning leads to rational behaviour in the neoclassical sense (optimization). Friedman's (1953) conviction that failure of inefficient firms makes rational behaviour inevitable can then be well-grounded. There is another reason that makes formalization difficult. Schumpeterian theory is a multi-facet theory. It is a theory of business fluctuations, of long waves, of technological change due to innovation and imitation in a context of oligopoly behaviour, of product innovations that entail a special kind of monopolistic competition (different from Chamberlin's), of the banking system as an essential ingredient for development. It is practically impossible to formalize all these different theoretical facets at the same time.

In fact, successful efforts have been made to formalize innovations and imitations and the subsequent evolution. We shall confine ourselves to mentioning a few contributions, which appear to be more relevant to the questions analysed in this paper: Fisher and Temin (1979), who showed the impossibility of establishing unique relations between firms' size, level of Research and Development Activity (R&D), and its rentability; Futia (1980), who outlined the peculiarities of Schumpeterian competition; Iwai (1984 a,b), who analysed the disequilibrating effects of innovations and the equilibrating ones of imitations; Soete and Turner (1984), who tried to deduce from the adoption and diffusion of new technologies the nebulous concept of the rate of technical change; Silverberg (1984) and Silverberg and Lehnert (1993), who explored emergence and effects of competition among technologies; Dosi (1988) and Chiaromonte and Dosi (1993), who investigated the links between technological innovations in a disequilibrium context, Pasinetti (1993), who studied the dynamics of Schumpterian innovations and the relationship with dynamics of consumptions.

21. COMPUTATIONAL ECONOMICS

Formalization has been pursued in the context of Newtonian philosophy. The model must state a general law arrived at by an axiomatic system. Schumpeterian theory, as indeed all theories dealing with complex systems and processes of evolution, can scarcely be interpreted by means of an axiomatic system conducing to *meaningful theorems* having general validity. Anyhow, two problems remain in the Newtonian approach: the problem of *computability* deemed relevant by some scientists, and the problem of *refutability*, a property that, according to Popper, qualifies scientific statements as compared with metaphysical ones. We dwelled a little on the first problem in Chapter 1. As to the second, I am sceptical about the Popperian criterion whereby science is distinguished from metaphysics. Could such a criterion be applied to economics, possibily most of our theories would no longer be considered scientific.

Developments in logic and mathematics along with the new techniques and tools provided by the computer age revolution make it possible for us to go beyond the Newtonian scientific approach. A new approach may be taken which could be labelled 'computational science'. Such an approach aims at producing *theoretical facts* to be explored in order to arrive at some meaningful generalizations, rather than analysing facts that are 'observed' and yet are always *theory-laden*. The models must be conceived in such a way as to allow simulations, by which for each set of initial conditions (values of parameters and kinds of relations) one or more sets of values (evolutions) is produced for the variables to be explained.

By saying that computational economics deals with *theoretical facts*, we do not mean to say that *empirical facts*, as are analysed by other methods (econometrics), are ignored. We can exploit all empirical knowledge in making the most appropriate quantitative hypotheses to implement a computational economics model. By simulation procedures we can obtain a large number of theoretical facts, whereas by observation we can only get a limited set of facts corresponding to the specific structural conditions of the system at the time the observation is made. From analysis of the theoretical facts, we can infer *hypothetical empirical laws* that are not constrained by the limited capability of nature to produce facts.

There is a link between *computational economics* and *computable economics* which we have mentioned in talking about rationality and equilibrium. A model to be used for computational economic analysis must pass the test of computability.

Computational economics may be helpful:

1. in investigating particular aspects of the workings of the system for which no adequate empirical data are available;
2. in producing suggestions for rebuilding the theoretical model: the cybernetic relations between theorizing and empirical observation can thus be replaced by a cybernetic relation between model-building and an assessment of the theoretical-empirical results of the processes of simulation. Simulation may suggest how to change *reaction chains*; may help in discriminating between different models produced by the same theory and thus clarify all implications of the theory;
3. in solving problems of economic policy by investigating, in more realistic contexts, the effects of government action;
4. in producing theoretical_empirical laws: that is the case if we note some uniformity in the correspondence between sets of initial conditions and dynamics of the relevant variables. Even when the model is such that a general mathematical solution can be computed, we can better understand the system by examining the results of simulations than by analysing the formula for the solution;
5. in stimulating the collection of new empirical data.

In computational economics, simulation is not confined to comparative statics (or dynamics). We can explore the properties of disequilibrium processes for the purpose of both analysing the transition to an equilibrium path and finding out the reasons why a transition is impossible under certain assumptions about initial conditions and coefficients. Thus, certain problems of economic policies may be stated, namely to determine changes that are capable of bringing the system close to equilibrium. Such explorations can offer suggestions:

1. for visualizing possible interactions - other than those that can be analysed by the model - between social and economic systems and between individuals' behaviour and the workings of the system;
2. for stating problems of economic policy afresh - in particular, for revising the goals entering into the definition of such problems - also in connection with the above-mentioned interactions;
3. for a better understanding of the mechanisms that prevent the economy from moving too far from equilibrium paths of growth;
4. for determining possible future scenarios and for stating the conditions that make each of them most likely to occur. Such an approach may be more useful than the usual forecasting methods.

As we have already noted, results of econometric research can be used; in fact, all information that can be obtained on concrete economic processes should be used to define sets of realistic values for the parameters and sets of reasonable initial conditions.

In Chapter 7 we shall apply the method of computational economics to investigate processes of evolution associated with Schumpeterian innovations

NOTES

1. By the utility function we can express the substitution and complementary relations existing between consumer goods. In the neoclassical analysis of equilibrium, it is assumed that substitution relations are prevailing: that may occur not only for technical reasons, but in consideration of the substitution that can be established between different goals (a reduction in the prices of compact disks may induce people to increase their consumption in this area at the expense of book consumption). The utility function has been applied also to explain the consumer's decision about the time to be devoted to labour rather than to leisure, on the assumption that consumption and leisure are connected by substitution relations. In fact most consumptions require time: which means that these consumptions are complementary to leisure.
2. Einstein was well convinced that a logical system can be considered as a physical theory even if not all statement can be interpreted and tested operationally.

3. We could be tempted to discover the short-run utility function by putting appropriate questions to the individual. There are quite a few reasons to be sceptical about the results of such interviews: they may not reveal the underlying preferences but only the preferences that individuals, more or less consciously, deem it convenient to have and express. Anyhow the utility function that can thereby be discovered is likely to be non-congruous and precarious.
4. See Gibbard and Harper (1978) for an analysis of the different implications and applications of the two concepts.
5. In fact:

$$\varepsilon_s = \frac{u'(c_{t_1})/u'(c_{t_2})}{c_{t_1}/c_{t_2}} \frac{d(c_{t_1}/c_{t_2})}{d[u'(c_{t_1})/u'(c_{t_2})]} = \sigma^{-1} \qquad (*)$$

6. We think that public goods should be distinguished from social services. The demand for the former requires political decisions; the demand for the latter could be expressed in the market; however, social preferences must prevail on individuals' tastes, since the community has an interest of its own that the needs involved shall be satisfied to a certain degree and in certain ways for everybody (health, education etc.).
7. In Lombardini (1971 pp. 223 ff.) the size of the firm is explained not on the basis of neoclassical arguments, but with reference to *barriers*: a technological barrier, arising because techniques entailing larger sizes are technically known but have not yet been experienced; and a management barrier, due to the fact that larger size requires a firm's reorganization. Thus learning processes may result in enlargment of the firm's size.
8. Dosi (1982 and 1988, p. 225) has proposed the term *technological paradigm* to 'define the technological opportunities for further innovations and some basic procedures on how to exploit them'. A technological paradigm is associated with engineering trajectories for certain products and production technologies.
9. This is in line with Schumpeter's thought:
Only a few people have these qualities of leadership and only a few in such a situation, that is a situation which is not itself already a boom, can succeed in this direction. However, if one or a few have advanced with success many of the difficulties disappear. Others can then follow these pioneers, as they will clearly do under the stimulus of the success now available. Their success again makes it easier ... for more people to follow suit, until finally the innovation becomes familiar and the acceptance of it a matter of free choice. (Schumpeter 1934a, p. 228)
10. According to Schumpeter (1934b, p. 75) facts justify two statements:
First, that innovations do not remain isolated events, and are not evenly distributed in time, but that on the contrary they tend to cluster, to come about in bunches, simply because first some, and then most, firms follow in the wake of successful innovations; second, that innovations are not at any time distributed over the whole economic system at random, but tend to concentrate in certain sectors and their surroundings.
11. For Schumpeter (1955a, pp. 89-3):
the personality of the capitalistic entrepreneur need not, and generally does not, answer to the idea most of us have of what a 'leader' looks like, so much so that there is some difficulty that he comes within the sociological category of leader at all. He 'leads' the means of production into new channels. But this he does, not by convincing people of the desirability of carrying out his plan or by creating confidence in his leading in the manner of a political leader – the only man he has to convince or to impress is the banker who is to finance him – but by buying them or their services, and then using them as he sees fit. He also leads in the sense that he draws other producers in his branch after him. But as they are his competitors, who first reduce and then annihilate his profit, this is, as it were, leadership against one's own will. ... In one sense, he may indeed be called

the most rational and the most egotistical of all. For ... conscious rationality enters much more into the carrying out of new plants, which themselves have to be worked out before they can be acted upon, that into the mere running of an established business, which is largerly a matter of routine. And the typical entrepreneur is more self-centred than other types, because he relies less than they do on tradition and connection and because his characteristic task ... consists precisely in breaking up old, and creating new, tradition.

12. As Freeman (1988 p. 334) remarks:
The Japanese system seems particularly well adapted to take advantage of the enormous potential of information technology for several reasons: 1) the system approach to process and product design; 2) the flexibility of the industrial structure; 3) the capacity to identify crucial areas of future technological advance at national and enterprise level; 4) the capacity to mobilise very large resources in technology and capital in pursuit of strategic priorities; 5) the horizontal flow of information within and between firms.

3. Models of Endogenous Growth

S. Lombardini and E. Canuto

1. DYNAMIC MAXIMIZATION OF UTILITY AND GROWTH

In the theories recalled in chapter 1, growth is induced:

1. By external factors (technological changes, increase in population) which, being *expected*, contribute in determining agents' behaviour. That is the case in the Walras-Pareto models of general equilibrium. In Harrod-Domar models, entrepreneurs' investments as justified by expectations of growth in demand, will cause the system to grow *provided some external factors - essentially population growth and technological progress of a peculiar type - are in operation.*
2. By firms' behaviour. In Smith's analysis entrepreneurs induce growth through accumulation and innovation: accumulation fosters innovations; innovations produce an increase in surplus and, thus, in the rate of accumulation. As we know, Schumpeter's concept of development is similar to Smith's, with one difference: it is innovations that, thanks to credit, can foster accumulation.

Von Neumann's model has opened the way to the analysis of optimal growth. It shows some essential features of the neoclassical theories, since optimality is attained through choice of techniques, but has a classical flavour in that growth is possible thanks to accumulation of surplus.

In all these approaches, growth is the result of two different kinds of agents' behaviour: they may either be seeking to increase their power (classical-Schumpterian view) or may be reacting to external factors (neoclassical view). In Schumpeter's analysis of the first kind of behaviour, the market context (oligopolistic competition) helps to explain *why* entrepreneurs are always trying to discover and implement new technologies and new products to be sold in the market, not *how*. The process is more akin to a neo-Darwinian process than to any optimization process over time. It is certainly possible - and indeed reasonable - to assume that entrepreneurs, once they have assessed the effects of their innovations after the reaction of other firms and of consumers, will change price and other decision variables (sales expenditures) to improve profit perspectives.

In models of *endogenous growth*, technological progress is not the result of any processes of Darwinian selection, but of the *consumers' and firms' strategies* entailing some kind of optimization over time. It is assumed that the effects of innovations can be envisaged, but only for external effects. Improvement in the quality of labour and most kinds of R&D, besides producing increases in revenue and reductions in cost for consumers and firms that have caused the changes, improve the general context and, thus, the positive effects of other agents' decisions. In Solow's model all factors causing changes in the production function - learning processes, innovations, improvements in education, more effective stimuli to entrepreneurial activity and all externalities - are lumped together: their effects are *regular* shifts in the production function. In other models the shifts are associated to external effects. Along an equilibrium path the shifts are correctly foreseen and help to determine the results of individual behaviour. For growth to be optimal individual decisions should be devised by taking into account their external effects, too. The features of the optimal path diverge from those of a steady growth path produced by a market mechanism. Then, specific institutions and fiscal policies shall be devised in order to remedy this market failure.

Two are the internal mechanisms that can produce growth: a) agents' optimization over time (which entails savings dynamics capable of producing growth); b) consumers' and firms' decisions that increase the productivity of labour, of the other production factors and of the firm as a whole. The two mechanisms have different implications.

Innovation activities may concern products: new products may be created and old ones be differentiated. We shall mention the Grossman and Helpman model (1991) in which innovation activities produce an increasing variety of consumer goods, with effects also on the efficiency of production because of the accumulation of knowledge. When technological progress concerns the products, endogenous growth models are inadequate. In fact, creation of new products makes the usual assumption of competition untenable and the concept of steady growth path disputable. Moreover it can hardly be separated from other firms' activities, mostly from sales promotion. Then a new link is established between firms and consumers. We think it more profitable to analyse the consequent process by reference to a Schumpeterian context; to simplify the analysis, we can assume that markets have the essential features of monopolistic competition.

2. VARIOUS KINDS OF ENDOGENOUS TECHNICAL PROGRESS

The theoretical development we are concerned with started with the well-known contribution by Solow (1956), which was followed by those of Romer (1986) and Lucas (1988).

In Solow's model, decisions producing technical progress are not specified: what the model analyses are the effects which are represented through shifts in the production function, being of the Cobb-Douglas type. In fact technical progress is the result of many decisions: those made by consumers improving their professional skills; by firms carrying on R&D activities; by the school system (universities in particular); by research centres and so on. In an equilibrium path of growth we can assume that the effects of all these activities can be foreseen. They result in a growth of the economy also in case of stationary population.

In Lucas's model, technical progress is mostly the result of decisions by consumers who devote some of their time to improving their professional skills, which they will then offer to firms in the form of qualified labour to be used for production purposes. To make the model manageable, Lucas does not assume different qualities of labour: labour is measured not in physical units, but in efficiency units, an efficiency unit being the product of the physical unit multiplied by a variable that expresses the effect of qualification. We can speak of *accumulation of human capital*. Labour qualification improves the general context; therefore we have a further positive effect that can be dealt with *after* Solow.

In Romer's model, technical progress is essentially the result of firms trying to enlarge the variety of intermediate goods (and thus change technologies). Capital is thus an increasing aggregate of intermediate commodities that enters into a production function, of a Cobb-Douglas type, together with labour not employed for the production of intermediate commodities. The continuous increase in the number of commodities making up capital causes the growth of general production.

Grossman and Helpman assume that technical progress consists essentially in enlarging the set of consumer goods and in the accumulation of knowledge that is thereby produced. The decisive factor for endogenous growth seems to be just the accumulation of knowledge.

When product variety changes, a problem of aggregation has to be faced.[1] We think it can be by-passed by extending Lucas' approach to *technological accumulation* - namely by assuming a capital good that increases in efficiency over time; production of the physical units does not undergo any change. This kind of technical progress is of the disembodied type. This is the approach we shall follow in the model presented in the next chapter.

3. ENDOGENOUS TECHNICAL PROGRESS. THE SOLOW MODEL

All models of endogenous growth have started from Solow's fundamental contribution in which the optimal evolution of the economy is analysed as it results from maximization of consumers' utility over time when growth is induced both by an increase in population and by technological progress. A special kind of technological progress is assumed: the one that can be represented by shifts in the production function being of the Cobb–Douglas type.

Technical progress occurs in a continuous way which justifies the assumption that it is foreseen by entrepreneurs as a continuous shift of their production functions. Prospects opened through technical progress are taken into account in the optimization process which refers to an immortal typical consumer.

In the economy there is one commodity only: consumers-workers are all alike, their number (N) increases over time at the rate λ. Firms do not enter explicitly into the model. The function of production is:

$$F(t) = A(t)K(t)^\varepsilon N(t)^{1-\varepsilon} \qquad (3.1)$$

where $0 < \varepsilon < 1$ represents the capitalists' income share, $1-\varepsilon$ the workers' share and K is the firm's capital ($\dot{K}$ being investments). $A(t)$ represents the effect of technical progress. We shall assume that the technological coefficient $A(t)$ can be expressed in the exponential form:

$$A(t) = e^{\mu t} \qquad (3.2)$$

The marginal productivity of capital is:

$$\frac{\partial F}{\partial K} = \varepsilon A K^{\varepsilon-1} N^{1-\varepsilon} \equiv \varepsilon \frac{F}{K} \equiv \varepsilon e^{\mu t}\left[\frac{K}{N}\right]^{\varepsilon-1} \qquad (3.3)$$

The consumer's utility function is of the type we have already considered in Chapter 2:

$$\int_0^\infty e^{-\rho t}\frac{1}{1-\sigma}[c(t)^{1-\sigma} - 1]dt \qquad (3.4)$$

where $c(t)$ denotes individual consumption.

The functional:

$$U(t) = \int_0^\infty e^{-\rho t}\left(\frac{1}{1-\sigma}[c(t)^{1-\sigma} - 1]\right)N(t)dt \qquad (3.5)$$

has to be maximized under the constraint:

$$\dot{K} = e^{\mu t}K(t)^\varepsilon N(t)^{1-\varepsilon} - N(t)c(t) \qquad (3.6)$$

$$\dot{N}(t) = \lambda N(t) \qquad (3.7)$$

K and N shall have initial values $K(0) = K_0$; $N(0) = N_0$.

Let us consider the per capita values, being $k = K/N$. Then we can express the two conditions by the equation:

$$\dot{k}(t) = -\lambda k + e^{\mu t} k^\varepsilon - c \qquad (3.8)$$

being $k(0) = K_0/N_0 = k_0$.

Since we are interested in the equilibrium path of growth being of an exponential type, we can state the condition for such an evolution to occur (the condition being the equality of the sum of the exponents entering into the products of the two sides of the general solution):

$$\kappa = \mu + \varepsilon\kappa \qquad (3.9)$$

namely:

$$\kappa = \frac{\mu}{1-\varepsilon} \qquad (3.9^*)$$

where κ is the rate of increase in consumption, equal to the rate of increase in per capita capital.

On the equilibrium path, per capita capital must grow at the same rate as per capita consumption. Being $\dot{K}(t)/K(t)$ constant, the ratio $N(t)c(t)/K(t)$ is constant too. By differentiating we get:

$$\frac{\dot{K}(t)}{K(t)} = \frac{\dot{N}(t)}{N(t)} + \frac{\dot{c}(t)}{c(t)} = \kappa + \lambda \qquad (3.10)$$

We can make a first important statement which only the equilibrium hypothesis entails: **1S: a) The rate of increase of per capita consumption depends only on the parameters of the production function; it is the higher, the higher is the rate of technical progress and the lower the ratio of income accruing to workers. Consumers' discount rate and their intertemporal elasticity of substitution do not affect the rate of growth of per capita consumption. Alternatively, we can say that the rate of increase in per capita consumption does not depend on any process of utility maximization; it depends only on technical progress and on income distribution. b) Capital must increase at a rate equal to the sum of the rates of increase of per capita consumption and of population. Such a sum can be considered as the global rate of growth.**

Let us now face the problem of utility maximization. This amounts to finding a specific value for $c(0)^\kappa$. To solve the problem we write the Hamiltonian:

$$H = e^{-\rho t}\left[\left(\frac{c(t)^{1-\sigma}-1}{1-\sigma}\right)N(t) + \theta\{A(t)K(t)^\varepsilon N(t)^{1-\varepsilon} - N(t)c(t)\}\right] \qquad (3.11)$$

Models of Endogenous Growth

The first order condition with respect to the decision variable is obtained by setting the derivative of the Hamiltonian with respect to *c(t)* equal to zero:

$$\theta(t) = c(t)^{-\sigma} \tag{3.12}$$

By differentiating and dividing both members by θ, being $\kappa = \dot{c}(t)/c(t)$, we get:

$$\frac{\dot{\theta}(t)}{\theta(t)} = -\sigma\kappa \tag{3.13}$$

We can formulate an important statement: **2S: At each instant of time the marginal utility of consumption must be equal to θ the shadow price of investments. The shadow price decreases at a rate which is the higher, the higher the rate of increase in consumption and the higher σ.**

The first order condition with respect to the costate is obtained by differentiating the Hamiltonian with respect to *K*:

$$\frac{\dot{\theta}(t)}{\theta(t)} = \rho - \frac{\partial F}{\partial K} \tag{3.14}$$

Since $\dot{\theta}/\theta$ is always negative because of equation 13, we can make a third statement: **3S: The marginal productivity of capital is always greater than the consumer's discount rate.**

By using both equation 13 and 14, we can write:

$$\rho = -\sigma\kappa + \varepsilon e^{\mu t}\left[\frac{K(t)}{N(t)}\right]^{\varepsilon-1} \tag{3.14*}$$

and therefore:

$$\varepsilon e^{\mu t} k_0^{\varepsilon-1} e^{(\varepsilon-1)\kappa t} = \rho + \sigma\kappa \tag{3.14**}$$

By substituting for κ, in the first member, its expression (3.9*), we get:

$$\frac{k_o^{\varepsilon}}{k_0} = \frac{\rho + \sigma\kappa}{\varepsilon} \tag{3.14***}$$

Let us now turn to equation (3.8) which we shall write:

$$\kappa k_0 e^{\kappa t} = -\lambda k_0 e^{\kappa t} + e^{\mu t} k_0^{\varepsilon} e^{\varepsilon\kappa t} - c_0 e^{\kappa t} \tag{3.15}$$

namely, using (3.9*):

$$\kappa k_0 = -\lambda k_0 + k_0^{\varepsilon} - c_0 \tag{3.15*}$$

Both k_0 and c_0 satisfying equations (3.14***) and equation (3.15*) are the optimal values (namely those obtained from utility maximization). From equation (3.14***) we get:

$$\bar{k}_0 = \left(\frac{\varepsilon}{\rho + \sigma\kappa}\right)^{\frac{1}{1-\varepsilon}} \qquad (3.16)$$

whereas equation (3.15*), if equation (3.16) is taken into account, allows us to write:

$$\bar{c}_0 = \left\{\frac{\rho + \sigma\kappa}{\varepsilon} - \kappa - \lambda\right\}\left(\frac{\varepsilon}{\rho + \sigma\kappa}\right)^{\frac{1}{1-\varepsilon}} \qquad (3.17)$$

We come to a fundamental statement: **4S: Since κ is determined uniquely by the rate of technical growth and the income distribution coefficient, represented by the exponent of capital in the production function, consumer's optimization amounts to determining the initial value of consumption.** Once the optimal initial value of per-capita consumption is given, the path of growth is uniquely determined by the equilibrium requirement imposed on the dynamics of the system.

Capital can never be negative, $K(t) \geq 0$. The transversality condition is:

$$\lim_{t \to \infty} e^{-\rho t}\theta(t)K(t) = 0 \qquad (3.18)$$

That means that consumption cannot be postponed indefinitely. For $e^{-\rho t}\theta(t)K(t)$ to converge to zero as time goes to infinity, the sum of the exponents for the expression evaluated at the equilibrium solutions must be less than zero. Therefore:

$$-\rho - \sigma\kappa + \kappa + \lambda < 0 \qquad (3.19)$$

By taking into account equation (3.9), we have:

$$\rho > \kappa(1-\sigma) + \lambda = \frac{\mu}{1-\varepsilon}(1-\sigma) + \lambda \qquad (3.20)$$

The relation between the consumer's discount rate and the rate of growth of population depends on the value of the intertemporal elasticity of substitution σ. **5Sa: In case σ < 1, the discount rate must be greater than the rate of growth of population. More precisely we must have:**

$$\rho > \lambda + \frac{\mu}{1-\varepsilon}(1-\sigma) \qquad (3.20*)$$

5Sb: In case σ > 1, the lower limit of the discount rate is less than the rate of growth of population. More precisely we must have:

$$\rho > \lambda - \frac{\mu}{1-\varepsilon}(\sigma-1) \qquad (3.20**)$$

5Sc: In the intermediate case (σ = 1) the discount rate is greater than the rate of increase in population:

$$\rho > \lambda \qquad (3.20^{***})$$

We can easily obtain the propensity to save:

$$\pi = \frac{\dot{K}(t)}{N(t)c(t)+\dot{K}(t)} = \frac{\varepsilon(\kappa+\lambda)}{\rho+\sigma\kappa} \qquad (3.21)$$

An important statement can be made: **6S: The propensity to save (net saving rate) is the higher, the higher are the rate of growth of per-capita consumption κ, the rate of growth of population, and the share of income growing to capital. It is the lower, the higher the consumers' discount rate and the intertemporal elasticity of substitution.** Consumers rate and σ affect the level of wealth. A society, being thrifty (namely having a low time preference) and having a large intertemporal elasticity of substitution will have a higher saving rate: it will be, in the long run, wealthier than a society which is less thrifty with a lower intertemporal elasticity of substitution.

We can express the optimal initial consumption in terms of the propensity to save:

$$\bar{c}_0 = \left[\frac{\pi}{(\kappa+\lambda)}\right]^{\frac{\varepsilon}{1-\varepsilon}} \cdot (1-\pi) \qquad (3.22)$$

7S: The optimal per-capita consumption is proportional to the propensity to consume (Keynesian factor), the factor of proportionality depending on the ratio between the intensity of accumulation, represented by the propensity to save, and the total rate of growth with an exponent reflecting the income distribution (neoclassical factor).

The path that has been determined is an *optimal path*. Does it correspond to the equilibrium path of a competitive economy? The answer by Solow is yes provided 'markets for every instant of time are available at the beginning of the problem, or else ... if everyone in this economy had an infinite perfect forecast' (Solow 1992, p. 4).

The two conditions have different implications. The first is meaningful if the problem is framing individuals' *optimal plans* mutually compatible *at a specific instant of time*. What we find is not an equilibrium path, but the equilibrium resulting at the initial instants of time for an economy in which individuals have made their decisions for all future instants and have implemented them in the infinite future markets. For transversality conditions, the same problem arises as was faced in Malinvaud (1953). Under the alternative condition we shall envisage an equilibrium path. The problem then arises of how expectations can be formed. If we are along the equilibrium path (namely if the initial per-capita consumption is the optimal one), the problem is irrelevant since individual expectations are similar to our expectations of sun eclipses. If we are not, then the problem of transition has to be faced.

4. HUMAN CAPITAL AND ENDOGENOUS GROWTH. THE LUCAS MODEL REVISITED

Lucas, with his well-known model, has made a further step in endogenizing technical progress, since he assumes that technical progress is induced by rational choices. These are the choices by which consumers allocate their time between production and qualification of their labour capacities. Human capital accumulation produces external economies that are expressed by a shift of the production function proportional to an exponential of the human capital qualification.

Lucas has warned us that by the term *human capital* he means to define

> an unobservable magnitude or force, with certain assumed properties, that I have postulated in order to account for some observable features of aggregative behaviour. If these features of behaviour were *all* the observable consequences of the idea of human capital, then I think it would make little difference if we simply re-named this force, say, the Protestant ethic or the Spirit of History or just 'factor X'. After all, we can no more directly measure the amount of human capital a society has, or the rate at which it is growing, than we can measure the degree to which a society is imbued with Protestant ethic. ... We can, after all, no more directly measure a society's holding of physical capital than we can its human capital. (1988, pp. 35-6)

Let us for the moment assume that we can measure labour qualification, consumers' propensity to work and the effect of some social activities (education) on the productivity of the activities carried on by consumers for their own qualification. Let us assume that in countries where all these variables have been measured a positive correlation between them is found. Then, by assuming *human capital* according to some proper definition, we can build a model aimed at explaining the effect on growth of all the factors just mentioned. However, the model does not provide a satisfactory explanation. There are state actions - or historical events - that can change the relevance of different factors, other than that which is specifically called *human capital*.

I Optimal path and market equilibrium path

Workers have different skills. Their productivity depends on their skills. Lucas has used the term *human capital* to indicate the general skill level of a worker, or, as we shall say, his *qualification* ($h(t)$): a worker whose skill level is twice as much as that of another workers has a productivity which is twice as high as the productivity of the other.

Let us assume that workers are all alike (and, thus, that we can refer to a representative consumer) and that their number $N(t)$ is growing at the rate λ: the level of workers *in efficiency units* is $h(t)N(t)$. The consumer can allocate his time between investing in human capital (increasing his qualification) and in producing commodities. Let u be the quota of labour employed by workers in production; $1-u$ is the quota invested in qualification.

Investing in human capital has two effects: it increases the qualification of the worker and, thereby, his income; it improves the technological context, the improvement causing a shift of the production function upwards. The latter is the *external* (global) effect. The path of development is an *optimal path*, if the choice of u and c is made by taking not only the direct advantage of the increase in human capital for the single worker, but also those associated with the external effect into account. We shall define as *market equilibrium path* the one resulting from consumers' choices aimed at maximizing their utilities over time (being all equal, we shall analyse the behaviour of the representative consumer). External effects are not considered in the maximization process; they are simply assumed as given. The consumer has his own expectation about the evolution of the external effect, which we shall indicate by $h_a^\xi(t)$. In order to arrive at *a market equilibrium path*, we must assume that market will operate in such a way as to make the individual estimate of the external effect equal to its true value; therefore in equilibrium $h_a = h$.

II The optimal path

When analysing the optimal path, we assume that $h_a = h$, *ab initio*. The external effect is the one that is obtained through the maximization of individual utility over time. Then, the production function is:

$$F(t) = A h(t)^\xi K(t)^\varepsilon [u(t)h(t)N(t)]^{1-\varepsilon} \qquad (3.23)$$

For population we have:

$$\dot{N}(t) = \lambda N(t) \qquad (3.24)$$

Being $N(0) = N_0$.

We can state the conditions for growth along an equilibrium path similar to condition (3.5) written for the Solow model:

$$\dot{K}(t) = F(t) - c(t)N(t) \qquad (3.25)$$

$c(t)$ being consumption per capita, or, by writing $k = K/N$:

$$\dot{k}(t) = -\lambda k + \frac{F(t)}{N(t)} - c \qquad (3.26)$$

being $K(0) = K_0; k(0) = K(0)/N(0) = k_0$.

As we already noted, along an equilibrium path per capita capital must grow at the same rate as consumption per capita. Being $\dot{K}(t)/K(t)$ constant, the ratio $N(t)c(t)/K(t)$ is constant too. Differentiating we get:

$$\frac{\dot{K}(t)}{K(t)} = \frac{\dot{N}(t)}{N(t)} + \frac{\dot{c}(t)}{c(t)} = \kappa + \lambda \tag{3.10}$$

Beside a production function for the commodity (the unique commodity used both for consumption and investment), we need a production function for human capital in order to assess the effect on the worker's skill of the labour invested for qualification. In line with Lucas we shall assume:

$$\dot{h}(t) = h(t)\gamma(1-u(t)) \qquad h(0) = h_0 \tag{3.27}$$

the rate of growth of $h(t)$ varying between two extremes: γ if all work is devoted to human qualification, 0 if all work is devoted to production.

Let $\bar{u}$ be the optimal value of the fraction of time to be allocated to production which we shall obtain through the process of consumer's optimization.

We can then state the condition for the equilibrium path of growth of an exponential type (the condition being the equality of the sum of the exponents entering into the products of the two sides of the general solutions):

$$\kappa = \varepsilon\kappa + \gamma(1-\bar{u})(1-\varepsilon+\xi) \tag{3.28}$$

being κ the rate of growth of consumption per capita. Equation (3.28) can be written:

$$\kappa = (1+\omega)\gamma(1-\bar{u}) \tag{3.28*}$$

where: $\omega = \xi/(1-\varepsilon)$. ω is the external effect per unitary share of income accruing to workers. In Solow's model κ is given by the structural conditions (rate of technical progress and share of wages in income); in Lucas it has one degree of freedom, inasmuch as it depends on the consumer's optimal decision about the share of his time to be allocated to production.

It is interesting to compare equation (3.28*) with equation (3.9*) obtained for the Solow model. In place of μ, the rate of technical progress we have $\gamma(1-\bar{u})$ which is the rate of human capital accumulation. In both formulas the rate of increase of consumption per capita is negatively correlated with the share of income going to workers; however, the relations between the two variables is different in the two formulas: in Lucas account is taken of the external effects which reduces the negative impact of an increase in the workers' share of income on the growth of consumption.

As we did for Solow's, we can make a first important statement, a little more complicated than 1S, which we can make on the basis of the mere equilibrium hypothesis: **1L: a) The relation between the rate of increase of per capita consumption and the consumer' decision variable u depends only on the parameters of the production function: κ is the higher, the** higher are the productivity of labour allocated to labour qualification, the external effects of technical progress and the lower the ratio of income accruing to workers. In the Lucas model, the effect of technical progress (being due to accumulation of human capital) is not independent from income distribution. b) **Capital must increase at a rate equal to the sum of the rates of increase of per capita consumption and of population.**

It we assume that the equilibrium path is attained through optimization, from the transversality condition, we shall express later on, $\bar{u}$ cannot be zero. It can be equal to 1: that means that all time is devoted to production. *In this case, in the Lucas model, we get the peculiar result of $\kappa = 0$.*

III Consumer Optimization

Total utility to be maximized, under constraints (3.21) and (3.24), is the same as in Solow's model:

$$U(t) = \int_0^\infty e^{-\rho t}\left(\frac{1}{1-\sigma}[c(t)^{1-\sigma} - 1]\right) N(t) dt \tag{3.5}$$

The Hamiltonian can be thus written:

$$H = e^{-\rho t}\left[\left(\frac{c(t)^{1-\sigma}-1}{1-\sigma}\right) N(t)\right] + \theta\{A K(t)^\varepsilon [u(t)h(t)N(t)]^{1-\varepsilon} h(t)^\xi - N(t)c(t)\}$$

$$+\phi[\gamma(t)h(t)(1-u(t))] \tag{3.29}$$

The two control (decision) variables are $c(t)$ and $u(t)$. In the optimal equilibrium path, we shall have $c(t) = c_0 e^{\kappa t}$ and $u(t) = \bar{u}$. Then we have two first-order conditions. The first is identical to the one already obtained for the Solow model:

$$\theta(t) = c(t)^{-\sigma} \tag{3.12}$$

which implies:

$$\frac{\dot{\theta}(t)}{\theta(t)} = -\sigma\kappa \tag{3.13}$$

We get a result similar to **2S: 2L: At each instant of time the marginal utility of consumption must be equal to θ the shadow price of production. The shadow price decreases at a rate which is the higher, the higher the rate of increase in consumption per capita and the higher σ.**

The first-order condition with respect to the second decision variable is:

$$\theta(t)\frac{\partial F(t)}{\partial u} = \phi(t)\gamma h(t) \tag{3.30}$$

The left hand side of equation (3.30) is the value of marginal productivity of labour employed in production of commodity (physical capital), whose shadow price is θ; the right hand side is the value of the increase in qualification (accumulation in human capital), whose price is φ, due to the unitary increase in the quota of labour devoted to it. Therefore we can state **3L: Labour must be allocated to the two uses - production and accumulation of human capital - in such a way as to equalize at the margin the value of physical accumulation and of accumulation in human capital.**

Let us now consider the two first-order conditions with respect to costates. The first is:

$$\frac{\dot{\theta}}{\theta} = \rho - \frac{\partial F}{\partial K} \tag{3.31}$$

The formula we get is similar to that obtained for the Solow model (equation 14).

The first-order condition with respect to the second costate is:

$$\dot{\phi} = \rho\phi - \theta\frac{\partial F}{\partial h} - \phi\gamma(1-\bar{u}) \tag{3.32}$$

By utilizing equation (3.30):

$$\frac{\dot{\phi}}{\phi} = \rho - \gamma h \frac{(\partial F/\partial h)}{(\partial F/\partial u)} - \gamma(1-\bar{u}) \tag{3.33}$$

Since:

$$\frac{(\partial F/\partial h)}{(\partial F/\partial u)} = \frac{\bar{u}(1-\varepsilon+\xi)}{h(1-\varepsilon)} = \frac{\bar{u}}{h}(1+\omega) \tag{3.34}$$

equation (3.33) can be written:

$$\frac{\dot{\phi}}{\phi} = \rho - \gamma\bar{u}(1+\omega) - \gamma(1-\bar{u}) \tag{3.35}$$

Let us substitute the steady growth values for the corresponding variables in equation (3.30), by taking into account equations (3.12) and (3.21). By equalizing the sum of exponents in the left side with the sum of those in the right side (3.30) we get: [2]

$$\frac{\dot{\phi}}{\phi} = \kappa(\varepsilon-\sigma) + \lambda + \gamma(1-\bar{u})(1-\varepsilon+\xi) - \gamma(1-\bar{u}) \tag{3.36}$$

By equating the right hand sides of equations (3.35) and (3.36) we get:

$$\kappa(\varepsilon-\sigma) + \lambda + \gamma(1-\bar{u})(1-\varepsilon+\xi) = \rho - \gamma\bar{u}(1+\omega) \tag{3.37}$$

and therefore:

$$\kappa(\varepsilon-\sigma) - \varepsilon(1+\omega)\gamma(1-\bar{u}) = \rho - \lambda - \gamma(1+\omega) \tag{3.37*}$$

Models of Endogenous Growth

Let us turn to the transversality conditions:

$$\lim_{t \to \infty} e^{-\rho t} \theta K = 0 \tag{3.38}$$

$$\lim_{t \to \infty} e^{-\rho t} \phi h = 0 \tag{3.39}$$

They imply:

$$\rho > \kappa(1-\sigma) + \lambda \tag{3.40}$$

$$\overline{u} > 0 \tag{3.41}$$

We can make an important statement: **4L: The consumers' discount rate must be sufficiently high: it must be greater than the sum of the rate of increase in population and of the complement to unity of the inverse of the intertemporal elasticity of substitution multiplied by the rate of growth. The time devoted to production must be positive.** We have already remarked on this last statement.

The value of the exponent of the law of growth of consumption per capita $c_0 e^{\kappa t}$ and the optimal value of the quota of labour to be allocated to production $\overline{u}$ can be obtained from equations (3.28*) and (3.37) which, in matrix forms, can be so written:

$$\begin{pmatrix} 1 & -\gamma(1+\omega) \\ \varepsilon-\sigma & -\gamma\varepsilon(1+\omega) \end{pmatrix} \cdot \begin{pmatrix} \kappa \\ 1-\overline{u} \end{pmatrix} = \begin{pmatrix} 0 \\ \rho-\lambda-\gamma(1+\omega) \end{pmatrix} \tag{3.42}$$

The determinant of the system must not vanish:

$$-\sigma\gamma(1+\omega) \neq 0 \quad \Rightarrow \quad \sigma \neq 0 \tag{3.43}$$

That means that marginal utility cannot be constant (see Chapter 2, p. 43). The solutions of the system are:

$$\kappa = \frac{\Omega - (\rho-\lambda)}{\sigma} \tag{3.44}$$

$$\overline{u} = \frac{(\sigma-1)\Omega + \rho - \lambda}{\sigma\Omega} \tag{3.45}$$

being $\Omega = \gamma(1+\omega)$.

For κ to be positive we must have:

$$\rho - \lambda < \gamma(1+\omega) \tag{3.46}$$

$\rho - \lambda$ can be considered as a *net discount rate*.

Statement 1L can be completed after optimization: **5L: κ is positively correlated not only with the productivity of labour allocated to labour qualification and the external effect of technical progress, but also with the rate of increase of population and the intertemporal elasticity of**

substitution; it is negatively correlated not only with the workers' income share, but also with the consumers' discount rate. As Lucas has remarked: 'Here at least is a connection between 'thriftiness' and growth!' (p. 23).

The conditions necessary for u to be positive are a little more complicated since they depends on the value of σ:

If $\sigma = 1$, then the net discount rate must be greater than 0. Taking into account (3.46), we can determinate the interval within which σ can vary:

$$0 < \rho - \lambda < \gamma(1+\omega) \tag{3.47}$$

If $\sigma < 1$, then the interval for the net discount rate is:

$$(1-\sigma)\gamma(1+\omega) < \rho - \lambda < \gamma(1+\omega) \tag{3.48}$$

If $\sigma > 1$, then the interval for the net discount rate is:

$$-(\sigma-1)\gamma(1+\omega) < \rho - \lambda < \gamma(1+\omega) \tag{3.49}$$

In this case, the net discount rate may be negative.

As for the optimal value of u we can state **6L: If $\sigma = 1$ the quota of labour allocated to production is the larger, the larger the discount rate and the workers' income share, and the lower the productivity of labour allocated to labour qualification and the external effect of technical progress.** It can easily be proved that u increases with the increase of σ and of the net discount rate. If $\sigma < 1$, u is negatively correlated with the productivity of labour in human capital accumulation; when $\sigma > 1$, u increases with the increase in λ.

Let us come back to equation (3.31) which has not been yet utilized. Based on equation (3.13) we can write:

$$\rho = -\sigma\kappa + \frac{\partial F}{\partial K} \tag{3.50}$$

which, after replacing the variables with their temporary evolution (in equilibrium), can be written:

$$\rho = -\sigma\kappa + \varepsilon A \left[\frac{k_o}{\overline{u}}\right]^{\varepsilon-1} \cdot h_0^{(1+\varepsilon+\xi)} \tag{3.51}$$

from which we get the initial value of k_0:

$$k_0 = u \left\{ \frac{\rho + \sigma\kappa}{\varepsilon A h_0^{(1-\varepsilon+\xi)}} \right\}^{\frac{1}{1-\varepsilon}} \tag{3.52}$$

We can easily get the initial *optimal* value of c:

$$c_0 = \left[\frac{\rho+\sigma}{\varepsilon} \overline{u}^{\varepsilon-1} - (\kappa+\lambda)\right] k_0 \tag{3.53}$$

8L: Initial capital per capita is the higher, the lower are the capital income share and the initial level of labour qualification and the higher are the discount rate, the intertemporal elasticity of substitution and the rate of increase of consumption per capita. The initial value of consumption per capita is a linear function of the initial per capita capital, the scalar being positively correlated to the rate of discount and the rate of growth of consumption per capita and negatively correlated with the rates of growth of population and the capital income share.

IV The market equilibrium path

Let us assume that consumers maximize utility on the basis of their expectation about the evolution of the external effect $h_a(t)$.

The transversality condition remains the same: u must always be positive.

Let us write the Hamiltonian, having introduced the consumer's expectation about the external effect:

$$H = e^{-\rho t}\left[\left(\frac{c(t)^{1-\sigma}-1}{1-\sigma}\right)N(t)\right] + \theta\{AK(t)^\varepsilon[u_m(t)h(t)N(t)]^{1-\varepsilon}h(t)_a^\xi - N(t)c_m(t)\}$$

$$+\phi[\gamma(t)h(t)(1-u_m(t))] \tag{3.54}$$

where we have put the subscript m to the two decision variables, to distinguish their market equilibrium values from their optimal ones.

The first order conditions with respect to the two decision variables are:

$$\theta(t) = c_m(t)^{-\sigma} \quad \Rightarrow \quad \frac{\dot\theta(t)}{\theta(t)} = -\sigma\kappa_m \tag{3.55}$$

$$\theta(t)\frac{\partial F(t)}{\partial u_m} = \phi(t)\gamma h(t) \tag{3.56}$$

Equation (3.55) is the same as equation (3.13). Equation (3.56) is reminiscent of equation (3.30); except for the expression $\partial F(t)/\partial u$ which, as we shall see, is different from the one of the optimal path.

The two first order conditions with respect to costates are:

$$\frac{\dot\theta(t)}{\theta(t)} = \rho - \frac{\partial F(t)}{\partial K(t)} \tag{3.57}$$

$$\frac{\dot\phi(t)}{\phi(t)} = \rho - \gamma h\frac{(\partial F/\partial h)}{(\partial F/\partial u_m)} - \gamma(1-\bar u_m) \tag{3.58}$$

Equations (3.57) and (3.58) are similar to equations (3.31) and (3.33) except for the partial derivatives that are different from the ones of the optimal path. In fact from the Hamiltonian we get

$$\frac{(\partial F(t)/\partial h)}{(\partial f(t)/\partial u_m)} = \frac{\overline{u}_m}{h} \tag{3.59}$$

Equation (3.59) is equal to equation (3.34) if the external effect is zero.
Then we can write equation (3.59):

$$\frac{\dot{\phi}(t)}{\phi(t)} = \rho - \gamma \tag{3.60}$$

Equation (3.60) is equal to equation (3.35) if the external effect is zero.

As we remarked, the market will operate in such a way as to make h_a equal to h. Then an equation is obtained similar to equation (3.28):

$$\kappa_m + \gamma(1+\omega)(1-\overline{u}_m) \tag{3.61}$$

whereas equation (3.56) becomes:

$$\frac{\dot{\phi}(t)}{\phi(t)} = \kappa_m(\varepsilon - \sigma) + \lambda + (\xi - \varepsilon)\gamma(1 - \overline{u}_m) \tag{3.62}$$

similar to equation (3.36).

By equalizing the right side of equations (3.60) and (3.62) we get:

$$\kappa_m(\varepsilon - \sigma) + \gamma(1 - \overline{u}_m)(\xi - \varepsilon) = \rho - \lambda - \gamma \tag{3.63}$$

The system composed by equations (3.61) and (3.62) can be written in matrix form:

$$\begin{pmatrix} 1 & -\gamma(1+\omega) \\ \varepsilon - \sigma & \gamma(\xi - \varepsilon) \end{pmatrix} \cdot \begin{pmatrix} \kappa_m \\ 1 - \overline{u}_m \end{pmatrix} = \begin{pmatrix} 0 \\ \rho - \lambda - \gamma \end{pmatrix} \tag{3.64}$$

For the system to have a solution the determinant must be different from zero:

$$\gamma[\omega(1-\sigma) - \sigma] \neq 0 \tag{3.65}$$

namely:

$$\omega \neq \frac{\sigma}{(1-\sigma)} \tag{3.66}$$

The solution of the system is:

$$\kappa_m = \frac{(1+\omega)(\rho - \lambda - \gamma)}{\omega - \sigma(1+\omega)} = \frac{\gamma + \lambda - \rho}{\sigma - \omega/(1+\omega)} \tag{3.67}$$

$$1 - \overline{u}_m = \frac{\rho - \lambda - \gamma}{\gamma[\omega - \sigma(1+\gamma)]} = \frac{\rho - \lambda - \gamma}{\gamma(1+\omega)[\omega/(1+\omega) - \sigma]} \tag{3.68}$$

We have written the rate of growth and the quota of labour devoted to production with the subscript m to indicate that they represent the market-equilibrium values.

It is interesting to note that, when there is no external effect, the optimal path solution is equal to that of the market equilibrium path.

Three cases shall be distinguished:

1. $\sigma > \omega/(1+\omega)$. In this case, for $\kappa_m \geq 0$ and $0 < \bar{u}_m < 1$, we must have:

$$0 \leq \gamma - (\rho - \lambda) < \gamma((1+\omega)(\sigma - A)) \tag{3.69}$$

2. $\sigma < \omega/(1+\omega)$. In this case, for $\kappa_m \geq 0$ and $0 < \bar{u}_m < 1$, we must have:

$$0 \leq \rho - \lambda - \gamma < \gamma((1+\omega)(A - \sigma)) \tag{3.70}$$

3. $\sigma = \omega/(1+\omega)$. Then a variable (let us say $\bar{u}_m$) can be assumed as given. We can determine κ:

$$\kappa_m = \gamma(1+\omega)(1-\bar{u}_m) \tag{3.71}$$

V Comparison between optimal path and market equilibrium path

Let us evaluate the difference between the optimum rate of growth of consumption per capita κ and the market equilibrium rate of growth κ_m:

$$\kappa - \kappa_m = \frac{\gamma(1+\omega) - (\rho - \lambda)}{\sigma} - \frac{\gamma + \lambda - \rho}{\sigma - \omega/(1+\omega)} =$$

$$= \frac{\omega}{(1+\omega)\sigma} \left\{ \gamma(1+\omega) - \frac{\gamma - (\rho - \lambda)}{\sigma - \omega/(1+\omega)} \right\} = \frac{\omega\gamma}{\sigma} \bar{u}_m \tag{3.72}$$

Let us now calculate the difference between the market-equilibrium value of the quota of labour devoted to production and the optimal value of u.

$$\bar{u}_m - \bar{u} = \frac{\omega}{(1+\omega)\sigma} \bar{u}_m \tag{3.73}$$

9L: Since u_m is always positive the optimal rate of growth is always greater than the market equilibrium rate. The difference between the two rates is the higher, the higher are the intertemporal elasticity of substitution, the productivity of labour devoted to human capital accumulation and the external effect, and the lower the workers' income share. The market-equilibrium value of the quota of labour devoted to production is always greater than the optimal value. The difference between the two variables is the higher, the higher the intertemporal elasticity of substitution and the external effect. It does not depend on the productivity of labour devoted to human capital accumulation.

5. IMPLEMENTATION OF OPTIMAL GROWTH AND SUSTAINABILITY OF MARKET EQUILIBRIUM

Let us consider the optimum rate of growth as can be achieved through global optimization. The problem arises how to get agents to take their decisions in such a way as to have the economy moving along the equilibrium path. We could suggest the Pigouvian way. However, as we have seen in Chapter 1, talking about the Chipman model of increasing returns (pp. 12-3), for a multi-sectors economy we could have different equilibrium paths. Any-way, we ought to assess in advance the optimal tax rates and/or subsidies to have people acting in the proper way. Thus the optimal equilibrium path remains an ideal path.

Let us now turn to the *market equilibrium path*. In Solow's model, the problem was how agents can take their decisions in line with the prospects of technological progress. Solow suggests two possibilities: either we assume an infinite set of future markets or we assume individuals having perfect rational expectations. We have already mentioned some of the difficulties to be faced. In the Lucas case there is a more serious logical difficulty, due to the external effect of human capital accumulation. According to Lucas, *market equilibrium path* can be envisaged if market mechanism can make consumers' expectations about the evolution of the external effect coincide with the true value of h. It is difficult to see any way through which this result can be achieved. In fact the two important problems that have not been faced are: the *transition* through which the system is brought along an equilibrium path and the stability of the path. Also the market-equilibrium path is likely to be an ideal path.

6. ENDOGENEOUS MECHANISM AND EVOLUTION

The models of endogenous growth have the merit of showing how technical progress induced by agents' decisions can frame the evolution of the economy together with the increase in population. Other mechanisms that can induce technical progress *from inside* can be considered:

1. Growth of demand can increase product differentiation if markets are of the monopolistic competition type.
2. Acceleration in the rate of increase in final demand may intensify the operation of self-sustained growth mentioned in Chapter 1, page 17. May we point out, in particular, processes of *learning by doing*. Both workers and entrepreneurs (managers as well as technical staff) can improve their capabilities through feasible experiences: some of them developed inside the firm and some by working in different firms. For the former we can

speak of *internal learning*, for the latter of *public learning*. We can speak of public learning also with reference to certain forms of cooperation between firms.
3. A similar effect can be produced by an increase in accumulation, provided final demand (either at home or in world markets) can expand at sufficiently high rates (Smithian process of development).

We can easily understand how increasing return, as well as the market form of monopolistic competition, may produce growth also in case of stationary population. In a market of monopolistic competition development occurs because the expansion of demand fostering competition causes a reduction in cost, while the availability of a larger number of product makes it possible to attain an increase in consumers'utility.

There are features of the social-economic system that can explain growth processes *from the inside*. The most important is the entrepreneurial greed for accumulation and entrepreneurs' propensity to innovate. We cannot deal with these factors by adopting Lucas' concept of human capital. The Schumpeterian process of development cannot be dealt with by models such as those recalled in this chapter or the one that will be presented in the next chapter. We shall try to explore evolutions produced by Schumpeter processes of innovations in Chapters 5 and 6.

SYMBOLS

See Chapter 4.

NOTES

1. This problem has been solved by Dixit and Stiglitz (1977).
2. Let us write the equilibrium values of the variables involved:

$$h(t) = h_0 e^{\gamma(1-u)t}$$

$$\theta(t) = \theta_0 e^{-\sigma\kappa t}$$

$$\frac{\partial F(t)}{\partial u} = a_0 e^{(\kappa+\lambda)\varepsilon + \lambda(1-\varepsilon) + (\xi+1-\varepsilon)\gamma(1-u)}$$

$$\theta(t) = e^{(t\dot\theta(t)/\theta)t}$$

Then we can write:

$$(\kappa+\lambda)\varepsilon + \lambda(1-\varepsilon) + (\xi+1-\varepsilon)\gamma(1-u) + \frac{\dot\theta(t)}{\theta(t)} = -\sigma\kappa + \gamma(1-u)$$

By simplifying we get equation (3.36).

4. Human-Capital and Technological Accumulation

S. Lombardini and E. Canuto

1. HUMAN CAPITAL, TECHNOLOGICAL ACCUMULATION AND GROWTH

In the Lucas model individual choices are required only for the purpose of labour qualification. Then the whole technological context is modified: the production function is shifted upwards. In Romer's, growth is assured by changes in the structure of capital goods which is more akin to what is usually assumed to be technological progress.

Indeed, technological progress is the result both of the consumers' decisions to improve their labour qualification and of the firms' decision to utilize a quota of the labour they employ in order to change capital goods. We can extend the concept of qualification, which Lucas has used for labour only, to capital, this being considered differently from Romer's as a commodity whose qualities are changed because of *technological accumulation*. With such a concept we can embrace also learning processes. To accumulation resulting from savings, we shall add the *human-capital accumulation* and the *technological accumulation*.

We shall define optimal growth as a strategy of evolution aimed at maximizing consumer's utility. However, we shall explicitly introduce the firm. The first objective of our analysis is to envisage a competitive market equilibrium path. Specific assumptions have to be made on agents' expectations so as to be able to analyse how their decisions can bring the economy to an equilibrium path (steady growth).

We shall follow Lucas in linking externalities of technical progress with human capital accumulation. In fact research is generally associated with accumulation in human capital and leads to innovation. Schools (universities in particular) produce both research and manpower qualifications. A firm uses resources to implement R&D programmes: research is the more effective the better qualified are the technicians the firm can employ.

Lucas has not explicitly faced the problem of how agents (consumers and firms) take their decisions, whether on the basis of *proper* expectations with market mechanisms assuring that an equilibrium path is reached, or through the co-ordination of individual behaviour under the hypothesis that expectations prove to be correct.

Thus, we shall distinguish the *competitive market equilibrium path* from the *optimal growth path*. More specifically we will concern ourselves with constant-rate-of-growth equilibrium paths. Only along these paths will capital, after being adjusted to obtain the best combination of the factors of production, increase together with production. Then, we shall examine whether such an equilibrium path can be produced by a competitive market mechanism as usually conceived. The problem remains how individual behaviour can be so affected as to ensure that the *optimal growth path* will be reached through the market mechanism. The problem may have a logical solution that can hardly be implemented. The state could enforce taxes and/or grant subsidies so as to induce individuals to take decisions that will optimize growth. But if this result is to be achieved, either the state will need to know the optimal path whereby to determine the right value of taxes and subsidies or we will have to think of a mechanism capable of changing subsidies and taxes so as to bring the economy along the optimal path growth.

The transition phase should be explored to find out whether and how the economy can be brought to an equilibrium path of growth (steady growth).

2. THE ECONOMY

We shall assume that only one commodity is produced, being used both as consumer and capital goods. Alongside the commodity market, there are the labour market and the capital market. The commodity plays the role of *numeraire*: its price is identically equal to 1. Wages are expressed in terms of the commodity: they are real wages.

At time t, there are $N(t)$ persons each consuming $c(t)$ of the commodity and supplying the share u of his potential work (being 1) to firms, the share $(1-u)$ being employed to qualify his working capacity (*human capital accumulation*).[1] All persons are alike and operate in the same environment with the same tastes.

To produce the commodity at time t, firms have to employ labour $L(t)$ and capital $K(t)$. The two factors of production entering into the production function are not the physical quantities of labour and of capital, but the *qualified labour* and the *qualified (technological developed) capital*. Let us indicate the level of qualification of one unit of labour at time t by $h(t)$: that means that if the firm employs $L(t)$ units, the quantity of the *labour factor* is $h(t)L(t)$. The variable $h(t)$ measures the accumulation in human capital. Firms employ the share v of the workers available to produce the commodity, the share $(1-v)$ being employed in qualifying capital (technological accumulation).

At time t, the technological improvement of one unit of capital is $g(t)$ which means that if the firm employs $K(t)$ units, the quantity of the *capital factor* is $g(t)K(t)$. The variable $g(t)$ measures the effect of technological accumulation.

Endogenous growth is thus produced by both the consumers' decisions that cause qualification of labour, and by firms' decisions that make capital goods more productive. Human capital accumulation causes upward shifts of production functions; the shifts being represented by a scalar factor: h^ξ.

3. EVOLUTION OF CAPITAL AND CONSUMPTION PER CAPITA

We can state the conditions for growth along an equilibrium path similar to condition (4.6), written for the Solow model, and to condition (4.25), written for the Lucas model in Chapter III:

$$\dot{K}(t) + c(t)N(t) = F(t) \qquad K(0) = K_0 \qquad N(0) = N_0 \qquad (4.1)$$

being:

$$F(t) = [h(t)]^\xi [g(t)K(t)]^\varepsilon [h(t)v(t)L(t)]^{1-\varepsilon} \qquad (4.2)$$

Let us express the equilibrium condition, in terms of capital per capita $k = K/N$ and consumption, similar to equation (4.26) in the Lucas model:

$$\dot{k}(t) = \frac{F(t)}{N(t)} - \lambda k - c \qquad k(0) = \frac{K_0}{N_0} = k_0 \qquad (4.3)$$

$c(t)$ being consumption per capita and $c(0) = c_0$.

On the equilibrium path we must have, as in Solow's and Lucas' models:

$$\frac{\dot{N}(t)}{N(t)} = \lambda \qquad (4.4)$$

$$\dot{h}(t) = h(t)\gamma(1 - u(t)) \qquad h(0) = h_0 \qquad (4.5)$$

to which we must add the condition for *technological accumulation*:

$$\dot{g}(t) = \eta(1 - v(t))g(t) \qquad g(0) = g_0 \qquad (4.6)$$

The equilibrium path is a steady growth path. Per-capita variables increase at the constant rate κ. In equilibrium $u(t)$ and $v(t)$ are constant: $\bar{u}, \bar{v}$.

The equilibrium conditions imply the following relation between the structural coefficients:[2]

$$\kappa = \psi\eta(1-\bar{v}) + \gamma(1+\omega)(1-\bar{u}) \tag{4.7}$$

being $\psi = \varepsilon/(1-\varepsilon)$ an *income distribution index* and $\omega = \xi/(1-\varepsilon)$ the *index of external effects on income distribution*.

It is interesting to compare equation (4.7) with equations (4.9*) and (4.28*) of Chapter III, obtained for the Solow and Lucas models. They can be written:

$$\kappa = \frac{\psi\mu}{\varepsilon} \tag{3.8*}$$

$$\kappa = \gamma(1+\omega)(1-\bar{u}) \tag{3.28*}$$

In (4.7) κ is the sum of two addenda. The second is the Lucas formula for κ, representing the contribution of the accumulation of human capital. The first reminds us of Solow's. In Solow the effect of technical progress is the product of μ/ε and the income distribution index ψ; in our formula, μ/ε is replaced by $\eta(1-\bar{v})$. We can say that in Solow the effect of technical progress does not depend on any decision variable (there is no degree of freedom); in Lucas it depends on one decision variable $\bar{u}$ (there is one degree of freedom); in our model it depends on two decision variables $\bar{u}, \bar{v}$ (there are two degrees of freedom).

4. THE COMPETITIVE EQUILIBRIUM ECONOMY

Let us now analyse the ways consumers' and firms' behaviour shape the structure of the competitive economy.

I The consumer

At time t, there are $N(t)$ individuals that are both consumers and workers. Their number grows at a constant rate λ. All individuals are alike.

Consumers act as one large family: knowing the rate of growth of population λ, each of them provides, pro quota, the wealth required for the new-born to be in the same condition as the old. If the consumer's wealth at time t is $p(t)$, the amount of individual savings required to equalize consumers' initial conditions is $\lambda p(t)$.

We shall consider the utility function appearing in Chapter 2:

$$U[c(t)] = \frac{1}{1-\sigma}[c(t)^{1-\sigma} - 1] \tag{4.8}$$

where σ is the coefficient of risk aversion. In our model which is of a deterministic type, no risk can arise; σ is the reciprocal of the intertemporal elasticity of substitution, which plays an important role in the evolution of the economy, still more relevant than in Lucas'.

Let us remind ourselves of the four cases seen in Chapter 2 (pp. 51-2):

$$1 \quad \sigma = 0 \Rightarrow U[c(t)] = c(t) - 1 \quad (4.9a)$$

In this case marginal utility is constant.

$$2 \quad \sigma = 1 \Rightarrow U[c(t)] = \ln c(t) \quad (4.9b)$$

$$3 \quad \sigma > 1 \Rightarrow U[c(t)] > 0$$

$$for \quad c > c_m > 0 \quad (4.9c)$$

In this case utility has the upper limit 1; consumptions at different dates are poor substitutes for one another.

$$4 \quad \sigma < 1 \quad (4.9d)$$

In this case utility has no upper limit. Consumers tend to substitute present consumption for future consumption.

In Chapter III, we have seen that $\sigma = 0$ is a critical value for Lucas' model; we shall see that $\sigma = 1$ is a critical value for ours; in a specific version the critical value is $\sigma = 1/2$.

Since, in order for the economy to be moving along a path of steady growth, all consumers must save in order to provide the same conditions for new consumers - all consumers, old and new, being alike - consumers' choice will be the result of the maximization of:

$$U_g = \int_0^\infty e^{-\rho t} \frac{1}{1-\sigma}[c(t)^{1-\sigma} - 1]N(t)dt \quad (4.10)$$

Human capital accumulation brings about increases in wages. The individual can increase future consumption either by increasing his wealth as represented by ownership of the firm capital on which interest accrues, or by increasing his qualification. In fact both *human capital accumulation*, governed by the consumers' decision variable u, and *technological accumulation*, governed by the firms' decision v, make it possible for consumption to be increased over time.

What we want to envisage is the equilibrium path along which consumers can move.

Consumers would not employ labour for training purposes unless they anticipate a larger labour income as a consequence of such higher qualifications. We shall assume that consumers expect:

$$u(t)w(t) = \alpha_w[u(t)h(t)] \quad (4.11)$$

We shall assume that consumers maximize utility under the budget constraint:

$$u(t)w(t)N(t) + i(t)P(t) = c(t)N(t) + \dot{P}(t) \qquad P(0) = P_0 \qquad (4.12)$$

Consumers have two control variables *c(t)* and *u(t)*. By increasing their wealth through savings, individuals can increase income represented by interest, whereas, by allocating some time to labour qualification (increasing human capital), they can expect higher wages. Consumers maximize utility by a proper choice of *c(t)* and *u(t)*.

Besides the budget constraint and the income-for-labour expectation (equation 4.5), we shall assume the following constraints:

$$\lim_{t \to \infty} P(t) = 0 \qquad (4.13)$$

$$0 \leq c(t)N(t) \leq i(t)P(t) + w(t)u(t)N(t) \qquad (4.14)$$

$$0 \leq u(t) \leq 1 \qquad (4.15)$$

To understand these constraints we must recall that we are interested in finding equilibrium paths. In an economy growing at a constant rate with consumers all alike, each of them choosing a stream of consumption maximizing expected utility, no consumer will change his consumption in a given period by borrowing money to be repaid in later periods. We thus have inequality (4.14). The meaning of inequality (4.15) is clear. Inequality (4.13) states that no consumer can permanently increase his consumption by borrowing money. No individual can behave like the state.

II The firms

We shall assume constant returns to scale for labour and capital. The production function, of a Cobb-Douglas type, is shifted upwards due to the external effects of human capital accumulation. Because of the constant returns to scale assumption, the number of firms is indeterminate. Since they are all alike, we can refer to the representative firm; inputs (and outputs) being expressed by global quantities utilized (and produced) by all firms. No firm will simply confine its behaviour to instant reactions to market signals. A firm has expectations and will seek strategies that can maximize profits over time, its horizon being infinite. Thus the firm's problem is logically akin to the consumer's. In fact, for a problem of optimization over time to arise, we must assume that the firm has definite expectations about its future finance, to implement investment programmes, and labour availability for futher growth, and also about possible increases in labour qualification and their effects on wages.

The structure of the economy is highly unstable. For the firms to remain price takers, the initial number of them must be sufficiently high. All firms are alike and have the same expectations; thus they make the same decisions and grow at the same rate: the one at which global quantities grow.

There are four sources for firms' profits. The first comes from optimization of combinations of labour and capital. The second is linked with human capital accumulation that changes the 'efficient units' of labour and shifts the production function upwards. The third is the firm's R&D activity that produces technological accumulation, changing the 'efficient units' of capital. The fourth comes from the increase in consumer demand resulting from an increase in wages and from population growth.

At time t, the firm employs labour and capital to produce the quantity of commodity $F(t)$. The increase in capital is provided for by individuals' savings.

The firm acquires labour:

1. to produce the commodity. The production function is of the Cobb-Douglas type, the fraction of labour utilized in production being $v(t)$;
2. to employs a fraction $(1 - v(t))$ to qualify capital (by R&D): capital in efficiency units being $g(t)K(t)$.

We shall then assume that the firm has the production function:

$$F(t) = [h(t)]^{\xi}[g(t)K(t)]^{\varepsilon}[h(t)v(t)L(t)]^{1-\varepsilon} \quad (4.16)$$

$L(t)$ and $K(t)$ being the quantities of labour and of capital employed and $h(t)^{\xi}$ the shifting effect of human capital accumulation ($\xi > 0$).

We can express the firm's expectations by the equations:

$$\dot{K} = \chi K \qquad K(0) = K_0 \quad (4.17)$$

$$\dot{L} = \alpha_l L \qquad L(0) = L_0 \quad (4.18)$$

$$w(t) = a_w(h) \quad (4.19)$$

$$\dot{h} = \alpha_h h \qquad h(0) = h_0 \quad (4.20)$$

$\dot{K}(t)$ being the investments made to increase production. In equation (4.17) χ can be given a different interpretation: it can represents the firm's attitude to grow.

We shall assume that the firm expects the rate of interest to remain constant.
The firm's profit:

$$\int_0^{\infty} e^{-\delta t}[F(t) - w(t)L(t) - i(t)K(t)]dt \quad (4.21)$$

has to be maximized under the constraints (4.6), (4.16)-(4.20) to which we must add:

$$\lim_{t \to \infty} K(t) = 0 \qquad (4.22)$$

$$\lim_{t \to \infty} L(t) = 0 \qquad (4.23)$$

The meaning of the constraints is clear. It is inefficient to take decisions that tend to get positive stocks of capital and labour no matter how far is the horizon.

The control variable of the firms is $v(t)$: it can vary between 0 and 1. Therefore we have the inequality:

$$0 \leq v(t) \leq 1 \qquad (4.24)$$

III The markets

The number of individuals $N(t)$ grows in time at the rate λ (see equation 4.4).

For the labour market to be in equilibrium the increase in the firm demand $\dot{L}(t)$ must be equal to the increase in consumers' supply:

$$\dot{L}(t) = \frac{d}{dt}(uN(t)) \qquad (4.25)$$

Since we are interested in finding equilibrium paths, at a constant and uniform rate of growth in the labour market stocks too must be equalized:

$$L(t) = u(t)N(t) \qquad (4.26)$$

The financial market is in equilibrium when:

$$\frac{dP(t)}{dt} = \dot{K} \qquad (4.27)$$

The commodity market is in equilibrium when:

$$F(t) = \dot{K}(t) + c(t)N(t) \qquad (4.1)$$

Being interested in the long-run equilibrium we must check that the following condition is satisfied:

$$F(t) - w(t)L(t) - i(t)K(t) = 0 \qquad (4.28)$$

From consumers' budget and financial and labour market equilibrium equations (4.25)-(4.27) we get:

$$\dot{K} = ip(t)N(t) + w(t)L(t) - c(t)N(t) \qquad (4.29)$$

which together with equation (4.27) entails (4.28). The value of production is thus equal to the sum of wages and interest paid.

5. CONSUMERS, FIRMS AND MARKET EQUILIBRIA IN STEADY GROWTH

We can now analyse the properties of the equilibrium path of growth. We shall not explore all solutions of course, but only those (and possibly the one) that entail a constant rate of growth (steady state solution).

I The consumers' equilibrium path

We start by writing the Hamiltonian:

$$H = e^{-pt}\{U_g[c(t)]N(t) + \theta(t)[iP(t) + \alpha_w[u(t)h(t)]N(t) \\ -c(t)N(t)] + \phi(t)\gamma[1-u(t)]h(t)\} \quad (4.30)$$

In the equation expressing the budget constraint we have substituted the expectation function (4.11) for labour income.

The first-order condition with regard to the decision variable c is:

$$\theta(t) = \frac{dU_g}{dc} \quad (4.31)$$

θ being the shadow price of a unitary increase in savings in terms of utility.

If we assume the utility function (4.10) we can get a specific expression for dU_g/dc and, therefore, for the shadow price:

$$\theta(t) = c(t)^{-\sigma} \quad (4.32)$$

Equation (4.32) is equal to equation (4.12) of the Solow and Lucas models. We can then state that: **LC1: Marginal utility of consumption must be equal to the shadow price of savings (in terms of utility).**

The first-order condition with regard to the decision variable u is:

$$\theta(t)\frac{\partial \alpha_w}{\partial u}N(t) = \phi(t)\gamma h(t) \quad (4.33)$$

We can easily note that $\partial \alpha_w/\partial u(t) = \partial[u(t)w(t)]/\partial u(t)$ is the marginal loss (or gain) in labour income due to a decrease (increase) in the time allocated to labour. Let us indicate it by $g_w(t)$. We can write the (4.33), having taken account of the expression for γ that can be derived from (4.5):

$$\theta(t)g_w(t)[1-u(t)]N(t) = \phi(t)\dot{h} \quad (4.34)$$

The first term of equation (4.34) expresses the marginal loss, in terms of utility, of the decrease in labour income due to the use of labour for qualification rather than for production. The second term expresses the value of the improvement in qualification, ϕ being the shadow price for better qualification. When condition (4.34) is satisfied, an optimal allocation of labour between production and qualification is obtained. Then, we can state: **LC2: Each consumer has efficiently allocated his time between production and qualification whenever the cost, in terms of utility, of the income lost is equal to the value of the improvement in qualification, on the basis of the shadow price for better qualification.**

The condition we have obtained is similar to the one in Lucas' model expressed by equation (4.13).

The two first-order conditions with regard to the costates are:

$$\frac{\dot{\theta}}{\theta} = \rho - i \qquad (4.35)$$

$$\dot{\phi}(t) = \rho\phi(t) - \theta(t)\frac{\partial\alpha_w}{\partial h}N(t) - \phi(t)\gamma[1 - u(t)] \qquad (4.36)$$

Equation (4.35) brings us back to equation (4.31) of Lucas' model except that here the productivity of capital is replaced by the rate of interest. **LC3: If the consumers' discount rate is greater than the interest rate, the shadow price of consumption increases over time.** Equation (4.36) recalls equation (4.32) in the Lucas model, where $\partial\alpha_w/\partial h N(t)$ takes the place of $\partial F/\partial h$.

If we assume the utility function (4.10), we get from equation (4.32):

$$\frac{\dot{\theta}}{\theta} = -\sigma\frac{\dot{c}(t)}{c(t)} \qquad (4.37)$$

From equations (4.35) and (4.37) we get:

$$\frac{\dot{c}(t)}{c(t)} = \frac{i - \rho}{\sigma} \qquad (4.38)$$

From equations (4.33) and (4.36), taking into account equation (4.11), we get:

$$\frac{\dot{\phi}}{\phi} = \rho - \gamma \qquad (4.39)$$

Equation (4.39) reverts to equation (4.35) of Lucas' model. In fact it is the same if we leave out the external effect.

We have thus reached the following important result: **LC4: The rate of change of the shadow price for labour qualification is equal to the difference between the consumers' discount rate and the productivity of labour allocated to qualification.**

This result is not surprising if we remember that ρ reflects the greed for current consumption, whereas the possibility of increasing future consumption depends on the value of γ, namely on the productivity of labour allocated to qualification.

Equation (4.33) allows us to state:

$$\frac{\dot{\phi}}{\phi} = \kappa(1-\sigma) + \lambda - \gamma(1-\bar{u}) \tag{4.40}$$

Because of constraint (4.13) we get the transversality condition:

$$\lim_{t \to \infty} e^{-\rho t}\theta(t)P(t) = 0 \tag{4.41}$$

which means that the value of the *final* capital, in terms of utility (beyond the infinite horizon), is zero.

In steady state the rate of interest is constant. Therefore:

$$c(t) = c_0 e^{\kappa t}$$

$$u(t) = \bar{u}$$

$$i(t) = \bar{i} \tag{4.42}$$

From equation (4.29), we get:

$$p(t) = p_0 e^{\kappa t} \tag{4.43}$$

$$w(t) = w_0 e^{\kappa t} \tag{4.44}$$

Recalling that the sum of the exponents of variables in the first member of an equation must be equal to the sum of those of the variables in the second member from equation (4.38) we get the relation:

$$\kappa\sigma = i - \rho \tag{4.45}$$

and from equation (4.39) and (4.40) the relation:

$$(1-\sigma)\kappa - \gamma(1-\bar{u}) = \rho - \gamma - \lambda \tag{4.46}$$

Equations (4.45) and (4.46) enable us to determine the value of the two unknowns $\kappa, \bar{u}$. In matrix form:

$$\begin{pmatrix} \sigma & 0 \\ 1-\sigma & -\gamma \end{pmatrix} \cdot \begin{pmatrix} \kappa \\ 1-\bar{u} \end{pmatrix} = \begin{pmatrix} i-\rho \\ \rho-\gamma-\lambda \end{pmatrix} \tag{4.47}$$

The determinant of the system $-\gamma\sigma$ is 0 only when $\sigma = 0$. Therefore 0 is a critical value for σ. The solutions are:

$$\kappa = \frac{i-\rho}{\sigma} \qquad (4.48)$$

$$\bar{u} = \frac{(\rho-\lambda)}{\gamma} + (\rho-i)\frac{(1-\sigma)}{\sigma\gamma} = \frac{i-\lambda}{\gamma} - \frac{\kappa}{\gamma} \qquad (4.49)$$

The constraint in κ ($\kappa \geq 0$) implies:

$$i-\lambda \geq \rho-\lambda \qquad (4.50)$$

The transversality condition entails that:

$$\rho-\lambda > \kappa(1-\sigma) = \frac{i-\rho}{\sigma}(1-\sigma) \qquad (4.51)$$

namely:

$$i-\lambda > \kappa \geq 0 \qquad (4.52)$$

The constraint on $\bar{u}$ ($0 < \bar{u} \leq 1$) implies:

$$\kappa < i-\lambda \leq \kappa+\gamma \qquad (4.53)$$

The left hand inequality is the same as that arising from the transversality condition.

In case $\sigma \leq 1$, the inequalities become:

$$0 \leq (1-\sigma)\kappa < \rho-\lambda \leq \gamma+(1-\sigma)\kappa \qquad (4.54)$$

We have already called the difference between the consumer's rate of discount ρ and the rate of population growth λ *consumer's net rate of discount*; we can talk of a net rate of discount with regard to the firm too; $i-\lambda$ is a net rate of interest. We can summarize the results expressed by equations (4.50)-(4.54):

LC5: The net interest rate must be non negative and greater than the rate of growth. Such a result is different from von Neumann's. The reason is that growth is not assured only by the choice of the best intertemporal process of production, but also by the accumulation of human capital. Moreover the net interest rate must not be less than the consumer's net rate of discount. If it is equal the rate of growth will be zero. In case $\sigma \leq 1$, the consumer's net rate of discount must be non negative and greater than $(1-\sigma)\kappa$. Changes in the values of ρ and/or in σ may have critical effects.

II The firm equilibrium

We start by writing the Hamiltonian:

$$H = e^{-\delta t}\{F(t) - w(t)L(t) - iK(t) + \beta_a(t)\chi K(t) +$$
$$\beta_l(t)\alpha_l L(t) + \beta_c(t)\eta[1 - v(t)]g(t)\} \quad (4.55)$$

The first-order condition with respect to the decision variable v is:

$$\frac{\partial F}{\partial v} - \beta_c \eta g(t) = 0 \quad (4.56)$$

Since from the production function we get:

$$\frac{\partial F}{\partial v} = (1 - \varepsilon)\frac{F}{v} \quad (4.57)$$

we can write:

$$(1 - \varepsilon)\frac{F(t)}{v(t)} = \beta_c \eta g(t) \quad (4.58)$$

By taking into account equation (4.6) we get:

$$\frac{\beta_c \dot{g}(t)}{1 - v(t)} = \frac{(1 - \varepsilon)F(t)}{v(t)} \quad (4.59)$$

The first member represents the marginal productivity of labour employed in research activity; the second the marginal productivity of labour employed in production. We have thus reached an important result: **LC6: The firm has efficiently allocated labour between production and research whenever the marginal productivity of labour employed in production is equal to the marginal productivity of labour employed in research**.

The first-order conditions with respect to costates are:

$$\dot{\beta}_a = \delta\beta_a - \frac{\partial F}{\partial K} + i - \beta_a \chi \quad (4.60)$$

$$\dot{\beta}_l = \delta\beta_l - \frac{\partial F}{\partial L} + w(t) - \beta_l \alpha_l \quad (4.61)$$

$$\dot{\beta}_c = \delta\beta_c - \frac{\partial F}{\partial g} - \beta_c \eta(1 - v(t)) \quad (4.62)$$

Because of constraints (4.22) we get the transversality conditions:

$$\lim_{t \to \infty} e^{-\delta t}\beta_a(t)K(t) = 0 \quad (4.63)$$

$$\lim_{t \to \infty} e^{-\delta t}\beta_l(t)L(t) = 0 \quad (4.64)$$

stating that at the end of the infinite horizon the value of labour and capital must be zero: a stronger statement than that entailed by inequalities (4.17).

In the steady state process $F(t)$ grows at the same rate as $K(t)$ and

$\partial F / \partial K = \varepsilon[F(t)/K(t)]$. Since in equation (4.60), i is constant, all other members must also be constant. Therefore β_a is constant. Then, from equation (4.60) we get:

$$\beta_a(t) = \overline{\beta_a} = \left\{\varepsilon\frac{F(t)}{K(t)} - i\right\} / (\delta - \chi) \tag{4.65}$$

The transversality condition (4.60) entails:

$$\delta > \chi \tag{4.66}$$

Then we can state: **LC7: The productivity of capital is greater than the rate of interest: the shadow price of accumulation is equal to the difference divided by the difference between the discount rate of the firm and the expected rate of growth of finance (alternatively we can say the desired rate of growth of capital).**

From equation (4.61), being $\dot{\beta}_l/\beta_l = \chi - \alpha_l$, we get:

$$(1+\varepsilon)\frac{F}{L} - w(t) = \beta_l(t)(\delta - \chi) \tag{4.67}$$

Therefore: **LC8: The marginal productivity of labour is always greater than wages. The difference is the greater, the higher the shadow price for labour and the firm's discount rate, and the lower the rate of growth of labour.**

As we shall see when turning to the conditions for markets equilibria, global long-run equilibrium requires equality between marginal productivity of labour (capital) and wages (rate of interest). That is produced by the market mechanism when it can be interpreted as inducing entry of new firms with the same features as the old ones. Alternatively we can interpret the final result as occurring as a consequence of both the firms' development strategies and their propensity to utilize financial resources to enlarge their production. Through their development strategies, firms will achieve profits, which means that they have the possibility of expanding production (we must remember that returns are constant). Optimal decisions by the firm will eventually cause profits to be eliminated.[3]

If we confine ourselves to an analysis of the firms' development strategies, we arrive at results that recall some Schumpeter's remarks on the process of economic development (requiring certain disequilibria: in our model the firms' tendency to break the equilibrium that is imposed by a *perfect* competitive market) and resemble Fanno's model of the process of growth after Cozzi's interpretation.[4]

From equation (4.62) and (4.58) we get that:

$$\frac{\dot{\beta}_c(t)}{\beta_c(t)} = \delta - \eta(1-\overline{v}) - \psi\eta\overline{v} = \delta - \eta + \eta(1-\psi)\overline{v} \tag{4.68}$$

is constant.

We can now evaluate the rate of growth of the variables by equating the exponents of the three variables F, β_c, g in equation (4.58). We get:

$$\chi + \psi\eta\bar{v} = \delta \qquad (4.69)$$

When considering the compatibility of the exponents in the production function we get another expression for v:[5]

$$\chi + \psi\eta\bar{v} = \alpha_l + \alpha_h(1+\omega) + \eta\psi \qquad (4.70)$$

From equation (4.70) we can state: **LC9: the rate of growth of production is the higher, the higher the rates of growth of population, of labour qualification and of the technological qualification of capital, and the higher is the capital income share.**

Since:

$$\delta = \alpha_l + \alpha_h(1+\omega) + \eta\psi \qquad (4.71)$$

we come to an important result: **LC10: The firm's discount rate is not arbitrary. It depends on: the firm's expectations concerning the growth of population, the growth of wages depending on the rate of growth of the level of qualification of labour h, the index of external effects of accumulation of human capital on income distribution and on the labour productivity in the qualification of capital multiplied by income distribution index.**

Let us turn to constraint (4.24). We can state that, because of equations (4.66) and (4.71):

$$\bar{v} > 0 \quad \text{since} \quad \delta - \chi > 0$$

$$\bar{v} \leq 1 \quad \Rightarrow \quad \delta - \chi \leq \eta\psi \qquad (4.72)$$

III Markets equilibria

A preliminary condition for markets equilibria is that firms' expectations shall be realized:

$$\alpha_l = \lambda \qquad (4.73)$$

$$\alpha_h = \gamma(1-\bar{u}) \qquad (4.74)$$

For the labour market to be in equilibrium the firm's demand for labour must be equal to the consumers' supply. Equation (4.25) must be satisfied.

$$L(t) = uN(t) \qquad (4.25)$$

For the capital market to be in equilibrium:

$$\frac{dK(t)}{dt} = \frac{d(p(t)N(t))}{dt} \qquad (4.75)$$

$$K(t) = p(t)N(t) \qquad (4.75^*)$$

If equations (4.1) and (4.28) are satisfied, we have a long-run equilibrium in the commodity market. Then:

$$\chi = \kappa + \lambda \qquad (4.76)$$

and equation (4.70) becomes:

$$\kappa = \eta\psi(1-\bar{v}) + \gamma(1-\bar{u})(1+\omega) \qquad (4.77)$$

From the consumers' utility maximization and from the firms' profit maximization we have obtained four equations: (4.45) and (4.46) for consumers; for firms, equation (4.70) which in equilibrium becomes (4.77), and equation (4.69) which in equilibrium becomes:

$$\kappa = \delta - \lambda - \psi\eta\bar{v} \qquad (4.78)$$

Remembering that the unknowns are $\kappa, \bar{u}, \bar{v}, i$, we can write the system of equations in matrix form:

$$\begin{pmatrix} 1 & -\gamma(1+\omega) & -\eta\psi & 0 \\ 1-\sigma & -\gamma & 0 & 0 \\ 1 & 0 & -\eta\psi & 0 \\ -\sigma & 0 & 0 & 1 \end{pmatrix} \cdot \begin{pmatrix} \kappa \\ 1-\bar{u} \\ 1-\bar{v} \\ \bar{i} \end{pmatrix} = \begin{pmatrix} 0 \\ A \\ B \\ \rho \end{pmatrix} \qquad (4.79)$$

where $A = \rho - \lambda - \gamma$; $B = \delta - \lambda - \eta\psi$; A expresses the difference between the excess of the consumers' rate of discount over the rate of growth of population (such a difference being considered the consumers' *net* rate of discount) and the productivity of labour allocated to human capital accumulation. B expresses the difference between the excess of the firms' rate of discount above the rate of growth of population (the difference being considered the firms' *net* rate of discount) and the productivity of labour allocated to technological accumulation, corrected by the income distribution index.

For the determinant of the system to be different from zero:

$$\eta\psi\gamma(\sigma - 1)(1+\omega) \neq 0 \qquad (4.80)$$

we must have:

$$\sigma \neq 1 \qquad (4.81)$$

In our model $\sigma = 1$ is a critical value, whereas in the Lucas model the critical value is $\sigma = 0$. As we shall see, if a specific relation holds among some structural coefficients, we can have a solution also when $\sigma = 1$: in such a case (labelled as pseudo-Sraffian case) the rate of interest is exogenously given.

The market equilibrium value of κ is:

$$\kappa = \frac{1}{(1-\sigma)} \cdot \left\{ \frac{B}{(1+\omega)} + A \right\} \qquad (4.82)$$

κ is positive if:

$$(\rho - \lambda)(1+\omega) + \delta > \gamma(1+\omega) + \eta\psi \qquad (4.83)$$

It is interesting to note: **LC11: The rate of growth of consumption is positive provided the sum of the discount rates - the consumers' one having been multiplied by a scalar depending on the external effect - is greater than the sum of productivities of labour employed in human and technological accumulations, γ having been multiplied by the same scalar and η by the income distribution index.**

If we compare the market equilibrium value of the rate of growth of individual consumption in our model with that of Lucas' we note: **LC12: The rate of growth of individual consumption depends on income distribution, both the consumers' and the firm's discount rates, the rates of increase of the labour productivity in human capital and technological accumulation. It is the higher, the higher the positive difference between the firm's discount rate and the rate of increase in population. If σ < 1, we can easily see that κ increases as σ tends to 1. It increases when the growth rate of population increases if σ > 1. It decreases as ρ increases.**

We can determine the quota of labour allocated to human capital accumulation and the quota of employment allocated to capital technological improvement:

$$1 - \bar{u} = \frac{B}{\gamma(1+\omega)} \qquad (4.84)$$

$$1 - \bar{v} = \frac{1}{\eta\psi(1-\sigma)} \cdot \left\{ A + B\left(\sigma - \frac{\omega}{1+\omega}\right) \right\} \qquad (4.85)$$

For the quota of labour allocated to human capital accumulation to be positive, the inequality $B \geq 0$, which can be written $\delta \geq \lambda + \eta\psi$, must be satisfied (this occurs when the rate of growth is positive). It is rather more complicated to state the condition necessary for the quota of employment allocated to capital technological improvement to be positive. What can instead be easily noted is the important role of σ.

The rate of interest depends only on σ, κ, ρ. In fact, We can note: **LC13: The rate of interest must be greater than the consumers' rate of discount. The difference is the higher, the higher are κ and σ.**

IV The case of $\delta = i$

We have assumed that the firm's discount rate is different from the rate of interest. In fact, such a rate can be given two interpretations: it can express the

Schumpeterian propensities of the entrepreneurs (an issue that will be considered in Chapters V and VI) or it can reflect the conditions of the financial market, in line with Fisher's approach. In the second interpretation it is reasonable to assume that $\delta = i$.

Let us go by this assumption. Then equation (4.45) enables us to determine δ as a function of κ:

$$i = \delta = \sigma\kappa + \rho \tag{4.86}$$

By adding the fourth to the third equation in (4.76), being $\bar{i} = \delta$, we get a system with three unknowns $\kappa, \bar{u}, \bar{v}$:

$$\begin{pmatrix} 1 & -\gamma(1+\omega) & -\eta\psi \\ 1-\sigma & -\gamma & 0 \\ 1-\sigma & 0 & -\eta\psi \end{pmatrix} \cdot \begin{pmatrix} \kappa \\ 1-\bar{u} \\ 1-\bar{v} \end{pmatrix} = \begin{pmatrix} 0 \\ A \\ B_\rho \end{pmatrix} \tag{4.87}$$

Where $B_\rho = \rho - \lambda - \eta\psi$ has the same meaning as B with one difference: the rate of discount is the consumers'.

To solve the system for all variables, the determinant must not be zero. Therefore:

$$\sigma - \frac{1+\omega}{2+\omega} \neq 0 \tag{4.88}$$

A relation is established between σ and the external effects.

We can easily solve for the three variables:

$$\kappa = \frac{\{(1+\omega)\gamma + \eta\psi\}/(2+\omega) - (\rho - \lambda)}{\sigma - (1+\omega)/(2+\omega)} \tag{4.89}$$

$$1 - \bar{u} = 1 - \frac{\rho - \lambda}{\gamma} + \frac{1-\sigma}{\gamma} \cdot \kappa \tag{4.90}$$

$$1 - \bar{v} = 1 - \frac{\rho - \lambda}{\eta\psi} + \frac{1-\sigma}{\eta\psi} \cdot \kappa \tag{4.91}$$

The rate of growth of per capita consumption can be easily compared with Lucas'. Let κ_l indicate the rate of growth of per-capita consumption in the Lucas model:

$$\kappa_l = \frac{(1+\omega)\gamma - (\rho - \lambda)}{\sigma} \tag{IV, 44*}$$

We can state: **LC14: Both in our model and in Lucas' the rate of increase in per-capita consumption is the higher, the higher is the difference between the consumers' rate of discount and the rate of increase in** population; in both it is the lower, the higher is sigma. κ depends both on the productivity of labour employed in human capital accumulation and on the productivity of labour employed by firms in technological accumulation, whereas κ_l depends only on the first of these two terms. The impact of the external effects, because of technological accumulation, is different in the two models. In ours it reduces the strength of the first term, but also the negative impact of σ. In fact, if external effects are disregarded, our formula can be easily confronted with Lucas'. κ is normally higher than κ_l because of technological accumulation and because the negative effect of σ is reduced by 1/2. Such positive effects on the level of κ are partially neutralized by the effect of human capital accumulation which is halved.

As for the time allocated to labour qualification by consumers and the quantity of labour available to the firms allocated to R&D, we can state: **LC13:** $1-\overline{u}$ **and** $1-\overline{v}$ **increase with the increase in** κ **if** σ **is less than 1.**

V Equilibrium and expectations

In our model, the competitive market mechanism is defined in a different way than that usually assumed for market equilibria in general equilibrium models. In the latter, demand and supply functions are arrived at and the price is supposed to make demand equal to supply. In our model the agents' decisions do not produce demand and supply functions but time strategies instead: the various strategies are mutually linked by market parameters. The market mechanism is assumed to operate in order to make the agents' expectations of these parameters compatible with one another.[6]

The general equilibrium is thus attained because of the assumption that expectations are fulfilled. We do not intend to discuss the mechanisms which, whenever the economy has strayed from equilibrium paths, will ultimately bring it back along some similar path, through changes in expectations: we shall confine ourselves to some hints to clarify the 'nature' of agents' expectations. We are, indeed, interested in analysing what logical possibilities there may be for expectations to be correct.

The labour market mechanism can assure the fulfilment of expectations regarding the rate of growth of population (labour) as stated by equation (4.77) (we must remember that the rate of growth of population is exogeneously given), provided disequilibria produce changes in wages that affect the consumers' and firms' expectations in such a way as to induce changes in u and v. Mechanisms can be conceived capable of bringing the capital market to equilibrium. Firms' investments are not affected by the rate of interest. For growth to occur, investments have to be decided on the basis of growth expectations. However, changes in the rate of interest, which we can suppose to occur when the capital market is not in equilibrium, can induce changes in firms' decisions when $i = \delta$. However, the model does not allow us to envisage a market mechanism capable of assuring consistency in expectations about the rate of growth of human capital, since there is no market for human capital. This means that: **LC15: In an economy as the one we are considering, the competitive equilibrium path is merely an ideal path. Rational expectations are practically impossible.**

6. REMARKS ON CONSUMERS' EQUILIBRIUM

In our model, the consumer's problem of optimization over time is different from Ramsey's inasmuch as consumer's income increases not only as a consequence of savings, but also because of the consumer's decision to allocate some of his time to qualification. Such a decision is a rational one only if consumers expect wages to be the higher, the higher is qualification.

The consumers' equilibria are characterized by two shadow prices: the shadow price for savings $\theta(t)$ and that for labour $\phi(t)$. Decisions about allocation of income between consumption and savings and about allocation of labour between productive activity and qualification are reached in accordance with marginalistic rules. The size of consumption is such as to make marginal utility of consumption equal to the shadow price of savings (see equation 4.32). The time is allocated in such a way as to make the value, in terms of utility, of the marginal decrease of labour income due to a unitary decrease in time allocated to labour equal to the value of the marginal improvement in qualification (see equation 4.34).

The rate of growth of the shadow price of savings is equal to the difference between the consumer's discount rate and the net rate of interest. We should remember that consumers must save a percentage of their income at least equal to the rate of growth of population to make it possible for the new-born to start out in the same conditions as active people in existence. If the discount rate is greater than the net rate of interest, the shadow price of savings increases over time; in the opposite case it decreases (equation 4.35).

The rate of growth of the shadow price for labour qualification is equal to the difference between the consumer's discount rate, which reflects the greed for day-to-day-consumption, and the productivity of labour allocated to qualification (equation 4.36).

We are now in a position to appreciate the role of the consumers' discount rate.

Both the rates of increase in consumption and in consumer wealth are positively correlated to the rate of interest and negatively to the rate of increase in population. In fact the relevant effect of changes in the rate of interest is the income effect. The rate of growth of consumption is negatively correlated to both the consumers' discount rate and the intertemporal substitution index σ. In our model, structural stability of income distribution is assured by a proper relation between labour income, wealth and consumption.

The quota of labour allocated to production is determined by equation (4.49). It is the higher, the higher are the growth rate and the intertemporal elasticity of substitution,[7] and the lower the higher are the productivity of labour in qualification and the rate of interest.

The intertemporal substitution index plays an important role in determining the solution of the model. It is interesting to note that changes in its value can cause abrupt changes in the rate of growth of income and in other variables. In fact, should we apply the model for analyses of comparative dynamics, we would find that evolution of the system is characterized by bifurcations.

7. REMARKS ON FIRMS' EQUILIBRIUM

From the analysis of the firms' equilibrium, we can infer some interesting considerations.

In the Hicksian equilibrium over time the economy is an adaptive system. Competition can be conceived in a rigorous neo-classical sense, firms being price takers. Evolution is caused by external factors: firms receive signals from markets and change their production plans. When growth does result from firms' strategy, the firm has to play a positive role in envisaging possible future developments of the economy. We let ourselves into some Knightian-Schumpeterian world. Still, we did hold on the assumption of firms being price takers: nonetheless, we had to assume that firms, in some ways, have expectations about the growth of capital, as provided by consumers' savings, and about future increases the labour availability. Such an assumption is necessary for a problem of optimization over time to be formulated, otherwise the firm could only try to make the most of current market conditions, as is assumed in the usual equilibrium models.

We cannot define the equilibrium position of the firm on the basis of equality between marginal productivity and factor price. For three reasons: the factors of production are *qualified labour* and *qualified capital*, the firm has to pay for qualification, conditions must be created for growth.

In fact, the marginal productivity of capital (labour) is higher than the rate of interest (wages); the rate of growth in wages is equal to the rate of growth of production less the rate of growth in population. However, as we have seen, free entry leads to long-run equilibrium in which the factor productivities are equal to their price.

Income distribution also depends on the effects of labour qualification as compared with those of capital qualification (technical progress). We are in a Smithian world.

8. THE PSEUDO-SRAFFIAN CASE

Let us now consider, in the general model, the critical case $\sigma = 1$. Let us recall the meaning of this assumption. We assume a unitary intertemporal elasticity: 10% decrease in present consumption can be compensated by 10% increase in future consumption. The instantaneous utility function is a logarithmic function. That entails that utility has no upper limit: it can increase for ever. This assumption frames a context which is different from Ramsey's and close to Sraffa's. We use the term *pseudo-Sraffian case*, being aware of the differences between Sraffa's model, aimed at analysing the interrelations between productive activities, and ours, akin to Solow's and Lucas' models where growth is the result of maximization of consumers' utility.

Let us multiply, in matrix (4.79), the second equation by $(1+\omega)$ and add it to the third equation. We then get the first equation, provided:

$$A(1+\omega) + B = 0 \tag{4.92}$$

having already defined $A = \rho - \lambda - \gamma$, $B = \delta - \lambda - \eta\psi$.

If condition (4.92) is satisfied, we can assume i as given. We then arrive at the system:

$$\begin{pmatrix} 0 & -\gamma & 0 \\ 1 & 0 & -\eta\psi \\ -1 & 0 & 0 \end{pmatrix} \cdot \begin{pmatrix} \kappa \\ 1-\bar{u} \\ 1-\bar{v} \end{pmatrix} = \begin{pmatrix} -B(1+\omega) \\ B \\ \rho - 1 \end{pmatrix} \tag{4.93}$$

Let us assume that the firm discount rate is equal to the rate of interest. Then, condition (4.89) can be written:

$$\gamma = (\rho - \lambda) + \frac{\eta\psi + \lambda - i}{1 - \omega} \tag{4.94}$$

For the Sraffian case to occur, γ must assume a specific value, which is the higher, the higher is the consumers' net rate of discount, the rate of growth of population and the productivity of labour devoted to technical accmulation, and the lower the external effect and the rate of interest.

Having assumed both discount rates equal to the rate of interest, we get the following solutions:

$$\kappa = i - \rho \tag{4.95}$$

$$1 - \bar{u} = 1 - \frac{\rho - \lambda}{\gamma} \tag{4.96}$$

$$1 - \bar{v} = 1 - \frac{\rho - \lambda}{\eta\psi} \tag{4.97}$$

We can thus state the following important result: **LC16: In the pseudo-Sraffian case, given the rate of interest, the rate of growth of per-capita consumption depends only on the consumers' discount rate. The lower the discount rate, the higher the rate of growth. The solution tends to approach the von Neumann solution (rate of growth equal to the rate of interest) as the discount rate tends to zero. The time devoted to human capital accumulation is the higher, the higher its productivity, and the lower the consumers' net discount rate. A similar relation holds for the time devoted to technical accumulation: the positive correlation is with its productivity corrected for the effect on income distribution.**

In von Neumann's model and in Sraffa's the rate of growth is determined by the technology and by the consumption coefficients. Technological and consumption coefficients are such as to make it possible to produce a surplus which is invested to expand production. Population is neither a brake nor a driving factor. The rate of growth of population adapts itself to the rate of growth of production. The philosophy is akin to Ricardo's. Ricardo has offered an explanation of how population dynamics is adjusted to the expansion of production. However Ricardo's analysis resembles the comparative statics. On the contrary, von Neumann's model is a dynamic model: the first model of optimal growth. Sraffa's model analyses the static interdependences of an economy capable of growing at a constant rate.

In our model, having assumed a given rate of growth of population, what remains to be determined in order to envisage the path of growth is the rate of increase in per-capita consumption. No wonder that such a rate depends on the greed of consumers, given the rate of interest. The economy must assume a coherent structure. And the coherence is produced by the appropriate values of the two decision variables u and v.

To isolate the effect of technological change on economic growth, it may be advisable to let the growth rate of labour supply adapt itself to the demand through migration. That is the approach taken in the models presented in Chapters 5 and 6.

The rate of increase in per-capita consumption depends on the consumers' net discount rate. Let us represent, in Figure 4.1, κ on ordinate and $\rho - \lambda$ on abscissa. Inequality (4.54) tells us that $0 < \rho - \lambda \leq +\gamma$. Equation (4.95) can be represented by a family of lines the intercept of which on the ordinates is i, the slope being -1. The admissable set corresponds to the interval $0 - \gamma$. If the productivity of labour allocated to human capital accumulation increases, the relations between κ and $\rho - \lambda$ do not change; however they are defined over a larger set. Stationary states correspond to the intercepts of the lines expressing this relation on the abscissa: the condition $\rho = i$ is satisfied.

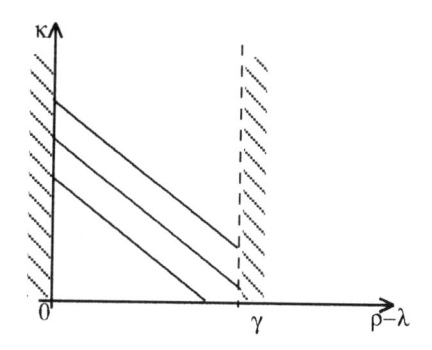

Figure 4.1

9. THE QUASI-STATIONARY STATE

In the stationary state the rate of growth is zero. What are the effects of the qualification of labour and of the technological accumulation which has been implemented? Our model can offer an answer to this question.

Let us consider the case $\delta = i$. Let us revert to:

$$\kappa = \frac{\{(1+\omega)\gamma + \eta\psi\}/(2+\omega) - (\rho-\lambda)}{\sigma - (1+\omega)/(2+\omega)} \quad (4.89)$$

It is easy to see that, when ρ becomes so high as to satisfy the equation:

$$\rho = \frac{(1+\omega)\gamma + \eta\psi}{(2+\omega)} + \lambda \quad (4.98)$$

then $\kappa = 0$. In that case, equation (4.45) tells us that $i = \rho$.

For equations (4.90) and (4.91), we have

$$(1-\bar{u}) = 1 - \frac{\rho-\lambda}{\gamma} \quad (4.96)$$

$$(1-\bar{v}) = 1 - \frac{\rho-\lambda}{\eta\psi} \quad (4.97)$$

which are the same values we have obtained in the Sraffian case when $\delta = i$.

This result is not surprising. When $\kappa = 0$, the values of $1 - \bar{u}$ and $1 - \bar{v}$ are independent of the value of σ, in particular they hold when $\sigma = 1$.

The constraints $\bar{u} \leq 1$, $\bar{v} \leq 1$ entail:

$$(\rho - \lambda) \leq \min(\gamma, \eta\psi) \qquad (4.99)$$

Since $\kappa = 0$, we must have $\rho - \lambda = \{(1+\omega)\gamma + \eta\psi\}/(2+\omega) \geq \min(\gamma, \eta\psi)$. This entails that the quasi-stationary state is only possible when $\gamma = \eta\psi$ and consequentially $\bar{u} = 1; \bar{v} = 1$.

LC17: In the quasi-stationary state, since the productivity of labour devoted to human capital accumulation is equal to that of labour devoted to technological accumulation (corrected by the index of income distribution), all workers are employed in production. Their level of qualification and the technological qualification of capital make it possible to achieve a high level of per-capita consumption which is kept constant over time.

10. THE ROLE OF CONSUMERS' DISCOUNT RATE WHEN $\delta = i$

κ can be considered a function of $\rho - \lambda$:

$$\kappa = RS - S(\rho - \lambda) \qquad (4.100)$$

where:

$R = \{[(1+\omega)\gamma + \eta\psi]/(2+\omega)\} \geq \min(\gamma, \eta\psi)$ and $S = 1/\{\sigma - (1+\omega)/(2+\omega)\}$.

The function is linear. Taking σ as a parameter, we have a family of functions. They all cross the abscissa for the value of $\rho - \lambda = R$, at which we have $\kappa = 0$, the stationary state. For $\sigma > (1+\omega)/(2+\omega)$ the line is negatively inclined: the slope increases as σ approaches $(1+\omega)/(2+\omega)$. For $\sigma < (1+\omega)/(2+\omega)$ the line is positively inclined. The admissible set is defined by the inequalities on $\bar{u}, \bar{v}$ which can be written:

$$0 < \rho - \lambda - (1-\sigma)\kappa < \gamma \qquad (4.101)$$

$$0 < \rho - \lambda - (1-\sigma)\kappa < \eta\psi \qquad (4.102)$$

When $\sigma = 1 > (1+\omega)/(2+\omega)$ the line VR represents the pseudo-Sraffian case for $\rho = i$. Along the Sraffian line, $1 - \bar{u}$ and $1 - \bar{v}$ assume the same values as in point R (see Figure 4.2).

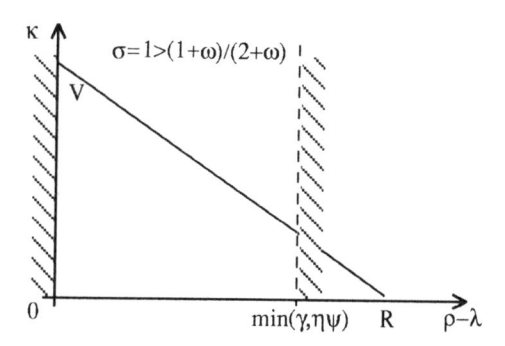

Figure 4.2

When $\sigma \leq 1$, in case $\sigma > (1 + \omega)/(2 + \omega)$, the lines negatively inclined which represent the relation between κ and $\rho - \lambda$ for different values of σ are partially in the admissable area; none of them being below the pseudo-Sraffian line (Figure 4.3).

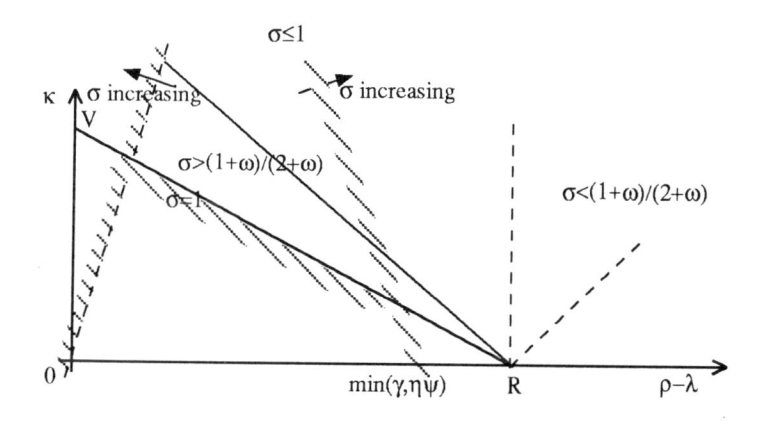

Figure 4.3

When $\sigma \geq 1$, in case $\sigma > (1 + \omega)/(2 + \omega)$, the lines negatively inclined which represent the relation between κ and $\rho - \lambda$ for different values of σ are partially in the admissable area; none of them being above the pseudo-Sraffian line (Figure 4.4).

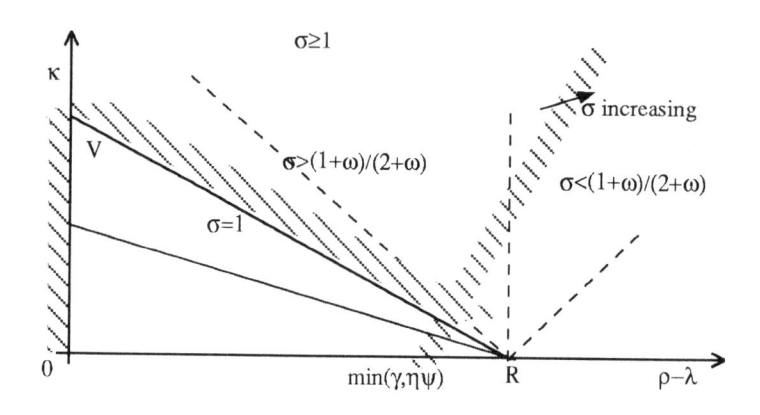

Figure 4.4

In case $\sigma < (1+\omega)/(2+\omega)$ the lines positively inclined are all outside the admissible region.

11. EXTERNALITIES, OPTIMAL GROWTH AND MARKET EQUILIBRIUM

In the general model, growth is the result of an external factor (population growth) and of two internal factors: the accumulation of human capital, resulting from individuals' choice about $u(t)$, and technical accumulation resulting from firms' choice about $v(t)$.

Consumers create an external economy for the firm through human capital accumulation. Then the *optimal growth path* may diverge from the equilibrium path.

To find the optimal path, we shall assume that all decisions – about $c(t)$, u and v – are taken by a planner in order to maximize consumers' utility over time. Thus, the external economy is internalized. Then, we shall compare the *optimal path* for the economy with the market equilibrium path we have analysed.

We have already remarked that externalities make the market incapable of bringing the economy to the optimal structure (or path). We shall not deal with the economic-policy problems which must be faced because of such a failure of the market.

Along the optimal path the relation (4.7) between the structural coefficients must hold:

$$\kappa = \psi\eta(1-\bar{v}) + \gamma(1+\omega)(1-\bar{u}) \tag{4.7}$$

To find the other relations defining the optimal path we have to maximize the utility of all consumers. The function to be maximized is the well-known utility function:

$$e(u) = \int_0^\infty e^{-\rho t}\left\{\frac{1}{1-\sigma}[c(t)^{1-\sigma} - 1]\right\}N(t)dt \tag{4.10}$$

Equation (4.10) shall be maximized under the constraints:

$$\dot{N}(t) = \lambda N(t) \qquad N(0) = N_o \tag{4.4}$$

$$\dot{h}(t) = \gamma[1-u(t)]h(t) \qquad h(0) = h_o \tag{4.5}$$

$$\dot{g}(t) = \eta[1-v(t)]g(t) \qquad g(0) = g_o \tag{4.6}$$

$$\dot{K}(t) + c(t)N(t) = F(t) \qquad K(0) = K_o \tag{4.1}$$

$$F(t) = h(t)^\xi [g(t)K(t)]^\varepsilon [h(t)u(t)v(t)N(t)]^{1-\varepsilon} \tag{4.2}$$

Let us write the Hamiltonian:

$$H = e^{-\rho t}\left\{\frac{1}{1-\sigma}(c(t)^{1-\sigma} - 1)N(t) + \theta([g(t)K(t)]^\varepsilon [h(t)vN(t)]^{1-\varepsilon}h(t)^\xi - c(t)N(t))\right\}$$

$$+ e^{-\rho t}\{\phi\gamma h(t)(1-u) + \beta\eta(1-v)g(t) + \alpha\lambda N(t)\} \tag{4.103}$$

The first-order condition with respect to the decision variable c is the same as that obtained in analysing the market equilibrium path:

$$\theta(t) = c(t)^{-\sigma} \tag{4.104}$$

which implies:

$$\frac{\dot{\theta}(t)}{\theta(t)} = -\sigma\kappa \tag{4.105}$$

The first-order conditions with respect to the variable u is:

$$\theta(t)\frac{\partial F(t)}{\partial u} = \phi(t)\gamma h(t) \tag{4.106}$$

The first-order conditions with respect to the variable v is:

$$\theta(t)\frac{\partial F(t)}{\partial v} = \beta(t)\eta g(t) \tag{4.107}$$

The first-order conditions with respect to the costates are:

$$\frac{\dot{\theta}(t)}{\theta(t)} = \rho - \frac{\partial F(t)}{\partial K(t)} \quad (4.108)$$

$$\frac{\dot{\phi}(t)}{\phi(t)} = \rho - \frac{\theta(t)}{\phi(t)} \cdot \frac{\partial F(t)}{\partial h(t)} - \gamma(1-u) \quad (4.109)$$

$$\frac{\dot{\beta}(t)}{\beta(t)} = \rho - \frac{\theta(t)}{\beta(t)} \cdot \frac{\partial F(t)}{\partial v} - \eta(1-v) \quad (4.110)$$

$$\frac{\dot{\alpha}(t)}{\alpha(t)} = \rho - \theta(t)\frac{\partial F(t)}{\partial N(t)} \quad (4.111)$$

From equations (4.105) and (4.108) we get:

$$\sigma\kappa = \tau - \rho \quad (4.112)$$

being $\partial F/\partial K = \varepsilon(F/K) = \varepsilon(F_0/K_0) \equiv \tau$.

τ is the interest rate which is equal to the productivity of capital.
From equation (4.106) and (4.109) we get:

$$\frac{\dot{\phi}(t)}{\phi(t)} = \rho - \gamma h(t)\frac{\partial F(t)}{\partial h(t)}/\frac{\partial F(t)}{\partial u} - \gamma(1-u) = \rho - \gamma(1+\omega)u - \gamma(1-u) \quad (4.113)$$

being $(\partial F/\partial h)/(\partial F/\partial u) = [(F/h)(1-\varepsilon+\xi)]/[(F/u)(1-\varepsilon)] = (1+\omega)(u/h)$.

By equalizing the sum of exponents in the left hand side with the sum of those in the right side of equation (4.106), after having substituted the steady growth values for the corresponding variables, we get:

$$-\sigma\kappa + \kappa + \lambda = \frac{\dot{\phi}}{\phi} + \gamma(1-\overline{u}) \quad (4.114)$$

By utilizing equation (4.113) we can write:

$$(1-\sigma)\kappa - (1+\omega)\gamma(1-\overline{u}) = \rho - \lambda - (1+\omega)\gamma \quad (4.115)$$

From equations (4.107) and (4.110) we get:

$$\frac{\dot{\beta}(t)}{\beta(t)} = \rho - \overline{v}\eta\psi - \eta(1-\overline{v}) \quad (4.116)$$

being $[\partial F/\partial g]/[\partial F/\partial v] = [\varepsilon(F/g)]/[(F/v)(1-\varepsilon)] = (v/g)\psi$.

By equalizing the sum of exponents in the left hand side with the sum of those in the right side of equation (4.107), after having substituted the steady growth values for the corresponding variables, we get:

$$-\sigma\kappa + \kappa + \lambda = \frac{\dot{\beta}}{\beta} + \eta(1-\overline{v}) \quad (4.117)$$

From equation (4.116) and (4.117) we get:

$$(1-\sigma)\kappa - \psi\eta(1-\bar{v}) = \rho - \lambda - \eta\psi \quad (4.118)$$

We can write the system of equations (4.7), (4.115), (4.118) and (4.112) in matrix form:

$$\begin{pmatrix} 1 & -(1+\omega)\gamma & -\eta\psi & 0 \\ (1-\sigma) & -(1+\omega)\gamma & 0 & 0 \\ (1-\sigma) & 0 & -\eta\psi & 0 \\ -\sigma & 0 & 0 & 1 \end{pmatrix} \cdot \begin{pmatrix} \kappa \\ 1-\bar{u} \\ 1-\bar{v} \\ \tau \end{pmatrix} = \begin{pmatrix} 0 \\ \rho-\lambda-(1+\omega)\gamma \\ \rho-\lambda-\eta\psi \\ \rho \end{pmatrix} \quad (4.119)$$

If we compare (4.119) with the corresponding system expressing the conditions for the market-equilibrium-growth path, we note that the second equation (4.115) is different from the corresponding equation in (4.76): the coefficient of $\gamma\bar{u}$ in the former is multiplied by ω. That is the result of the fact that in *global optimization* we take the external effect into account.

The determinant of the system is:

$$\eta\psi(1+\omega)\gamma(2\sigma-1) \quad (4.120)$$

It is equal to zero when:

$$\sigma = \frac{1}{2} \quad (4.121)$$

The value of the variables are:

$$\kappa^o = \frac{[(1+\omega)\gamma + \eta\psi]/2 - (\rho-\lambda)}{\sigma - 1/2} \quad (4.122)$$

$$1-\bar{u} = 1 - \frac{\rho-\lambda}{(1+\omega)\gamma} + \frac{1-\sigma}{(1+\omega)\gamma} \cdot \kappa \quad (4.123)$$

$$1-\bar{v} = 1 - \frac{\rho-\lambda}{\eta\psi} + \frac{1-\sigma}{\eta\psi} \cdot \kappa \quad (4.124)$$

Let us compare equation (4.116) with the corresponding equation that has been obtained in case $\delta = i$:

$$\kappa = \frac{\{(1+\omega)\gamma + \eta\psi\}/(2+\omega) - (\rho-\lambda)}{\sigma - (1+\omega)/(2+\omega)} \quad (4.89)$$

It will be easily noticed that the two equations coincide when the external effect is zero, namely $\omega = 0$.

κ^o is 0 when: $\rho - \lambda = [(1+\omega) + \eta\psi]/2$. We can consider κ^o as a function of $\rho - \lambda$ and represent the family of the lines corresponding to different values of σ. The stationary state occurs at a value of $\rho - \lambda$ smaller than that to which a stationary state corresponds in the market equilibrium path. The change of slope occurs when $\sigma = 1/2$. The slope of the line changes only when σ changes, whereas in market equilibrium path it changes also when ω changes. The family of lines can be represented by families similar to Figures 4.2 and 4.3.

Let us point out a difference between the analysis of the market equilibrium path and the optimization problem: in the latter we have only one rate of discount ρ.

12. OPTIMAL GROWTH AND COMPETITIVE PATH

Let us compare the competitive equilibrium path, being $\delta = i$, with the optimal growth path.

Let us calculate the derivatives of κ and κ_o with respect to the productivity rate of labour employed in qualification and research:

$$\frac{\partial \kappa}{\partial \gamma} = \frac{1+\omega}{2\sigma - 1 + \omega(\sigma - 1)} \qquad \frac{\partial \kappa_o}{\partial \gamma} = \frac{1+\omega}{2\sigma - 1} \qquad (4.125)$$

$$\frac{\partial \kappa}{\partial \eta} = \frac{\psi}{2\sigma - 1 + \omega(\sigma - 1)} \qquad \frac{\partial \kappa_o}{\partial \eta} = \frac{\psi}{2\sigma - 1} \qquad (4.126)$$

We can establish **LC18: The effects of increases in productivity of labour employed in qualification and research are larger in the optimum path than in the equilibrium path. In both paths the effects of the increase in productivity of labour employed in qualification on the rate of growth is the larger, the larger is the index of external effects of human capital accumulation, whereas the effects of an increase in the productivity of labour employed in research depend on the index of income distribution.**

Let us now examine how κ and κ_o change with changes in ω. As we have already remarked, when $\omega = 0$, namely when there is no external economy, κ and κ_o are equal.

Let us calculate the derivative of κ with respect to ω:

$$\frac{\partial \kappa}{\partial \omega} = \frac{[\gamma - (\rho - \lambda)]\sigma - [\eta\psi - (\rho - \lambda)](\sigma - 1)}{[\sigma(2+\omega) - (1+\omega)]^2} \qquad (4.127)$$

In the optimal path the rate of growth of production (κ_o) is a linear function of ω (l_o in Figure 4.5).

In case of $\sigma > 1$, in market equilibrium κ has an asymptote:

$$\lim_{1+\omega \to \infty} \kappa = \frac{\gamma - (\rho - \lambda)}{\sigma - 1} \qquad (4.128)$$

We need now to distinguish between two cases:

Human-Capital and Technological Accumulation

$$a) \quad \frac{\gamma-(\rho-\lambda)}{\psi\eta-(\rho-\lambda)} > \frac{\sigma-1}{\sigma}$$

$$b) \quad \frac{\gamma-(\rho-\lambda)}{\psi\eta-(\rho-\lambda)} < \frac{\sigma-1}{\sigma} \qquad (4.129)$$

being:

$$0 < \frac{\sigma-1}{\sigma} < 1 \qquad (4.130)$$

$\gamma-(\rho-\lambda)$ can be considered as the actualized productivity of labour allocated to qualification, whereas $\psi\eta-(\rho-\lambda)$ is the actualized productivity of labour allocated to research, weighted with the income-distribution index. We can say that case *a)* holds when the actualized productivity of labour allocated to qualification is sufficiently small in comparison with the actualized productivity of labour in research. Case *b)* would occur in the opposite case. The analysis of the constraints on the values of parameters enables us to state that the latter case is not admissible.

It is easy to show that in case *a)* κ increases as ω increases.

We can then state **LC19: For steady state evolution to be possible, the actualized productivity of labour allocated to qualification must be sufficiently strong and/or the actualized productivity of labour allocated to research sufficiently weak: such a statement is reinforced if σ is augmented.**

Such a result is not surprising. To enhance capital productivity we need to use labour that will thus be no longer available either for labour qualification or for production. To have a steady growth in which the rate of growth increases with the external effects produced by labour qualification, we need a sufficiently strong productivity of the qualification activity and/or a small consumer rate of discount.

An upper limit can be found for κ^o in correspondence to the upper limit of $\overline{v}$ which is equal to 1. The optimal rate of growth cannot be greater than: $(\psi\eta-\rho)/(\sigma-1)$ corresponding to $\omega = \omega_m$. After reaching this value, the optimal rate of growth remains constant.

If:

$$\frac{\psi\eta-(\rho-\lambda)}{\sigma-1} \geq \frac{\gamma-(\rho-\lambda)}{\sigma-1} \qquad (4.131)$$

the second term of the inequality being the asymptote of κ, κ can increase indefinitely, remaining always lower than κ_o (case a_1 in Figure 4.5).

If:

128 *Growth and Economic Development*

$$\frac{\psi\eta - (\rho - \lambda)}{\sigma - 1} < \frac{\gamma - (\rho - \lambda)}{\sigma - 1} \qquad (4.132)$$

it can then be shown that there is a limit for κ. At the superior value, the equilibrium rate of growth is equal to the optimal rate of growth (case a_2).

As we can easily check, the intercept of the lines expressing the rate of growth (of the equilibrium path and of the optimal path) as a function of ω moves upwards when both the productivity of labour employed in qualification and that of labour employed in research increases, whereas the slope increases only when the former increases. This is due to the external effect.

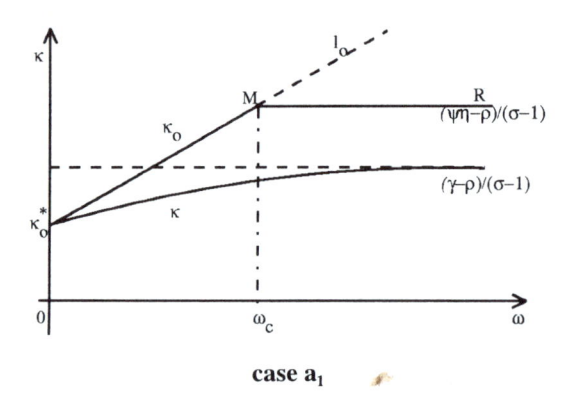

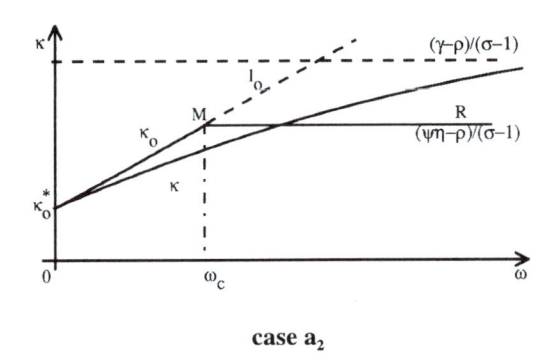

case a_1

case a_2

Figure 4.5

Let us now turn to the case of $\sigma = 1$. In the admissible case, the relation between κ and ω is a line with a positive slope lying always below the line of the optimal growth that has no superior limit. (See Figure 4.6)

We can express the difference between the optimal rate of growth and the market-equilibrium rate in terms of $\overline{u}$:

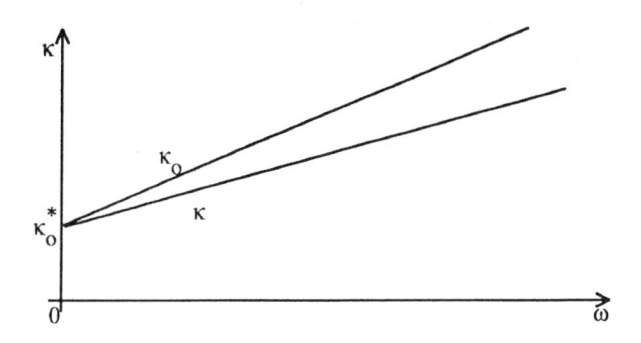

Figure 4.6

$$\kappa^o - \kappa = \frac{\gamma\omega}{2(\sigma - 1/2)} \, \bar{u} \qquad (4.133)$$

When $\sigma > 1/2$ the optimal rate of growth is always greater than the market-equilibrium rate.

13. FINAL REMARKS

When agents make their choices by optimizing over time (with an infinite horizon), the system is no longer an adaptive system. Then competition cannot be interpreted as mere adjustments of price takers to signals coming from markets. All agents must have definite expectations. Optimization means looking for a strategy and implementing it. That has remarkable effects on the way a competitive market can be conceived.

In such a framework, the steady growth requires some structural features. We have dwelt on the consumer's features, mainly on those concerning the intertemporal substitution index.

In our model the effects of changes in productivity are more complex than in other models, mostly because of the feedback effects of the external economy on income distribution. The importance of the qualification of labour compared with that of research has relevant effects on income distribution which can affect the rate of growth in different ways.

If we turn to problems of comparative dynamics, our analysis will run into the difficulties caused by several bifurcations. Small changes in some critical values of some parameters such as σ for instance, may cause changes in the trajectories.

Solow's and Lucas' models were intended mostly to explain divergencies and convergence of the rates of growth in different countries. We think that economic theories may contribute to explain historical facts provided they are combined with proper considerations of the different institutional and social set-ups that may help classifying the countries to be examined. However, it is our opinion that a prior and indeed more significant claim of endogenous growth analysis should be to clarify some theoretical issues concerning the agents' time strategies as compared with their myopic point optimizations, the role of expectations, the different optimality criteria and the market failures. The problem of optimality of growth will appear more intricate when we turn to Schumpterian processes of development. Then, the market will be found to take on a role that cannot be properly assessed in equilibrium path analysis, the more important effect of competition being a kind of Darwinian selection.

SYMBOLS

Parameters

ρ: consumer's discount rate
σ: consumer's risk aversion coefficient (σ^{-1}: intertemporal elasticity of substitution)
γ: labour productivity in labour qualification
α_w: expected effect of labour qualification on wages
α_l: expected rate of growth of population
α_h: expected rate of growth of human capital
χ: expected rate of growth of finance: propensity to grow
λ: rate of increase in population
μ: rate of technical progress in Solow's model
η: labour productivity in qualification of capital
ξ: external effect of labour qualification
ε: capital coefficient in production function
δ: firm's rate of discount

Variables

$c(t)$: individual consumption at time t
$u(t)$: quota of labour allocated by consumer to production
U: utility
$h(t)$: human capital qualification

$h(t)_a$: global human capital qualification expected by each firm in Lucas' model
$w(t)$: wages
$i(t)$: rate of interest
$p(t)$: consumer's wealth
π: propensity to save
$s(t)$: per-capita savings
$A(t)$: shift of production function due to technical progress (in Solow's model)
μ: rate of technical progress in Solow's model
v: rate of increase of labour qualification in Lucas' model
$g(t)$: technical qualification of capital
$v(t)$: quota of labour allocated by firm to production
$K(t)$: firm's capital
$L(t)$: labour employed by firm
$F(t)$: quantity of commodity produced
$N(t)$: population
θ: shadow price of a unitary increase in savings (of investments in Solow's and Lucas' models)
ϕ: shadow price of a unitary increase in labour qualification
i: interest rate
ι: interest rate in global optimization (LC model)
κ: rate of growth of consumption, wages and consumer's wealth
β_c: shadow price of a unitary increase in the qualification of capital
β_a: shadow price of accumulation
β_l: shadow price of labour
$\psi = \varepsilon/(1-\varepsilon)$: income distribution index
$\omega = \xi/(1-\varepsilon)$: external effect per unitary share of income accruing to workers.

NOTES

1. As is well known, a fraction of population is inactive. If this fraction of inactive population is p, it follows that each member of the active population can provide the economy with $(1+p)$ unit of work.
2. By substituting the equilibrium value for the variables in equation (4.2), taking into account equation (4.1), we get:
$$e^{(\kappa+\lambda)t} = h_0^{\gamma(1-u)(\xi+1-\varepsilon)t} \cdot g_0^{\varepsilon\eta(1-v)t} \cdot K_0 e^{(\kappa+\lambda)\varepsilon t} \cdot vL_0 e^{\lambda(1-\varepsilon)t}$$
Therefore we must have:
$$\kappa+\lambda = \gamma(1-u)(\xi+1-\varepsilon) + \varepsilon\eta(1-v) + (\kappa+\lambda)\varepsilon + \lambda(1-\varepsilon)$$
By simplifying this expression we get equation (4.7)

3. Also in static analysis of market equilibrium, we distinguish two moments of the result: the first depends only on the solution of the firm's problem (the short run necessary condition for profit maximization: marginal cost equal to marginal revenue); the second is produced by free entry (the long run condition for market equilibrium: marginal cost equal to average cost).
4. According to Fanno a firm will be willing to adopt a strategy of growth only if it can expect positive profits. In the model of endogenous growth, a weak point is the assumption that such a strategy is adopted in spite of the fact that the firm knows that profits will disappear. Such an assumption will be dropped in the Schumpeterian models (see Chapter V and VI).
5. In the steady-growth path we must have:

$$F_0 e^{\chi t} = h_0 e^{\alpha_h(1-\varepsilon+\xi)t} \cdot l_0 e^{\alpha_l(1-\varepsilon)} \cdot g_0 e^{\varepsilon\eta(1-v)t} \cdot K_0 e^{\varepsilon\chi t}$$

Therefore:

$$\chi = \alpha_l + \alpha_h((1+\omega) + \psi\eta(1-\bar{v})$$

6. Such a procedure is logically equivalent to the one based on von Neumann's model. The equilibrium concept reminds us of the Hayek's.
7. From equation (4.49) we get: $\partial \bar{u}/\partial \sigma = \frac{(i-\rho)}{\sigma^2_Y} = \frac{\kappa}{\sigma_Y} \geq 0$

5. A Schumpeterian Path of Economic Development

S. Lombardini and F. Donati

1. THE SCHUMPETERIAN PROCESS OF INNOVATION

Schumpeterian processes of innovation require some disequilibria in various markets and tend to produce new disequilibria. Credit expansion makes it possible to exploit the former and partly contributes in producing the latter. What we are interested in, by now, is to analyse *how Schumpeterian innovations may produce growth*. Technical progress is assumed to be endogenous in a sense different from the one that has been clarified by the models of Chapters 3 and 4. It is endogenous inasmuch as it results from the entrepreneurs' propensity to innovate and not from 'rational' calculation of consumers and firms. However, we shall assume that some *Deus ex machina* assures equilibrium in commodity markets. In the labour market supply is always adjusted to demand through immigration or emigration. In fact, the main result we aim at is showing how innovations can be the essential factor for growth, accumulation being induced by the same growth process. The growing economy tends to a quasi-equilibrium growth path with particular properties as compared with the neoclassical and the Keynesian ones.

In neoclassical analysis, consumer demand functions are derived by a utility maximization process. The essential assumption is that consumers' *tastes* are given. Most innovations entail some product differentiation or creation of new products. Thus, consumers' reactions are not independent from firms' choices.[1] In fact the alternatives offered to consumers are changed after the innovation strategy of firms. The consequence is changes in tastes correlated with the creation of new products and differentiation of old ones. Thanks to sales promotion, consumers may be more inclined to consume and more willing to work. The assumption of consumers maximizing their utility presupposes a given number of well-defined and well-known products. A product is a specific subset of a set of properties, all relevant to the consumer: the subset changes with changes in other commodities and products available.

One could consider defining the utility function not in the commodity space but in that of the *properties* of commodities. But also the set of properties changes after entrepreneurs' innovations.

Therefore, Research and Development (R&D) covers both technological research in its standard sense and *commercial activity* (search for new products, product differentiation and sales promotion). Consumers' tastes can no longer be assumed as given: the notion of utility function must be put aside.

2. QUASI-SCHUMPETERIAN MODELS

Schumpeter's theory is deemed too vague by certain economists. However, we can single out and analyse some features of the Schumpeterian process of economic development by formalized models: the results can be usefully compared with those arrived at by means of endogenous growth models. As we have already remarked, economists cannot explain economic development by a general (unique) model; various tools can be produced which can be useful to understand some features of the economic process in specific conditions. Critical reasoning is then required for an efficient use of the tools in order to explain real processes.

The models presented in this and in the following chapter are quasi-Schumpeterian models aiming at analysing a set of relevant features of the process of economic development.

1. No production function is assumed. Input coefficients decrease in time after innovation. A demand function is assumed for each product.
2. R&D covers both the search for new processes of production and new products. For the sake of simplicity, being interested only in certain economic effects, we shall assume that the effects of R&D depend only on its level (we could consider also the rate of change). Innovators start from different initial conditions; the effects of their activity are uncertain. We shall express these features of the process by associating each entrepreneur with a set of personal parameters and, possibly, by introducing stochastic parameters in the relations by which the effects of R&D are determined.
3. Innovation occurs in the production of both consumer goods and capital good. Innovation is fostered by competition which, in Schumpeterian analysis, is of the oligopolistic type: it is different from the neoclassical concept. However, we think that the effects on development can be analysed by disregarding oligopolistic interdependence and assuming the conceptual framework of monopolistic competition. More precisely, we shall assume that the consumers' choice out of the set of the different consumer goods produced by all the firms in the economy is assimilated to that made by the consumers out of the products offered in a monopolistic competition market. Should we consider the oligopolistic interdependences between

innovating firms, the analysis of the structure of the whole economy, as it results from the interrelations between production, consumption and income distribution, would become too difficult to be dealt with. The relations between innovations in machines and innovations in the production of commodities for which machines are utilized will not be considered.
4. In the Schumpeterian models substitution between commodities occurring after changes in prices and reflecting *consumers' evaluations given their tastes* can be disregarded. Attention will be concentrated on those substitutions occurring after *changes in tastes induced by product innovation and sales promotion activity*. Demand is assumed to be a function of the purchasing power of wages in terms of the price of the commodity. The demand functions is shifted by sales promotion activities. The effects of commercial R&D are different for the various products; their prices undergo different changes. Therefore consumptions of various commodities increase at different rates.
5. One of the effects of commercial activity is reductions in consumers' savings. Firm's investments in machines and in R&D can be financed out of their profits. Alternatively firms can finance their development by issuing bonds or asking for loans.
6. Firms establish price by putting a mark-up on labour costs.
7. Consumers' supply of labour depends on real wages. If labour supply exceeds demand some people will emigrate; in the opposite case immigration may occur.
8. The commodity markets are in continuous equilibrium. In the labour market supply is made equal to demand.
9. The banking system decides the *monetary flow* and firms decide their strategy of development, namely the distribution of labour between accumulation and research. Alternately, we could assume that money supply is decided from outside to affect the agents decisions. However, in order to properly assess the role of such a positive monetary policy we should need a more complex model, as it is required to deal with the country's relations with other economies and the fiscal policy. In our model we shall assume that the banking system supplies the money required and fixes the rate of interest.

We intend to single out the effect of firms' R&D strategies on development. Therefore, we shall disregard the other factor accounting for development: in particular population growth.

In this chapter we shall consider a simple neo-Schumpeterian model that can be compared with models of endogenous growth. We shall concentrate our attention on the effects of innovation, rather than on those produced by competitions among firms, on the structure of the whole economic system.

We can thus make the simplifying assumption that all firms are alike and that only one product is produced. Therefore assumptions **b, c** and **d** are simplified since we have one entrepreneur and one commodity only.

Let us stress the main Schumpeterian features of this model: **a)** It is innovation and not the increase in population that produces growth. **b)** Saving evolution is adapted to the growth requirement by the increase in labour productivity and in profits.[2] Changes in wages, in input coefficients and in mark-up are reflected in price changes. What we shall try to show in this model are the effects of the different development strategies of the firm.

3. THE EQUATIONS OF THE MODEL

Since firms are all alike, no firm can improve its position through sales promotion activity. However, such activities contribute to growth, inasmuch as they cause increases in demand for commodity and in the supply of labour. Thus we have two endogenous factors for growth: the increase in productivity (reductions in input coefficients) and the increase in willingness to work.

Let us simplify the model by assuming a single firm and let us indicate the variables which we shall assume varying continuously:

p the price of consumer commodity
p_t^k the price of capital good at time t
l_t^p the labour employed in the production of consumer good at time t
l_t^k the labour employed in the production of capital good at time t
l_t^r the labour employed for R&D at time t
l_t the total labour employed at time t
q_t the quantity of consumer good produced at time t
w_t wage rate at time t
i_t interest rate at time t
P_t the amount of consumer credit or debit at time t
M_t the amount of firm credit or debit at time t

Let us list the equations of the model:

Price:

$$p = \mu_t w_t \lambda_t^p \qquad (5.1)$$

$$p_t^k = w_t \lambda_t^k \qquad (5.2)$$

A Schumpeterian Path of Economic Development

Since financial flow is endogenously determined, we shall attribute the role of numeraire to the consumer good.[3] Therefore wages are real wages and increase over time. We shall keep p to indicate the price of the commodity. Because of the assumption just made $p = 1$.

LD1: Labour input coefficient λ_t^p decreases over time. Therefore, either p_t decreases or w_t increases in time.

Demand for labour and capital required:

$$l_t^p = \lambda_t^p q_t \tag{5.3}$$

$$l_t^k = \lambda_t^k k_t \tag{5.4}$$

$$k_t = \kappa_t q_t \tag{5.5}$$

total labour employed being

$$l_t = l_t^p + l_t^k + l_t^r \tag{5.6}$$

Consumer demand equal to quantity supplied (q):

$$\frac{q_t}{l_t} = a_t + b \frac{w_t}{p} \tag{5.7}$$

a_t being affected by the research activity (see equation (5.13).

Labour supply equal to labour demanded (l_t):

$$l_t = n_t + m \frac{w_t}{p} \tag{5.8}$$

n_t being affected by the research activity (see equation (5.14).

Consumers' budget equation determining the change in financial assets (money):

$$w_t l_t + i P_t = q_t p_t + \dot{P}_t \tag{5.9}$$

Effects of the research activity (on input coefficients, consumption and supply of labour):

$$\frac{\dot{\lambda}^p_t}{\lambda^p_t} = -\alpha^p_1(l^r)^{\varepsilon_p} - \alpha^p_2 \frac{\dot{l}^r_t}{l^r_t} \tag{5.10}$$

$$\frac{\dot{\lambda}^k_t}{\lambda^k_t} = -\alpha^s_1(l^r)^{\varepsilon_s} - \alpha^s_2 \frac{\dot{l}^r_t}{l^r_t} \tag{5.11}$$

$$\frac{\dot{\kappa}_t}{\kappa_t} = -\alpha^k_1(l^r)^{\varepsilon_k} - \alpha^k_2 \frac{\dot{l}^r_t}{l^r_t} \tag{5.12}$$

$$\frac{\dot{a}_t}{a_t} = \alpha^a_1(l^r)^{\varepsilon_a} + \alpha^a_2 \frac{\dot{l}^r_t}{l^r_t} \tag{5.13}$$

$$\frac{\dot{n}_t}{n_t} = \alpha^n_1(l^r)^{\varepsilon_a} + \alpha^n_2 \frac{\dot{l}^r_t}{l^r_t} \tag{5.14}$$

Firm's rentability:

$$r_t = \frac{pq_t - w_t l^p_t}{p^k_t k_t} \tag{5.15}$$

$\lambda^k_t k_t$ represents the quantity of labour that is embodied in the capital employed. Therefore, we can consider the ratio $(\lambda^k_t k_t)/l^p$ as a *mechanization index* $\omega_t = l^k_t/l^p_t$. The firm's rentability can be expressed in terms of the *monopoly power* $(\mu - 1)$ and of the mechanization index:

$$r_t = \frac{\mu_t - 1}{\omega_t} \tag{5.15bis}$$

LD2: The firm's rentability is higher, the higher is market power and the lower is mechanization.

The firm's investments resulting from equation (5.2) and (5.4):

$$I_t \equiv w_t l^k_t = p^k_t \dot{k}_t \tag{5.16}$$

The firm's financial flow:

$$\dot{M}_t - i_t M_t = pq_t - w_t l_t \tag{5.17}$$

Equations (5.9) and (5.17) tell us that consumers' net saving (dissaving) is equal to the negative (positive) firm's financial flow, namely the *(net) monetary flow* (ϕ_t):

$$\phi_t = \dot{P} - iP \equiv -(\dot{M} - iM) \tag{5.18}$$

A Schumpeterian Path of Economic Development

We can state that: **LD3: An increase in the rate of interest has the mere effect of decreasing the impact on development of a given increase in money ($\dot{M}$) by reducing the corresponding monetary flow.** Thus, the rate of interest is a variable associated with monetary policy. It is interesting for us to evaluate the effects of increases in ϕ_t.

Equations (5.1), (5.3), (5.17) and (5,18) allows us to write:

$$\mu = \frac{wl_t - \phi}{wl_t^p} = 1 + \frac{w(l_t^k + l_t^r) - \phi}{wl^p} \quad (5.19)$$

It is easy to state that $\mu > 0$ only if:

$$w_t l_t > \phi_t \quad (5.19)$$

Then: **LD4a: For μ to be positive it is necessary that the financial flow is smaller than the wages paid by firms.**

We can easily see that $\mu > 1$ only if:

$$w_t(l_t^k + l_{to}^r) > \phi_t \quad (5.20)$$

Therefore **LD4b: For $\mu > 1$ the financial flow must be smaller than the wages paid to workers employed in research and in accumulation.**

A sufficient conditions for $\mu = 1$ is:

$$l_t^k + l_t^r = 0 \qquad \phi_t = 0 \quad (5.21)$$

LD5: If all workers are employed in production (namely if no R&D and no accumulation take place) and financial flow is zero (namely all income is spent in consumption), mark-up is zero. No profits accrue to firms. As we shall better see later on, such a condition is realized in the stationary state.

Alternatively we can state: **LD5bis: For growth to occur, the firm must enjoy a market power, such a condition being associated to another one: that a part of labour be employed in R&D and in accumulation.**

Thus the permanent growth factor is research activity associated with accumulation. The *firm's propensity to accumulate* (ρ can be expressed by the ratio between labour employed in producing capital goods and labour employed for both accumulation and research activity):

$$\rho = l^k / (l^k + l^r) \quad (5.22)$$

ρ is exogenously given: it expresses the entrepreneurs' animal spirits.

Equations (5.19) can be written:

$$\mu_t = 1 + \frac{l_t^k}{\rho l^p} - \frac{\phi}{w_t l^p} \quad (5.23)$$

We can state that: **LD6: The lower are the entrepreneurs' animal spirits, the higher must be the mark-up, given the allocation of labour and the financial flow, or the higher must be the financial flow given the mark-up and the allocation of labour. If the market power is high, a high financial flow is required, given the entrepreneurs' propensity to grow and the allocation of labour.** In fact, the entrepreneurs' propensity to expand their activity (the only means being research and innovation), namely the more Schumpeterian is the entrepreneur, the less monopolistic is the market (we have a more competitive oligopolistic structure). If banks increase finance to firms, a lower market power is required. Market power is linked to the development process, as it should be according to Schumpeter's philosophy.

Let us visualize the relations between the three agents: consumers-workers, firms and banks (Figure 5.1), to better appreciate the role of credit. Consumers-workers deposit their savings at banks which utilize them to supply finance (money) to firms. Consumers receive wages from firms and pay back money to purchase the final commodity. Thus, firms are normally indebted with banks.

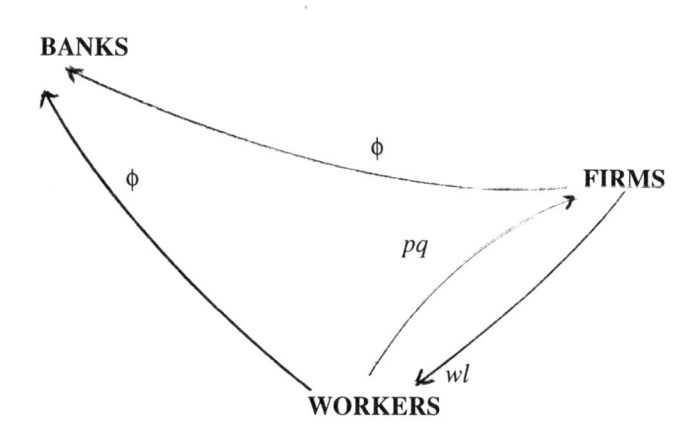

Figure 5.1

Let us explore the consequences of different firms' strategies. By this way, we shall get some clues as to how growth can be affected by the strategies of the firms competing with one another and having a finite horizon for development strategy.

The state variables are: $P, M, k, \lambda^p, \lambda^k, \lambda^r, \kappa, a, n$: their dynamics engender growth. The role of *control variables* is played by ϕ, ρ. In our model ϕ is assumed to adapt to the dynamics of the economy, whereas ρ reflects the *animal spirits* of entrepreneurs, as we have already remarked. The other variables are $q, l^p, l^k, l^r, l, w, \mu, p_t^k$ (under our assumptions p is given and equal to 1). Thus, we have eight variables that can be obtained from equations (5.1), (5.2), (5.3), (5.4), (5.5), (5.6), (5.7) (5.8), by utilizing the other equations, in terms of the state equations.

For the sake of simplicity we have assumed linearity in both the equations determining the quantities of labour and capital employed and in the relations expressing the effects of innovations. Therefore, the evolutions that can be envisaged look rather distorted and unreal. In the real world innovations cannot produce unlimited development for all firms. The possibility of bifurcations should be considered even in the firms' strategies. However, since our essential aim is to show how far innovations can produce growth of the economy, we can take advantage of the simplifying linearity assumptions. Then, we shall be able to visualize an asymptote for evolution which is an ideal one.

4. THE STATIONARY STATE (SCHUMPETERIAN CIRCULAR FLOW)

In Schumpeter theory the starting point of the analysis is the *circular flow*, that is obtained in the *stationary state*. Let us try to envisage it in our model.

From equations (5.7) and (5.8) we get:

$$q_t = \frac{b}{m} l_t^2 + \left(a_t - \frac{bn_t}{m} \right) l_t \qquad (5.24)$$

The parameter a_t defines a family of parabolas crossing the origin. For $a_t = bn_t/l$ the parabola has the minimum at the origin; for $a_t > bn_t/l$ the minimum occurs at a negative value of l_t (the parabola has a positive intercept on the quantity axis); the contrary in the opposite case.

Let us plot in Figure 5.2, where we have represented a family of parabolas (5.24), equation (5.3), which we shall write:

$$q_t = \frac{1}{\lambda_t^p} l^p \qquad (5.3bis)$$

and let us assume that: $l_t^p = l_t$.

For l^* to be positive the following inequality must hold:

$$a < \frac{1}{\lambda} + \frac{bn}{m} \qquad (5.25)$$

From equation (5.24) and (5.3*bis*) we get the quantity of labour (*l**) that, being all employed in production, allow us to reach the maximum quantity of consumer good that can be produced (*q**):

$$l^* = \frac{m}{\lambda b} - \frac{am - bn}{b} \tag{5.26}$$

The *stationary state* is the one corresponding to the maximum quantity that can be produced (*q**). Then, all labour being employed in production, neither accumulation nor research activity can occur. The maximum quantity *q** (and the associated *optimal capital*) is reminiscent of the Ramsey *bliss* or *turnpike* level in Samuelson's interpretation (see Samuelson 1967, p. 271). The rate of interest is zero at the bliss level.

If production is smaller that *q**, labour is employed in part to produce capital goods: accumulation occurs.

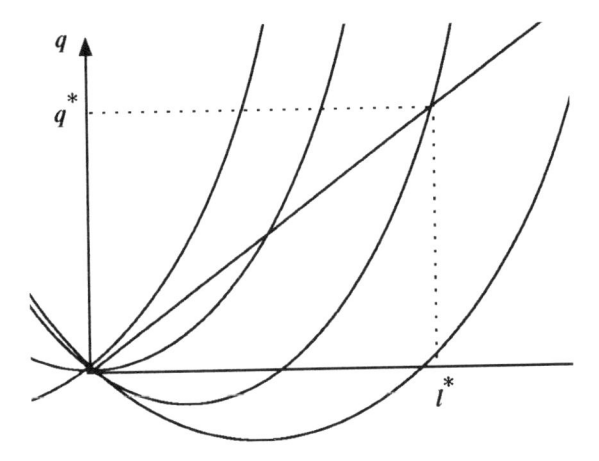

Figure 5.2

In the stationary state, the quantity of labour depends on the quantity of capital. We can get labour as a function of capital by utilizing equations (5.5) and (5.24):

$$l = \frac{1}{2}\left\{ n - \frac{am}{b} + \sqrt{\left(\frac{n-am}{b}\right)^2 + \frac{4mk}{b\kappa}} \right\} \tag{5.27}$$

Let us now outline the main features of the stationary state. Consumers spend all their income, represented only by wages, on consumption. Firms have no market power: $\mu = 1$. Stationary state does not allow for profits; no interest has to be paid. All income accrues to labour, since there are no natural resources (land). We have pictured the Schumpeterian circular flow.

Let us investigate the relations which must occur between labour productivity and the coefficients of the demand function to get just the stationary state, namely a state in which no surplus is produced. We can easily find out such relations. From equation (5.9) we get the real wages at stationary state:

$$\frac{w^*}{p^*} = \frac{q^*}{l^*} \tag{5.28}$$

From equations (5.3*bis*), (5.7) and (5.28) we get the condition that must be satisfied for the economy to be in a stationary state:

$$\frac{1}{\lambda^{p^*}} = \frac{a}{1-b} \tag{5.29}$$

A condition can be derived for b:

$$b3 < 1 \tag{5.29}$$

LD7: In the stationary state the demand function is related to the productivity of labour $1/\lambda_t^{p^*}$. The productivity of labour must be just equal to the ratio between the constant term in the demand function and the one expressing the sensitivity of the demand for the real wage. If labour productivity is higher than such a ratio, the economy is capable of producing more than is required to satisfy the present demand: the economy grows. If it is smaller the labour productivity is not enough to satisfy the potential demand: the economy will eventually shrink. Alternatively we can say that if the labour productivity increases, the stationary state is maintained if the demand function is shifted upwards and/or become flatter.

5. A PROCESS LEADING TO THE STATIONARY STATE

Let us now consider a process by which the stationary state can be reached starting from certain initial conditions. Let us remember that in Ricardo's and Mill's analyses stationary state is arrived at because of land scarcity, technical progress being lacking.

At the beginning of the process, equality (5.25) is satisfied, but capital is lower than the quantity required for the economy to be in a stationary state. Let us assume that firms can finance accumulation out of profits and that consumption is financed by banks where profits are deposited.[4] Then capital is increased.

For such a process to occur, rentability must be positive. Not all workers can be employed to produce final commodity. As time goes on, accumulation tends to zero: all labour tends to be employed in final production; rentability tends to zero; capital tends to the level required for the stationary state. When the stationary state is reached, consumers will have a debt towards banks equal to the credit that firms have acquired by depositing profits. In the stationary state (the Schumpeterian circular flow) the rate of interest must be zero. Consumers debt, equal to firms' credit, represent only a historical accident linked to the transition process.

Let us assume the following initial conditions: $k = 100.000$; $a = 2$, $b = .9$; $n = 20.000$, $m = 3.000$, $l^p = .05$, $l^k = 4$, $\kappa = 2$. Initial consumer wealth (and thus firms' initial debts towards banks) are zero.[5] We can compute the evolution of endogenous variables.

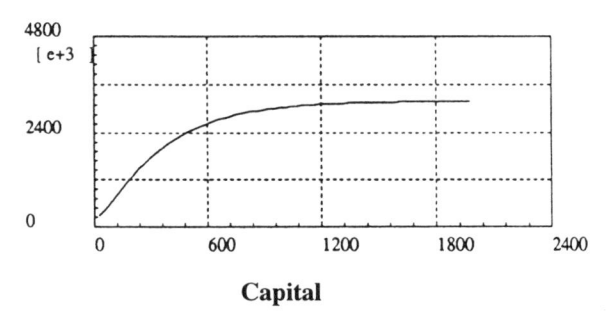

Capital

Figure 5.3

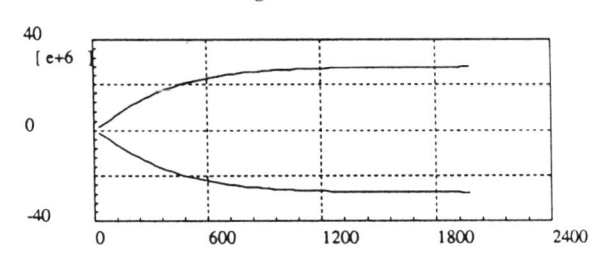

Consumers' wealth and firms' debt

Figure 5.4

Some of them are represented in Figures 5.3–5.8. We can see how capital tends, *through the transition process*, to the stationary value: the final capital, congruous to stationary equilibrium, is 3.2 million. The evolution of consumers wealth (money assets) is specular to that of firms' debts: both consumers' wealth and firms debt tend towards the stationary equilibrium values. Total

A Schumpeterian Path of Economic Development

production increases to reach the maximum value (the stationary value). The same occurs for employment: the equilibrium number of total workers is equal to the equilibrium number of workers employed in production. In the stationary equilibrium the per capita final production is equal to real wages it has increased from the initial value of 2.35 to the stationary equilibrium value of 20; the number of workers, initially 21,200, settles at 80,000. Rentability decreases and tends to zero.

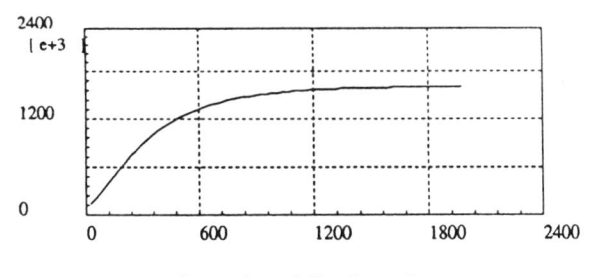

Quantity of final good

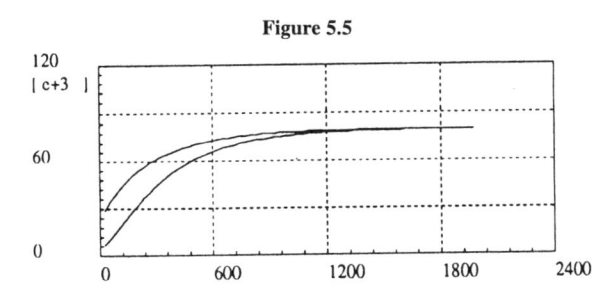

Figure 5.5

Total workers and workers in production

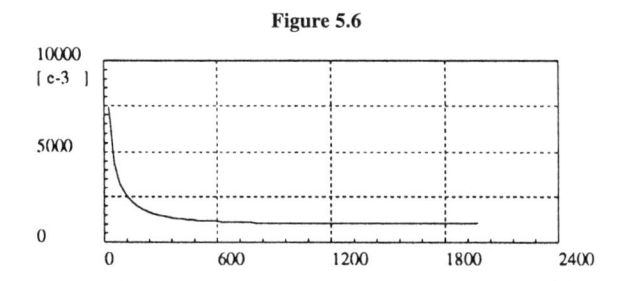

Figure 5.6

Rentability

Figure 5.7

146   *Growth and Economic Development*

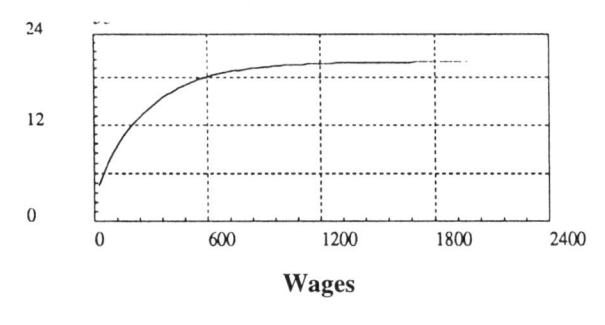

Wages

Figure 5.8

We can label the process of growth required to reach the stationary state as a Millian process of growth. In the economy, referring to which the model has been built, accumulation can only bring to the stationary state. Growth can continue after the critical point represented by the stationary state only if technical progress and expansion of consumption is produced by innovations (technical progress). This is in line with Ricardo's and Mill's thought. In their analyses, technical progress is required to offset the effect of the land scarcity. In our model for growth to occur beyond the stationary state two conditions must be realized: an adequate surplus, namely a sufficiently high labour productivity (Smithian condition) and a sufficient entrepreneurs' propensity to expand their activity (Schumpeterian condition). Because of the assumptions of continuity and linearity, we have obtained unusual numerical figures: the model is a *stylized theory*.

6. A GROWING ECONOMY

In our model R&D is the engine of continuous growth. Let remind us that R&D activity causes an increase in a_t associated with an increase in n_t and a decrease in λ^p.

Let us visualize these effects by means of the family of parabolas defined by equation (5.24) and of the line representing equation (5.3*bis*): the *production line*. Let $0P_1$ be the parabola that crosses the production line at the quantity of labour available, all being employed in production, at a given value of a. An increase in a_t shifts the parabola towards the left (Figure 5.9a): this entails a reduction of the maximum quantity that can is produced. An increase in n_t causes the parabola to move to the right (Figure 5.9b): this entails an increase of the maximum quantity that can be produced. Thus sale promotion activity has a positive effect on growth if the increase in the utility of the final commodity is associated with a more relevant decrease in the utility of leisure.

A Schumpeterian Path of Economic Development

Because of technological innovations the maximum quantity that can be produced is increased (Figure 5.9c). In fact, growth occurs because the production frontier is continuously moved by innovation.

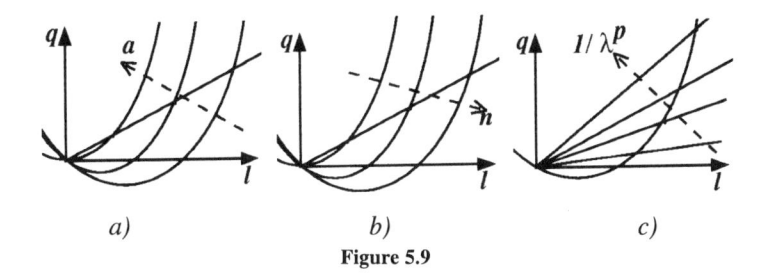

Figure 5.9

Remembering equations (5.9), (5.24) and (5.30) we can write:

$$p = \phi_t \left(l_t \frac{w_t}{p} - q_t \right)^{-1} \tag{5.30}$$

$$p = \phi \left\{ l_t \frac{w_t}{p} - \frac{b}{m} l_t^2 - \left(a_t - \frac{bn_t}{m} \right) l_t \right\} \tag{5.31}$$

From equations (5.7) and (5.27) we get:

$$\frac{b}{m} l_t^2 + \left(a_t - \frac{bn_t}{m} \right) l_t = l_t \left(a_t + b \frac{w_t}{p} \right) \tag{5.32}$$

Equations (5.31) and (5.32) allow us to envisage the evolution of labour and of real wages, being p exogenously given. Knowing the strategy of the firm we can determine both labour employed in the production of capital good and in research:

$$l_t^k = \rho_t (l_t - l^p) \tag{5.21bis}$$

$$l_t^r = (1 - \rho_t)(l_t - l^p) \tag{5.21ter}$$

q_t can be determined on the basis of (5.24), then we can get the value of l_t^p on the basis of equation (5.3). Then, once the firm has fixed its strategy ρ_t, we can determine both the quantities of labour to be devoted to accumulation and to research. We can compute both the amount of capital and the price of the capital good.

The price of the capital good in terms of the price of the final commodity (numeraire) can be determined on the basis of equations (5.1) and (5.3):

$$\frac{p}{\bar{p}} = \frac{1}{\mu_t} \frac{\lambda_t^k}{\lambda_t^p} \qquad (5.33)$$

$$k_t = \kappa \left\{ \frac{b}{m} l_t^2 + \left(a_t - \frac{bn_t}{m} \right) l_t \right\} \qquad (5.34)$$

$$k_t = \frac{l_t^k}{\lambda_t^k} \qquad (5.35)$$

We are left with three equations to determine μ_t, k_t, p_t^k. The price of the capital good and μ must be such as to make the capital produced (equation 5.33) equal to the capital required (equation 5.35).

Now, we are able to assess the fundamental role played in the process of growth by l^r_t. It causes changes in the input coefficients and in the constant terms of the demand equation and of the labour supply equation. As we shall show in the next paragraph **LD8: the system tends to move towards a quasi-equilibrium growth path that depends essentially on the resources devoted to research, namely on the firm's strategy variable ρ. Its main features are:**

1. **The number of workers employed in the production of the capital good and in research remains constant: the ratio between the former and the latter is equal to ρ and the number of workers utilized for accumulation and research ($l^k + l^r$) increases with the increase in ρ.**
2. **The price of capital remains constant.**
3. **Mark-up settles at the value of 1.**
4. **Rentability remains constant: its value increases as R&D increases.** [6]
5. **The quantity of the final commodity, capital and labour, increase at a constant rate.**
6. **Consumer savings tends to zero. In fact, since firms attain a surplus, consumers are found to be indebted. However, as we move towards the the quasi-equilibrium path (asymptote of evolution), the ratio ϕ/wl tends continuously to zero. ϕ/l tends to a constant value, which is higher, the larger research activity is.**

Now, we can clearly see, how growth is related only to R&D. Real wages increase after the increase in productivity. The increase in real wages induces an increase in labour (population). Therefore, capital grows in spite of the increase in capital productivity.

The quasi-equilibrium growth path is only an *ideal asymptote* of evolution, due to the fact that in our stylized theory, as time goes on, input coefficients tend to zero while the constant terms of the consumer good demand and of the labour supply tend to infinity.

7. A SIMULATION OF THE GROWTH PROCESS

Let us assume, for the sake of simplicity, that the effects of R&D depend only on the level of research activity (all α_2 are equal to zero), and let us put all α_1 equal to .0001 and all ε equal to .3. At time 0 $k = 100.000$. At the beginning of the process consumers have no capital.[7] Consumers save to enable banks to finance firms.

Let assume the following initial conditions:

$\alpha_1 = .0001$	$\varepsilon = .3$	$a = 2$
$n = 20.000$	$b = .9$	$m = 3.000$
$k = 100.000$	$P = -M = 1$	$i = .01$
$\lambda^p = .05$	$\lambda^k = 4$	$\kappa = 2$

$\rho = .7$ and $\phi = 1$.

The evolutions of l_t^k, l_t^r and of $P(=-M)$ are represented in Figures 5.10-11; in Figure 5.12-13 the evolution of rentability and mark-up are depicted; in Figure 5.14-15 that of price of capital good and ϕ. In Figure 5.16 the evolution of consumption pro capita is represented, that of wages being similar.

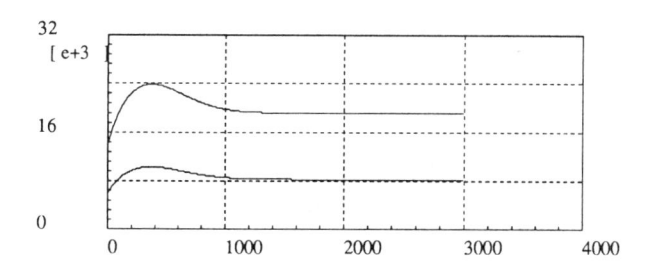

Workers in production and in research

Figure 5.10

150   *Growth and Economic Development*

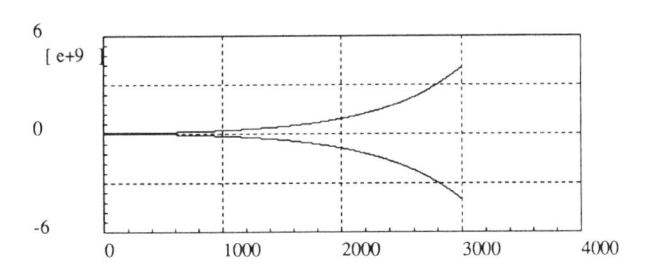

Consumers' wealth and firms' debts

Figure 5.11

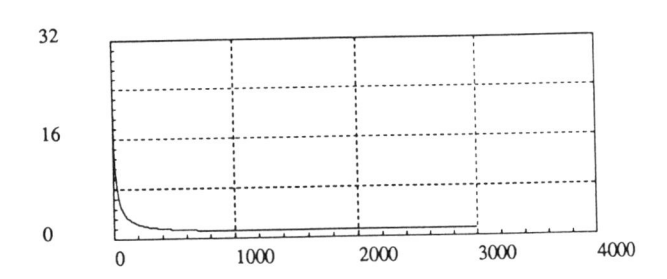

Rentability

Figure 5.12

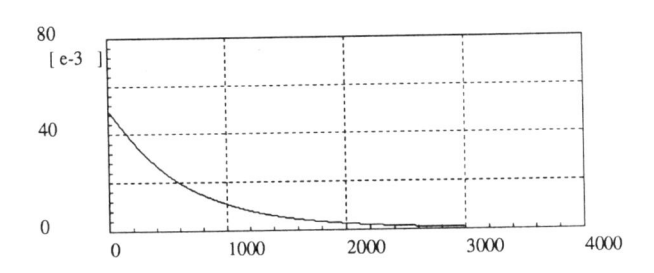

Mark-up

Figure 5.13

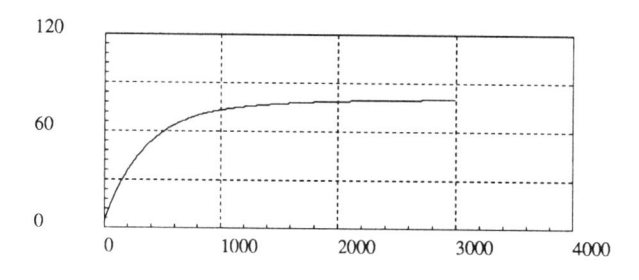

Price of capital good

Figure 5.14

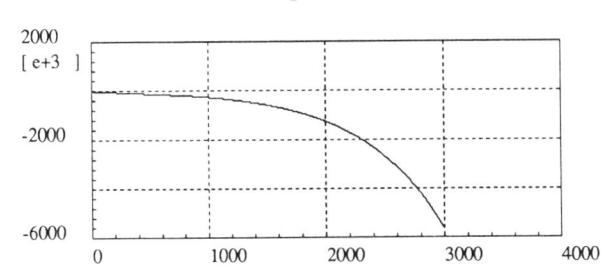

Financial flow

Figure 5.15

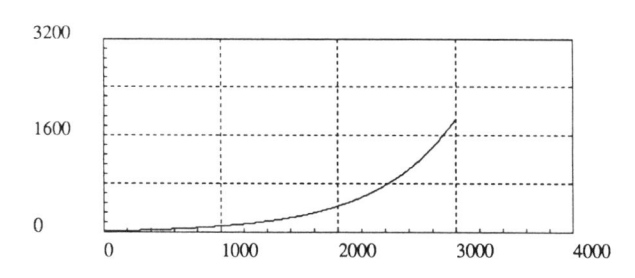

Consumption per capita

Figure 5.16

Let us evaluate the dynamics of the endogenous variables for ρ varying from 0 to 1 and. We can see that rentability increases as ρ decreases (namely as research activity increases) tending to constant values.

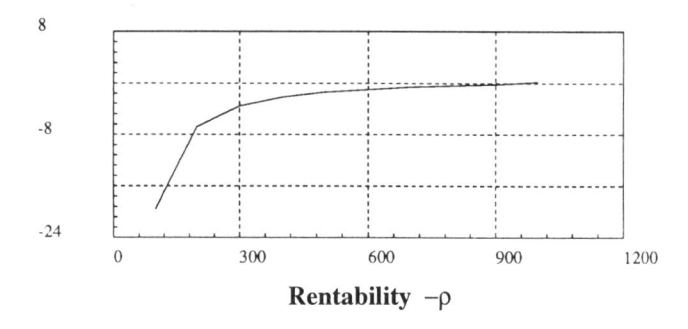

Figure 5.17

8. CONCLUDING REMARKS

This growth process induced only by innovations has completely different features from the neo-classical and the neo-Keynesian ones (Harrod, Kaldor) where technical progress is assumed to occur outside the economy: agents are offered the possibility to move towards different, more favourable equilibria. In neoclassical models, the rate of interest is established at the level that make investments equal to savings resulting from the choices of consumers maximizing their utility function. In Keynesian analysis, a causal relation is established between investments and savings. In fact savings result from the increase in income caused by the increase in investment: equilibrium is attained when savings are equal to investments required for a congruous increase of income (Domar-Harrod models).

In both Keynesian and Schumpeterian theories, savings are not the promoter of growth. In Keynesian models autonomous demand engendering growth can be generated by fiscal policies or spurred by monetary policies; for Schumpeter growth is induced by innovations which can be enhanced by an increase in the monetary flow. According to Schumpeter's philosophy growth produced by innovations generates sufficient savings through increase in productivity; increases in labour (population) are subsequent phenomena.

In our model we consider innovations both in techniques of production and in products themselves. The increase in consumption is a consequence, being due to the increase in consumers' willingness to work and in their propensity to consume: hence savings tend to decrease. In our model consumers get indebted; this is the condition allowing firms to increase wages, the ratio of debt to wages tending to zero. These are some of the main results of our analysis:

1. In many historical processes of development, inflation has played a positive role. According to Schumpeter's view, this may occur because inflation is a surrogate for the consumers being financed by banks. The other, more common, surrogate has been credit expansion which, together with speculation, has allowed firms to increase their capital at the cost of consumers-savers.
2. Insofar as processes of growth are enhanced by sales promotions, a reduction in the propensity to save is produced.

In a growing economy firms enjoy some market power due to innovations. In the asymptote of evolution we reach a pure competitive oligopolistic structure in which market power disappears. Through the solution of the model we can distinguish a *transition phase* from the phase in which the economy approaches the asymptote of evolution (the *quasi-equilibrium path*).[8] In the transition phase (in which accumulation occurs) structural changes are largely affected by initial conditions. If no research activity is undertaken, transition will eventually lead to a stationary economy. If innovations take place, then a process of growth occurs that tends to bring the economy closer and closer to the quasi-equilibrium path that will never be attained, as it is only an ideal path. However, innovations cannot occur indefinitely according to a given strategy. Because of the quasi-equilibrium context and the hypothesis of firms all alike, we cannot analyse some important issues raised by Schumpeterian theory.

NOTES

1. 'We will - Schumpeter writes (1934a, p. 47) - ... act on the assumption that consumers' initiative in changing their tastes ... is negligible and that all change in consumers' tastes is incidental to, and brought about by, producers' action'.
2. In fact, saving is considered an effect of economic development, rather than a prerequisite for it. As Schumpeter has remarked (1934a, p. 167) 'whatever the definition of saving the reader adopts, it is clear that most of its sources, as well as most of the motives for it, would be absent in a stationary state.'
3. Should we assume that banks have a strategy for increasing the *monetary flow* over time, money could play the role of numeraire, prices resulting from the evolution of the system as it has been affected by monetary policy.
4. This calls to mind the theory of *monetary circuit* (see Godley 1990 and Graziani 1989).
5. For computational reasons we shall assume a small consumers' wealth (=1).
6. Here comes a limit due to linearity assumptions: the asymptotic value of rentability cannot be inferred from equation (5.15) since the input coefficients tend to zero.
7. For computational reasons we have assumed a very small consumers' wealth (=1).
8. The convergence towards equilibrium paths for neoclassical and Keynesian processes of growth has been analysed by Cozzi (1966).

6. Selection, Innovation and Economic Development. Computational Economics Analysis

S. Lombardini and F. Donati

1. A MORE GENERAL VIEW OF THE SCHUMPETERIAN PROCESS OF DEVELOPMENT

In the previous chapter, we have analysed how far a mere process of Schumpeterian innovation can produce growth. The model is a quasi-equilibrium model. However it is different from the models of endogenous growth: the role of entrepreneurs is decisive even in the evolution of demand.

We shall now try to take some further steps towards the Schumpeterian theory. Two aspects of the Schumpeterian theory will be analysed in this chapter. The first is the effect of competition which has been disregarded in the simple model exposed in the previous chapter. The second aspect regards the role of the social system and that of historical contingency. The first will be considered by assuming a function of investment which reflects the aggressiveness and the optimism of entrepreneurs; the second by a stochastic scheme. In fact Schumpeterian processes are essentially linked with selection processes resembling the Darwinian natural selection. Schumpeterian processes require specific social systems, as we have shown in chapter 2.

What we shall try to do in this chapter is to explore the effects of selection and innovations in a context that allows the analysis of the general structure of the economy where equilibrium is attained only in commodities markets and not in the labour market. In fact, processes generated by innovations intertwine with selection processes contributing to evolution. Both innovations and selection processes interact with accumulation. As we shall see, in the long run, accumulation is the essential engine for development. Thus our approach may be said to reconcile Schumpeter's analysis with Smith's.[1]

2. FIRMS' SELECTION IN THE PROCESS OF ECONOMIC DEVELOPMENT

In neoclassical analysis the number of firms is either given or determined by conditions of the long-run equilibrium if perfect freedom of entry is assumed (the production function being the same for both operating and potential firms). Similar results have been obtained by the model of chapter 4. When we turn to the Schumpeterian process of development, the number of firms is a historical accident affected by the strategy of the firms operating in various markets, by the socio-cultural and institutional contexts and by monetary policies. However, certain aspects of the evolution in the number and in the features of the firms can be analysed by assuming that a selection process occurs, resembling the Darwinian natural selection and being connected with firms' competition linked to innovation.

Prima facie, Darwin's theory of selection seems completely alien to Schumpeter's thought. In fact, pure Darwinian theory makes evolution depend essentially upon stochastic processes. In effect, Darwin did not have in mind any concept of stocastic processes as the one that has become popular today among scientists. Mutations are assumed to occur because of causes that cannot be investigated; for our purpose they are casual (see Roger 1985). In such a context, probability can be considered, after Laplace, as an instrument allowing us to describe real processes in spite of our ignorance.[2] In Schumpeter theory, evolution is the result of entrepreneurs' deliberate activities which, for the reasons we shall consider later on, can be considered rational, in spite of the impossibility of leading them back to optimization.

Natural selection is now given an interpretation that, though still conceived essentially in a Darwinian way, does allows for a positive role of individuals in determining the species evolution, as it leaves room for Lamark's argument concerning the possibility that improvements realized by individuals, may be transmitted to other individuals as well. In fact, in the Schumpeterian concept improvements are transmitted because of imitations.

Such an 'adjustment' in the Darwinian theory of natural selection is required if some logical difficulties entailed by the concept of adaptation of species to environment are to be avoided.

3. INDIVIDUALS AND ENVIRONMENT

Some remarks on the relationship between individuals and environment may be useful to better understand how innovation intertwines with natural selection.

1. Environment is always a complex system. Some features may have negative as well positive implications. The variety of local conditions makes complex interactions possible between individuals and environment. Being a system, environment can be perceived through a few specific parameters.
2. To some extent, individuals choose their environment. That happens also in a social system: individuals can change environment by emigration.
3. Environment changes. Certain changes are assumed to occur after exogenous (as compared to *micro-evolution*) events. Changes in environment may occur because some species affect environment both by depleting resources and by deteriorating it (through wastes). Certain species may achieve some adaptation of the environment to their own needs: that is the most striking peculiarities of man.[3] Changes in environment may also occur because *all* species adapt themselves to environment. Each species produces micro-changes in environment. The sum of micro-changes may account for a macro-change: changes produced by man can have a macro-relevance. The theory of natural selection, in so far as it tries to explain how species adaptation occurs, is a *partial* theory in the sense that it explains only certain phenomena, *coeteris paribus*.
4. Environment may produce changes in individuals.

Evolution is therefore a complex phenomenon in which both individuals and environment play interacting roles.

4. ADAPTATION, SELECTION AND EVOLUTION

Some remarks on the process of individual mutations and speciacion, which is considered to have been the central moment of evolution, may help our analysis.

1. We must distinguish evolution from the diachronic features of the system. The system can change in time because of its diachronic features. Laplace's concept of universe is essentially based on his conviction that, at least potentially, all changes can be interpreted by reference to the diachronic features of the system. Thus changes are foreseeable. On the contrary, true evolution can be assessed only ex post.[4]
2. Evolution related to natural selection depends both on the variety of certain characteristics of the units of the species and on the adaptations processes. The characteristics are transmitted through reproduction which is a result of sexual activities. The increasing frequency of those characteristic that are more suitable for adaptations is the essential feature of natural selection.

3. Sexual activities entail a mix of solidarity and competition. They are often associated with the operation of a social system. Then all activities are related to both the social system and the larger system called environment. In fact, sexual activities are not merely functional to the survival of species; they contribute to the meaning and scope of social life. For some species of birds, (peacock) the large tail feathers stimulate sexual activities and procreation, but represent a waste of energy. A species of deer has disappeared because their horns, helpful for reproduction (in that they put certain males in a dominant position), grew larger and larger after evolution and ultimately hamper mobility. It is a fact that individuals have different goals that are not always compatible with each other. Darwin has already remarked on the anomaly of altruism, namely of those behaviours that do not help those who adopt them, but other elements. Selection among groups may account for that: sacrifices of altruists help the group survival. I think we can more convincingly refer to the essential features of sexual activities and those herewith associated (to the *heros* in the Jungianan sense).
4. Adaptation is always goal-oriented. It cannot be explained only on the basis of the features of environment. Natural selection has been explained essentially on the basis of the need to *survive*. However, we cannot define adaptation merely in terms of the need to survive: that entails a logical circle.[5] Adaptation needs a reference to an external context which is assumed as given and the definition of a criterion of rationality.
5. The external context is *environment*. As we have seen, environment is a complex system difficult to be defined. What are the relevant features of environment? Does environment change? Why and how? These are still open issues.
6. Even more difficult is to define the rational criterion entailed in the notion of adaptation. Lotka assumes that orientation in evolution can be singled out on the basis of the principle that humans as well as non-humans try to develop and avail themselves of the least costly means for leaving, namely those that minimize energy. Therefore nature selects the most efficient users of energy (Khalil 1992, p. 37). Such a principle offers no solution to the problem of establishing what are the goals in view of which energy is to be minimized. In some cases (as in the case of certain birds that undergo long migrations), natural selection appears as a goal in itself.
7. Means are defined in relation to goals. However, the use of certain means may induce changes in goals. Therefore where we say that adaptation occurs according to an economic principle, we must specify the time context. From a short-run viewpoint, goals can be assumed as given and constant. Then, saying that means are optimized (consumption of energy is minimized) has a sense. In the long-run perspective, however, we cannot assume goals as given. How can we then formulate the *economic* criterion? It might be that goals themselves are changed in order to make a better use

of means possible (to preserve certain features of the environment, eventually by minimizing consumption of energy). Adaptation as well as optimization is defined *locally*, and *coeteris paribus*. As Elster (1989) has remarked, if the relation between the quantity dimension of a character has a local maximum smaller (in terms of fitness of adjustment) than the global maximum, and the actual value of the character is close to the local maximum, natural selection will bring it to such a relative optimum and the absolute optimum will never be attained.

8. Given environment and individual goals, we can conceive of an optimal structure. In evolution, optimal adaptation is not only difficult to assess; it is also difficult to be conceived. First, for the reason we have just pointed out: because, at best, a local optimum is obtained. Second, because in evolution a cybernetic relation appears between goals mutations and means utilization. Third, because adjustment processes are gradual. Fourth, because *external events* are likely to occur that change the terms of the optimization problem. It seems reasonable to assume that they obey to a *sufficiency* criterion. In fact, as Lorenz has shown, should we plan the structure of a frog, the result would be better than that produced by natural selection (the heart would be better adapted to other organs). Should we know in advance all possible evolutions related to the set of external events and to different effects of interactions and adaptations, we could envisage an optimal process of adaptation. However, in uncertain contexts, processes of adaptation on the basis of certain sufficiency criterion may lead to future states better than those which could be attained through planned processes.

9. Adaptation may be helpful for individuals but not for the group. As Elster reminds us, mutations may increase the probability of survival, by making it easier for some fish to move to the centre of the cluster; but that also makes the job of predators easier to the detriment of the group as a whole.

10. Are goals definable only with reference to individuals or can they be conceived also with reference to the system as a whole (to environment and possibly to the entire cosmos)? This is a question that we will never be able to answer satisfactorily, for the simple reason that we can elaborate only *partial views* of the system as a whole. In social science, according to a prevailing methodology (methodological individualism) only individual goals are relevant, since society is not a separate entity. In fact, even in social science, individual behaviour cannot be explained without making non-reducible-to-individual assumptions about society. Anyhow, in natural science, nobody will deny that the cosmos is an entity in its own right. Let us assume, not being able either to prove or to disprove, that the cosmos has some goals of its own, or at least some orientations not resulting from the behaviour of single elements and yet affecting individual behaviours. Then evolution becomes an awfully complex process

resulting from double interacting processes between the formation of the goals of cosmos and individuals and the use of means (adaptation being involved in and affecting both processes). Gould and Eldredge (1993, p. 224) talk, after Stanley, of *decoupling macro from micro-evolution.*

Decoupling is not a claim for the falseness or irrelevancy of micro-evolutionary mechanisms, especially natural selection, but a recognition that Darwinian extrapolation cannot fully explain large-scale change in the history of life. ... Darwin's location of causality in organism must be superseded by a hierarchical model of selection, with simultaneous and important action of genic, organismal and taxic levels.

11. Some characteristics are preserved in spite of the fact that they are not required for survival. It might be that the characteristic which looks useless and perhaps harmful may be required for attaining some goals that have not yet been elicited by scientists.
12. According to the classical conceptualization, evolutionary changes occurred both very slowly and very steadily. The dominant model has been that of *phyletic gradualism.* New species result from continuous, gradual mutations in individuals of an original species, which affect almost all individuals in most of the areas where they are located. Such a model has been challenged by that of *punctuated equilibrium.* Evolution may actually be characterized by long periods of no alteration (*stasis*) punctuated by relatively brief periods of very rapid modifications. Stasis becomes 'punctuated equilibrium'. In fact, new species appear through separation of some evolutionary lines, separation producing discontinuities: the resulting evolution being a rapid one. Long stases in evolution, which have in fact been observed, can then be explained.
13. Mutations can occur in order to assure structural stability. In fact, it may be that some mutations are justified because they help in preserving some properties of certain organic structures. Then assessment is made by referring to certain structural-stability-requirements rather than to evolution. Such situations are rather common in economics. In fact, they are the only relevant type of mutations according to neoclassical economists. Mutations that may appear as adaptations to environment in the short run, in a long-run perspective may instead appear as necessary to maintain certain essential features of the organism in the face of possible mutations in the environment. But when can we assess such a perspective *ex post*? In biology, modules have been discovered that keep their essential properties constant in evolutionary processes; mutations occur because of changes in the combination of such stable elements.

14. According to Gould and Eldredge (1993, p. 225), 'stasis might just be a lull in anagenetic gradualism'. At a better scrutiny, stasis may appear as such with reference to the model letting us perceive mutations. Mutations may occur that do not change features that are both relevant and apparent after the model available. However, hidden features may change; the changes producing discontinuous, more or less abrupt, evolution *according* to our model. Such a possibility is more relevant with respect to the economic and social systems since more or less gradual changes in the social-cultural system may cause discontinuous changes in the economy and in the socio-institutional system. Let us remember that both continuity and discontinuity are related to different forms of our ignorance.
15. The study of evolution cannot be constrained to suit a scientific paradigm, whichever it might be. As Sober (1993, p. 7) remarks: 'Evolution matters because history matters. Evolutionary theory is the most historical subject in the biological sciences, in the sense that its problems possess the longest time scale'. In fact, both in biology and in economics, historical scientific explorations (and understanding) can help to single out problems for scientific research and to get hints about possible solutions of those that what is considered positive science cannot face. Historical processes make it difficult to set up and apply scientific paradigms. As Sober reminds us: 'selection tends to destroy the variation on which it acts ... This raises an epistemological difficulty since we must know about ancestral variation if we are to reconstruct the history of a selection process. Selection tends to cover its own tracks, so to speak' (1993, p. 69).

5. PECULIARITIES OF SOCIAL SELECTION AND EVOLUTION

Let us try to find out analogies between social and natural processes that can justify extension and applications of the biological theory of natural selection and evolution to economics.

We can make firms (and entrepreneurs) to correspond to the individual of a species. A species may be characterized by social and cultural features. If entrepreneurs are considered, we can make their social-cultural-psychological characteristic correspond to the genes. If firms are considered, then the features of technology and organization become relevant in defining the variety of individuals.

Individual activities are motivated both by individual goals and by the need for adaptations. Individual goals can, to a large extent, be related to some notion of power to be pursued through accumulation, innovation and the control of economic and political systems. Individual activities have some peculiarities as compared with the life of biological individuals: learning,[6] programming, changing goals (objectives). Thus, selection results from both the individual activities related to individual goals and adaptation capabilities. An entrepreneur may fail because the advantages of being successful in pursuing his goals (and possibly acquiring power) is more than offset by its incapability of adapting to environment. However, a large firm may change environment by using its power; then it can avoid some processes of adaptation.

In the different *social species*, power is differently defined and is related to different mix of solidarities and competition. The economy of Japan is a different 'species' as compared to that of United States.

Environment can be conceived at four levels: market, national economy, national institutions, international set-up. In the model we shall present environment is essentially defined with reference to the national economy.

Interaction between agents' activities and environment presents certain peculiarities when considering social systems. In economic evolution, entrepreneurs are *conscious* of their interactions with environment. In fact, some interactions can and must be considered in framing the best strategy for development. The Cournot process of adjustment which allows us to envisage equilibrium in oligopolistic markets, seems unsatisfactory for purposes of interpreting such conscious interactions.

More difficult is to define transmission of relevant characteristics to the 'sons'. Two ways can be considered: the creation of new firms by a successful firms (this may be a relevant way when we consider the international set-up); imitation of successful firms by other firms.

To stress the analogy between biology and economics we shall speak of births and deaths of firms.[7] It is open to debate how the results of learning processes are biologically transmitted. They may entail some Lamarckian processes. In the social system we can have a similar processes through changes in what has been called collective unconscious (Jung).[8] Learning processes are produced as external effects of certain firms' activities. However, the results of some learning processes (know-hows) cannot be transmitted through the second way. A direct participation of the old firm, which has acquired the non transmissible capabilities in the creation of the new firm is, at least, required.

The consideration we made about the comparison between optimal processes and spontaneous ones is more relevant for economic systems. If planning is considered with regard to initial conditions, we cannot say that results that are (or could be) obtained by planning are always better than those produced by selection. Planning makes it possible to consider certain interactions in a horizon larger than those within which market choices are made. However, changes − as those in goals actually pursued − occurring *after* evolution are intrinsically unforeseeable. Moreover, planning may produce systematic errors and is likely to hinder entrepreneurship, thus curbing selection processes. As we shall see, the implementation of long-run strategies by a firm may entail also an accumulation of errors that can cause its death.[9] Efficiency is indeed assured by proper interactions between system and individuals: strategies can then be adapted after external changes and acquisition of new information.

Specific problems arise with regard to evolution as it is interpreted by Schumpeter's theory of economic development, since it depends not only on the efforts of single entrepreneurs, each striving first for survival and then for acquiring more power through a better control of environment, but also on interactions between strategies of different entrepreneurs. As we have already noted, a similar problem arises also when dealing with the species natural selection. In the environment with regard to which evolution of a species can be analysed, we must include also the other species. That entails interactions between the evolution of species; in such a complex process, environment can no longer be considered external. However, in natural selection processes as far as they can be investigated by man, these interactions could be interpreted as 'adjustment processes'. In fact, since most mutations play a neutral role in determining evolution, as can be interpreted in a *partial* context, the possibility of a teleological orientation of the process as a whole cannot be discarded, as we have already observed: should we be able to envisage such orientations, certain mutations could no longer appear neutral. Moreover, certain relevant mutations might then no longer look like random ones. Unfortunately, since *global orientation*, though not impossible, is beyond our capacity of investigation, we are in no position to prove or disprove teleological assumptions referred to the whole. It is for this reason that recourse to probability schemes may be inevitable, even if there are no persuasive arguments in favour of sheer chance. If we consider the economic system in its connection with the political one, global goals become relevant.

We can interpret Schumpeterian processes of innovation from a different stand-point. We have already noted (by referring to the migration of some birds) that natural selection may be a goal in itself. To some economists, Schumpeter appears to be closer to Nietzsche's philosophy than to Darwin's concept of natural selection. The Nietzschian component will be taken into account by starting from *historical given* coefficients of entrepreneurial greed.

Paradigms of natural selection and evolution have had a more extensive and more specific applications in sociology and even in philosophy. Veblen perhaps was the first to think of sociology from a point of view quite similar to that of Darwinian biology. As Hodgson (1993 p. 288) notes:

Veblen ... clearly saw institutions as well as individuals as units of evolutionary selection. With modern hindsight, this suggests the notion that the information transmitted through learning or imitation to institutions or individuals was analogous, but different from, the transmission of genetic information in the process of biological evolution. As a consequence, institutions are both replicators and the units of selection in socio-economic evolution.

As Boulding has remarked:

The greatest difference between social and biological species ... is that biological species carry their own genetic instructions within the phenotype, but the social species do not. This separation of the phenotype from the genetic instructions which initiated and guided its production can give societal evolution some very different characteristics from biological evolution. (1992, p. 55)

The role of the phenotype can be played by what can be differently termed as the collective unconscious, culture (the expression of fundamental propensities) and so on.

A direct link between biological evolution and social selection needs to be mentioned. Men have different qualities, partly inherited from their parents. Also their initial economic and social conditions are different. Buican (1989, p. 153), quoting Charles Richet stresses the effect that the unequal conditions at birth have on social evolution. We can notice that if the fathers succeed in accumulating wealth because of their superior capabilities, the positive effects of the Darwinian process of social selection may be strengthened. Such an assumption is doubtful. Moreover, wealths inherited, while improving the perspectives of the sons of successful fathers, represents an obstacle for the numerous capable people born from poor parents. Buican's remark deserves attention.

In Schumpeter's view, innovations entail discontinuities in technical progress. We can note some resemblance with the punctuated equilibrium theory of evolution. (Barkley Rosser Jr., 1992, uses the term saltationalism in talking about Schumpeter theory.) In fact, evolution is the result of innovations as well as of adjustment processes: continuous changes (as are those engendered by learning processes) may be disturbed by more or less abrupt, discontinuous, ones (as are qualitative structural change, see Day 1975, 1983 and Day and Walter 1989). Lotka (1925, pp. 407-8) has suggested that at some point of the evolutionary process human beings may face unstable orbits: then an imperceptible deviation may cause a change in the orbit. The possibility of chaotic movements may make it difficult to translate historical observation into a coherent relatively simple theory.

6. BIRTH AND DEATH OF FIRMS: COMPETITIVE SELECTION

The analogies we have noted between biology and sociology allow us to speak of selection in interpreting economic evolution.

An essential feature of economic evolution is represented by the births and deaths of firms, which cannot be 'explained' by any scientific model (in the common sense), just as there is no accounting for the mutation of genes (in the sense of building some functional, not necessarily causal, relations). Nor can we explain why some entrepreneurs are more optimistic or more energetic than others. The historian will be able to tell us why a specific firm, rather than a different one, has entered the market in specific conditions. Psychologists, on the other hand, may help us to understand why an entrepreneur is more aggressive than others. However, in the context of economic analysis these events can only be considered stochastic as the same mutations of genes. It is, therefore, only for analytical purposes that we can adopt a stochastic framework.

We have already noted that survival is not the only - nor the primary - goal of individuals. Acquiring power because of the gratification directly derived from being powerful has in economic life a role similar to sexual activities in social life. That is not always functional to survival. In fact, one of the results of our model is to show how firms striving to increase their power may go bankrupt.

Elster is right in noting that natural selection improves the reproductive capacity of single individuals, whereas in economics we cannot speak of reproduction by single individuals. New firms are different agents as compared with old ones.[10] Moreover, environment, to which firms become adjusted through selection processes, changes continuously. And yet, as Elster himself notes, firms (we prefer to speak of entrepreneurs), are characterized by behavioural routines (we prefer to speak of entrepreneur's personality features) which play a role similar to genes subjected to stochastic changes (mutations being replaced by variety improving through competition in the Schumpeterian sense).

Evolution can be analysed in terms of agents (entrepreneurs) promoting evolution, as we have just mentioned, or in terms of changes in the cultural and sociological system (including associated institutions). These approaches are alternative to one another for certain aspects of evolution and complementary for others. In fact, the origin of evolution is not reducible to mere stochastic processes (we can thus refer to agents); at the same time evolution creates objective conditions, so that we can say that it is transmitted. In Schumpeterian theory transmission occurs mostly through imitations. This is not the only way. Innovations can contribute to evolution also by creating the proper climate. That may have two different consequences. It may encourage optimism and aggressiveness among entrepreneurs, which can be assimilated to changes in genes. Or it may improve scientific and technical knowledge and thereby make new innovation easier. This is a change in environment.[11] It also entails changes in the orientation of evolution. Suffice it to think of the effects of the railway and motor car innovations on social life as well as on social ideals.

Among the few economists who have considered social evolution, beside Veblen who has already been recalled, we shall mention Hayek (1983). Veblen thinks of social evolution as a global phenomenon, it resulting mostly in *cultural evolution*.[12] The process cannot be properly analyzed by any neoclassical economic paradigm, evolution being incompatible with equilibrium resulting from agents' optimization. As Nelson and Winter (1982, p. 142) have remarked

> in models involving an extended process of selection among an initial set of behavioural routines, firms whose behaviour would be profit-maximizing under conditions of a given time may be eliminated by competition at an earlier stage, under conditions for which their behaviour was not optimal.

In fact, optimization is obtained both through selection of optimal choice on the basis of market parameters and entrepreneur's expectations and by adjustments after the results of other agents' optimal choices have affected the market. Thus, equilibrium can be envisaged through a process of adjustment (when such a process is conceivable, we say that equilibrium is stable). However, as changes arise in the initial conditions whereby equilibrium was defined, the entrepreneur will need to change his optimal choice *while he is adjusting the old choice to reach the old equilibrium*. Thus, the most successful entrepreneur is not necessarily the one who has made the best choice; it might be the one that has chosen a process which proves to be more in line with subsequent changes.

As Matthews (1984, p. 115) has remarked 'competitive selection is an entirely different kind of process from optimization'. Hayek (1985) appears to have released economic analysis from the cage represented by the notion of equilibrium only to replace that concept with his notion of *order*. Order is not the result of any *design*, but of natural rules that account for unintentional results of intentional behaviour. The neoclassical theory of competition intends to offer the key to understanding how that can occur. But, as Hirshleifer (1978) notes: 'The Invisible Hand ... requires a severely constrained form of competition; vying to engage in exchange with third parties, and doing so only by offering better terms under an ideal system of property and law' (p. 240). Thus, it is not clear how order, which entails some normal structure and is therefore akin in some essential aspects to equilibrium, can be compatible with evolution.[13] On this point Hayek's concept departs from Veblen's. According to Hayek, in economics we have processes resembling 'autopoiesis' (an assumption put forward by some biologists and also adapted in cybernetics, according to which living organisms reproduce themselves through self-organization); accordingly the functions of the components of cells or organisms would tend to adjust to each other. Evolution is a spontaneous process that cannot be foreseen, at least in its long-run manifestations, and in fact, Schumpeterian development and the associated structural changes (evolution) are, to a large extent, unforeseeable. Notwithstanding it can be considered the result of firms' strategies. It is unforeseeable because the strategies are not uniquely determined by what are considered to be objective conditions (as, in neoclassical models, are individual tastes, techniques of productions, resources available), and because the adjustment of individual decisions cannot reach such a degree of perfection as to make it possible for individuals to predict the outcome of their alternative choices.

7. RATIONALITY AND PREDICTABILITY

Some scientists (see for instance Khalil, 1992, pp. 31 ff.), think that rationality is not peculiar to man; it can be found also in non-human animals [14]. Optimizing behaviour assumptions proved to be a useful tool even to explain physical processes. However, human rationality, inasmuch as is revealed by conscious choices in uncertain contexts, differs from the *mechanical rationality* not only for the reasons pointed out by Simon (1976), but also for its creative content.

This remark leads us to consider a peculiarity of social and economic evolution. Evolution as produced by men is of the *exosomatic* type. As Georgescu-Roegen (1986, p. 249) noted

> man transgressed the biological evolution by entering into a far faster evolutionary rhythm [exosomatic evolution] - the evolution in which organs are manufactured, instead of being inherited somatically.

Mayumi, in quoting such a sentence by Georgescu-Roegen, adds: 'Our exosomatic rhythm of evolution has been accelerated ever since the industrial revolution' (Mayumi 1993, p. 91).[15]

When analysing selection in economic and social life and that occurring through species evolution a fundamental difference needs to be mentioned. Natural selection theories are based on observation of fossils and of other features of the natural environment. Models built in order to analyse the effect of social selection linked with innovations propose to envisage *ex ante* possible evolutions; in particular their aim is to single out the main factors and assess their effects. The shortcoming of the *Darwinian approach* lies in its inability to visualize any specific possible future evolution.[16] Past experience can, of course, help in framing *computational-economics analyses*. However, no formalized theory can give an adequate account of past evolutions: economic analysis needs to be integrated by historical investigation.

In spite of these differences, we may appropriately extend to the economic analysis of evolution the following remarks by Gould and Eldredge (1993, p. 227):

> In summarizing the impact of recent theories upon human concepts of nature's order, we cannot yet know whether we have witnessed a mighty gain in insight about the natural world (against anthropocentric hopes and biases that always hold us down), or just another transient blip in the history of correspondence between misperceptions of nature and prevailing social realities of war and uncertainty. Nonetheless, contemporary science has massively substituted notions of indeterminacy, historical contingency, chaos and punctuation for previous convictions about gradual, progressive, predictable, determinism.

Scientific analyses cannot provide an explanation of *external facts* (except in trivial cases such as the assessment of the effects of certain drugs). They can only offer tools whereby facts can be identified and explored in order to better describe past experiences and envisage possible future scenarios. Critical discernment (we can talk of *critical reason*) does not merely represent the propellant of the machines built by scientists; it lies with the driver who ultimately must choose both the machine and the road. Computational economics can then be of some help in utilizing different machines in order to explore different roads. This remark may have clarified why uncertainty is essential for human rationality and why human rationality essentially has a creative content.

In chapter 1 (pp. 8-12), we have seen how development of the theory of games has led to re-thinking rational behaviour by stressing the need for some kind of procedural rationality. By studying learning processes and evolution we can better see how strategies are conceived, implemented and adjusted. As Binmore notes 'What distinguishes eductive theory from evolutive theory is that, in the former, evolution operates *at one remove*. In evolutive theory, evolutionary processes work *directly* on the strategies in *one specific game*' (1988, II, p. 16). If evolution is considered, then Nash equilibrium loses much of its relevance.

One reason for rejecting Nash equilibrium is that, if one master-program (or set of closely related master programs) wins out in the evolutionary struggle, then, towards the end of the struggle, there will be a high probability that such a master-program *will be playing itself* (or a close relative or relatives) when called upon to play. Given that it is the 'welfare' of the master-program, rather than the 'welfare' of any particular host or hosts carrying the master-program, that matters for evolutionary success or failure, it is clear that a master-program, playing itself, has a *one-person* decision problem to solve rather than a multi-person problem. A mechanism therefore exists for the evolution of *co-operative behaviour*, as described, for example, by Axelrod (1984). Biologists refer to this as kin selection. A gene which generates behaviour which favours relatives, generates behaviour which favours itself, because the gene has a good chance of being replicated in the body of a relative.

There is yet another aspect of evolution to which game-theorists should pay attention. In the process of evolution the individual changes. As Pareto himself has noted, environment may favour some attitudes that are relevant in explaining economic evolution. For the reasons pointed out in section 6 of Chapter 1, such an evolution is important in understanding how games are conceived and played. Environment may be a contributory factor in framing communications possibility (Binmore and Dasgupta 1987).

8. COMPETITION AND INNOVATIONS

Innovation is linked to evolution *via* competition. In fact, evolution can result from competitive selection in Matthews' sense. The neoclassical concept of competition is inadequate for two reasons: 1) If we stick to the neoclassical notion of competition, we must conceive the economy, after Pareto, as an adaptable system whose evolution can be explained only by external factors; 2) If innovations are considered, we cannot refer to neoclassical competition as the necessary context to assess the efficiency of the economy. As Schumpeter (1942, p. 106) has pointed out '... in this respect, perfect competition is not only impossible but inferior, and has no little to be set up as a model of ideal efficiency'.

The problem of whether competition or monopoly favour innovations has been debated long since Smith. Smith has recognized that in some cases expectations of monopoly power may encourage innovations. In Schumpeter's theory innovation is largely associated with large firms. In fact, for Schumpeter, the most favourable context for innovation is oligopolistic competition, or to use his term, *industry monopolistically competitive* (Schumpeter 1934b, p. 312). Innovation is an essential ingredient of such kind of competition. As

Schumpeter remarks (1942, pp. 84-5) 'in capitalist reality as distinguished from its textbook picture, it is not [price] competition which counts but the competition from the new commodities, the new technology, the new source of supply'.

Competition is not always associated to innovation. Competition is, first of all, the essential manifestation of entrepreneur greed for power, innovation being the main way competitive strategies are implemented. Power can also be achieved by increasing the barriers to entry through collusion with other firms, with banks or financial institutions, or with the political power. In Schumpeter's theory, physiological competition is that occurring through innovation. A by-product of competition is an increase in the firm's size, which entails acquisition of monopoly power. Some firm's decisions having these effects are assimilated to innovations: for instance 'mergers must ... be listed among the innovations ...' (Schumpeter 1934b, p. 251). In any case, a question does arise: is monopoly power *per se* favourable to innovations?

The answer provided by Arrow (1962) is no: profits to be expected due to a change in costs may be smaller if the firm enjoys a monopoly power before innovation. However, more relevant than the level of profits are: the firm's organization,[17] the propensity to growth of the entrepreneur (or of the top managers), the alternatives offered to the firm. Monopoly power is not determined by conditions of demand and supply in equilibrium, it reflects entrepreneur's aggressiveness and expectations: it may be adjusted, as we shall assume in our model, after market experience.

9. SCHUMPETERIAN INNOVATION AND EVOLUTION

Innovation produces growth not merely because it entails technical progress. Technical progress can be dealt with - as it has been - by models of endogenous growth, being the result of optimizing the behaviour of firms which, by taking appropriate action, can change some features of labour and capital and thus increase their productivities (chapters 3 and 4). Schumpeterian innovation produces growth because it creates *new* market conditions entailing structural changes. It is, therefore, essentially linked with selection.

In Chapter 5, by assuming a single firm, we could isolate the effects of Schumpeterian innovation from those produced by competition (a kind of monopolistic competition) and selection on development.

Evolution can be the result of selection because *technological competition* will drive the less efficient firms out of the market and will cause new firms to enter; the new firms being more efficient because they imitate the best ones. Iwai (1984 a,b) has analysed how new technologies being introduced will cause structural changes, and how imitations tend to bring the economy into equilibrium. Silverberg, in his essay of 1984 and in the one written with Lehnert in 1993, has proposed a criterion whereby to determine whether a new technology, initially introduced in a small quantity, will ultimately displace an existing technology.

Schumpeterian competition is more pervasive than technological competition, since it concerns not only techniques of production but also products, as technological innovations are mostly associated with product innovations. In analysing technological innovations and imitations, we can ignore evolution of demand. When product innovation is considered, competition ceases to resemble the classical type of competition (which, for price takers, is equivalent to the neoclassical perfect competition with no barriers to entry).

Economic development produced by Schumpeterian competition can be considered as a specification of what has been called 'economic development' by Boulding: 'a process essentially in the evolution of human artifacts - that is in the development first of all of the new know-how which has the capacity for producing artifacts which have a niche in the total ecosystem' (1992, p. 66). The evolution of human artifacts does not fill any potentially existing niche in a given ecosystem. It contribute to changes of the ecosystem as a result of which new potential niches are created, while old ones collapse. That is why some tension can be created between the social ecosystem and the natural one. The social evolution may bring about some catastrophic effects on the natural ecosystem, and negatively affect the outlook for the social ecosystem as a result.

10. A COMPUTATIONAL ECONOMIC MODEL FOR THE ANALYSIS OF INNOVATIONS AND SELECTION

In this paper, we present a multi-firms model whereby to analyse the effect both of innovation activities and of the selection process which, as we said, occurs because of the death of some firms and of the birth of new ones; the latter being more efficient than the average thanks to imitation. As in the model presented in the previous chapter, growth is not produced by the dynamics of external factors, such as population, but by the internal mechanism of the economy, mostly by some entrepreneurs' inclinations and competition properly defined, and by improvements resulting from selection. The process is, indeed, a *development* process since structural changes are produced that can hardly be foreseen and that induce adjustment processes. The term evolution is used in a more specific sense than Pareto's: it implies economic development.

The model has been conceived as a *computational-economic model* (see section 21 of chapter 2).

Entrepreneurs enter into the model with their Schumpeterian features. However, hypotheses of procedural rationality are made. Processes of learning after choices have been made, mostly on the basis of propensities and expectations, and adjustments, tend to rationalize the entrepreneurs' behaviour as well as the consumers'.

To isolate the effects of innovations and selection we shall assume that labour supply is always adjusted, through immigrations and emigrations, to the demand for labour.

The factors we consider in analyzing the evolution of the system are those that, given proper structural and initial conditions, will cause growth to accelerate. Factors checking the process of growth operate as well. We shall mention them at the end of the chapter.

11. FIRMS, ENTREPRENEURS AND THE ECONOMY

In neoclassical economic analysis, the economic process is split into the configuration of a potential structure (*equilibrium*) having some efficiency properties and being the result of the agents' optimizing behaviour, and an adjustment process by which the actual structure is shifted to correspond to the potential one and equilibrium is moved after changes in exogenous variables. The New Classical Macroeconomics has attempted to integrate the two moments of the economic process, whereas models of endogenous growth have converted into endogenous some factors producing growth that were assumed to be exogenously given. In any case, the problem is to established how the market mechanism that makes the agents' optimizing behaviours compatible with each other, can achieved the best allocation of available resources, *given consumers' tastes and firms' technologies*. Such an approach is incompatible with evolution. Hayek, as we have recalled, conceives social evolution as a process similar to natural evolution in that it is produced in the same way as *order*. However it is not clear what kind of *invisible hand* is at work in establishing order and what in promoting innovation.

In most neoclassical analyses the entrepreneur is a robot whose only function is to produce the best output from inputs which essentially consist of information. A noteworthy exception is Marshall's theory of the firm. For Marshall, a firm's development is hampered by its passage from the efficient father who founded it, to his less efficient sons. In line with Schumpeter's thought, we shall not consider the entrepreneur as the personification of the firm, but rather the firm as a product of the entrepreneur who is characterized by specific socio-cultural and psychological features. We shall summarize such features by a set of *entrepreneurial coefficients*. Initially they are assumed to be drawn randomly from given populations; they will change after the entrepreneur's experience. As has been already noted, such an assumption does not ascribe the assignment of a role to pure chance as in Monod's interpretation of evolution and life appearance. In fact, probability can better be considered as a tool that helps us in building models in spite of our *limited information* about the factors involved in the process.[18] Some of these limitations are unremovable; which of the limitations shall be considered removable being an impossible fact to establish *a priori*.

The Schumpeterian entrepreneur is more akin to Nietzsche's superman than to a robot. He strives for power. He does not infer the best decisions from *given* market data. He does his best to change the market conditions, so as to make most profitable actions possible. Profit is the raw material for power. Power may be used to increase profits. Such a possibility is limited by competition induced by innovations and imitations.

In most analyses, the unit of the economy is the firm. Economy structure and firm organization are related to each other. The concept of firm, as it emerges from certain developments of economic theory, cannot enlighten such relationship. In fact, the firm cannot be assumed to be an efficient mechanism created in order to reduce costs of transactions or merely as a nexus of contracts. The firms is an entity that changes the context in which transactions are conceived and implemented. Firm is not the mere reflect of objective market or technological relations. As has been suggested by Khalil, we should distinguish economic organization from economic structure.

> As an organization, the economy is a more-or-less stable division of labour ordered by trust, property rights, purposeful initiatives, and the commanding state taking the role of entrepreneurial leadership. As a structure, the economy is the collection of chaotic markets ordered by autocatalytic mechanisms which give rise, *inter alia*, to business cycles and geographic core-periphery bifurcations. Such cycles and bifurcations are ultimately ruled by equilibrium forces. In contrast, evolutionary processes are the property of the economy as an organization. (1993, p. 35)

The firm is the link between organization and structure, since it is the agent that pursues organization goals that are justified by expectations regarding the whole economy. The actions by which the firm pursues its goals produce the structure.

Evolution is a complex matter because it covers phenomena taking place both within and outside the firm. We need to simplify our analysis. We shall therefore be speaking of the entrepreneur in tune with Schumpeter approach.

12. INNOVATIONS. TECHNOLOGICAL ORIENTATIONS

It may be useful to keep the distinction between innovations and imitations.[19] A new technology or a new product is an innovation. Technology innovation entails some product innovations. In section 17 of chapter 2 we have recalled some classifications of innovation.

Dosi (1984, p. 14) has introduced the concept of *technological paradigm* which resembles the notion of 'scientific research program': it 'could be approximately defined as an "outlook" which states the relevant problems, a "model" and a "pattern" of inquiry'. Within a paradigm it is possible to define 'strong prescriptions on the *directions* of technical change to pursue and those to neglect', in other words to visualize *technological trajectories*. In so far as innovations are the result of planned research activity both notions are useful to explain structural changes produced by innovations. Again as Dosi (1984 pp. 166–67) notes, technological paradigms

> are likely to be linked to an 'organization sociology', built on or around them, which routinizes and promotes advances along a technological trajectory, while inducing relative blindness and institutional resistance with respect to radical change.

Innovations are not always the result of planned activity. Sometimes they result as sub-products of other activities. In fact, it is difficult to distinguish innovation from changes of techniques that were all previously available (as represented by the neoclassical production function). As Robinson (1956, p. 156) has remarked

> In reality techniques are not fully blueprinted before they are about to be used. The spectrum of techniques is a real phenomenon, but a very amorphous one. The possibility of using less or more mechanized techniques than those actually being operated is known only in a vague and general way. When a new technique is to be applied it requires adaptation and a period of 'teething troubles' quite as much when it is introduced in response to a change in costs as when it follows from a new discovery.

We cannot, thus, but agree with Scott (1989) when he asserts that investment activity itself entails some innovation.

What we want to stress is the role of *entrepreneur*. For this purpose, we will then set aside the interesting problems of the interactions between firm's organization and innovation activity and place more emphasis on psychological-cultural factors than on sociological-institutional ones. In this same context, we can also introduce notions similar to Dosi's. We could more appropriately talk of *technological orientation*. This depends on what Nelson and Winter (1974) have named 'selection environment'. Many factors go to determine it. Relative prices of factors of production can play a relevant role. Suffice it to think of the different agricultural technologies applied in a country where land is abundant, as compared with those applied in countries where land is scarce. Different combinations of productive factors may be the result not of choices of techniques within sets available at a given moment of time (production functions), but rather of research orientation (and thus of innovations) towards techniques more suitable to the structure of relative prices of production factors. Technological orientations may reflect prejudices. Suffice it to recall the orientations prevailing in the USSR in favour of mechanization in agriculture (neglecting the opportunities that could be opened up by biology which in fact have been amply exploited in the United States). Technological orientations may disregard technological possibilities because of long-established economic interests. We can thus understand why treatment of illness is more relevant in orienting research and innovation than prevention is. Cultural orientation may contribute to technological orientation. Should concern for ecological equilibria be more widespread, preservation of the environment could become a business and different technological orientations could emerge. The political structure and its aims may have a strong influence on technological orientation, as it appears when we reflect on the development of technology in the electronic and telecommunications sectors in the USSR. When a big group assumes employment as one of its goals - as it occurs in Japan - orientation may be more articulated.

Technological orientation is not sufficient for forecasting the direction of future innovations. Innovation depends on the creative capacity of entrepreneurs, on their idiosyncrasies, on their expectations. In fact, we can speak of orientations of innovations with reference to single entrepreneurs.

Innovation depends to some extent on some services (school system, university in particular) both because a precondition for innovation is qualified human capital and because scientific research is, to a large extent, carried on in universities. Innovations in turn create favourable conditions for research. Firms' innovations entail a fall-out of which everybody can take advantage.

Innovations can occur in clusters for essentially three reasons: a) any *revolutionary discovery* will usually open the way to a large set of potential innovations (think of the steam engine and of the explosion engine, of discoveries in electronics and information technology); b) special conditions are achieved that favour innovations; c) some hard innovations will open the way to a large set of soft innovations and induce vast imitations and adjustment processes. Innovations following a revolutionary discovery may have a much larger impact, since they affect the cultural system, land and urban organization as well as social propensities. Schumpeterian long waves have much to do with these occurrences. Clusters occurring for the second reason may explain how an economy gets out of depression.

We can think of cluster as establishing *space connections* between innovations, whereas technological orientations tend to establish *time connections*. In our model we shall not consider these connections, since our purpose is to stress the role of the entrepreneur competing with other entrepreneurs to secure larger market shares through better and less costly products.

13. INNOVATION, OPTIMIZATION AND FIRM'S DEATH

We are now in a position to better understand why innovation is incompatible with substantial rationality as defined by neoclassical economists. Two are the main reasons:

1. Intensity and orientation of innovation activities depend to a large extent on the *entrepreneurial coefficients*;
2. The results of innovations are not foreseeable to such an extent as to make the calculations presupposed by neoclassical optimization possible.

Asserting that when innovation is allowed for, paradigms of substantial rationality cannot be applied, does not mean to say that the innovating process reflects only the animal spirits of entrepreneurs and their more or less rational expectations. As Simon long ago suggested efficient behaviour can result from *procedural rationality*. We shall in fact assume a *learning process* that leads the entrepreneur to identify his best price policy. In our assumptions, the learning process develops within a given framework, on the basis of objective data concerning rentability, financial conditions and stocks dynamics. This procedural optimization is a medium-long term process which interacts with the adjustment process. Adjustment consists of short period phenomena expressing the firm's reactions to abrupt imbalances.

In the opinion of many economists (Friedman's for instance), a firm's death occurs because of its non-rational behaviour. If rational behaviour cannot be reduced to any mechanical application of well-established rules, the firms being adequately informed, firms' death cannot be explained this way. At a closer scrutiny, a shortcoming of economics appears to be its basic inability to explain firms' death.

As Khalil (1992, p. 38) reminds us, senescence has been given different explanations. He considers the two approaches that have been labelled as *genetic programming* vs *error accumulation*; the first relates to the conviction that 'there are direct or indirect selective advantages to limiting life space though senescence'.

In contrast the error accumulation approach argues that the main aging event is stochastic, governed by chance, and expresses itself by accumulation of errors in DNA RNA, protein, or in a combination of the three.

In our theoretical context, death may occur both because the process of learning, while improving the firm's capacity to exploit the advantage of the technological trajectory that has been opened up by its research programme (more generally its innovations orientation), makes the firm less capable of imitating other innovations that have opened different trajectories or are in tune with different orientations. This possibility is not analysed in our model since, as previously noted, the space and time connections between innovations are not taken into consideration.

The second reason can be described as *learning limitations and lack of negative feedbacks*. The propensity to grow is not adjusted as a result of a learning process, nor are there any negative feedbacks that will eventually curb the firm's development. Our firms are extrovert in Jung's sense of the word. The first assumption of a propensity to grow that is not adjusted after learning processes can have institutional and sociological grounds; the assumption of inadequate negative feedbacks is justified for the sake of simplicity.

In fact two different feedbacks could be produced by growth. A negative one: the reaction of the financial system. Because of our assumption of endogenous money, which will be explained below, and of a direct link between firms and families, we are not able to analyse such a feedback. A positive one: the capacity of the firm to strengthen its control of the market (and indeed its connection with banks and financial institutions) and the *political power* it acquires, being thus able to further its growth even when this is not justified by any fundamentals. An interesting example has been provided by the United States Steel Corporation and the calculator manufacturer Facit AB, recalled by Wiskovatoff (1993, p. 75).

If negative feedbacks are as efficient as the positive ones, our approach is not so unreasonable as it may seem to be.

14. ENTRY AND EXIT OF FIRMS. THE SELECTION PROCESS

In the Schumpeterian process, firms die when they go bankrupt. New firms will then enter the market. The selection process results from this evolution since the new firms will try to imitate the best techniques and to produce commodities having features similar to those of the most successful ones. Imitation occurs on the basis of partial informations. The problem can thus be framed in two ways:

1. By assuming that the populations of *entrepreneurial coefficients*, as well as of the other magnitudes that initially are attributed randomly to the firms, change after the exit of the less efficient firms, so that the coefficients randomly drawn for the new firms are, as *averages*, better than those previously included in the populations. We can assume that the coefficients for the new firms are the more likely to be drawn, the better they are, just because of *imitations*.
2. By assuming that the probability distributions of the parameters initially attributed to firms are asymmetrical, the skewness expressing the intensity of imitation.

In our model we have adopted the first approach.

Some of the new firms are born after the failure of old firms. In this case, part of the equipment belonging to the old firms is transferred to the new ones; only part of their capital (in the financial form) is kept; the rest is lost.

New firms can enter the market independently from the failure of old ones. That is an important feature of the Schumpeterian theory of development. It is the banking system that makes such an evolution possible, through credit expansion. In our model, since we consider money as internal money, firms enter only to replace the failing ones.

Different entrepreneurial coefficients and different expectations entail different firms' decisions, even if they operate in similar conditions. The degree of success will be different for the various firms. This is the premise of the selection process having features similar to natural selection processes and specific peculiar ones due to the more relevant and open interactions between the elements of mutation (which can defined in different ways) and environment.

The selection process may produce growth since the new firms are more efficient than those that die, provided entrepreneurs are sufficiently *growth minded*. In fact, one feature of the Schumpeterian entrepreneur is his motivation to invest with a view to producing growth: *power*. Such a motivation is revealed by the entrepreneur's propensity to risk and by his aggressiveness as can be inferred from his investment projects. The peculiar features of entrepreneurs are relevant also in explaining their sales promotion and technical innovation activities.

Both innovation and the selection process resulting from imitations by new firms produce growth. It is not induced by external factors. However, we shall not speak of endogenous growth, since the economy's evolution is a development process of the Schumpeterian type. This is affected by external conditions (entrepreneurial innovations are linked with research carried on in non economic institutions, universities in particular) and it entails structural changes that are, to some extent, unforeseeable, as we have already noted.

15. CONSUMPTION, SAVINGS AND POPULATION GROWTH

For Smith, savings (frugality) is an essential prerequisite for growth and development. In models of the Harrod type, as well as in endogenous growth models, savings and investments, as decided independently by consumers and firms, are made to correspond to each other so that the economy can move along an equilibrium path. As we have already noted, in Schumpeter's theory of development, savings is not the prerequisite for development but rather one of its products. Keynes comes to a similar conclusion by a different argument. For Keynes the prerequisite for growth is demand that may come both from consumers and from the state. Savings is a residual variable. Frugality, far from being a factor of growth, may actually hamper it.

Consumption has a role also in Schumpeter model. But in Schumpeter's conception consumption is not of the type considered in neoclassical model – i.e. resulting from consumers' utility maximization – nor can it be interpreted by behaviour equations. Consumers' rationality can only be procedural rationality (see Simon 1976). It results from adjustments in consumption after changes in income, in price and in wealth.

As we have already remarked, technological innovations are generally associated with changes in product. Product change and the invention of new products may be the main objective of the entrepreneur's innovative activity and are usually associated with his activity aiming at spurring sales. We shall aggregate all these activities by talking of *sales promotion*. Sales promotion is interwoven with *technological research*. However, we shall distinguish between them since their implementations are not necessarily correlated. Sometimes it is convenient for the entrepreneur to foster technological research, sometimes sales promotion is instead deemed to be more useful to improve the firm's profitability. Both activities constitute Research and Development (R&D).

A factor for growth, which is usually assumed as external, is population growth. In fact, such a factor is, to some degree, endogenous too. Think of the United States whose population has immigrated from abroad, attracted by the country's rapidly growing economy. Of course population growth often plays the role of exogenous factor. Then development results from the interweaving of endogenous and exogeneous factors.

To isolate the effects of selection on development from those of external factors, we shall assume that labour supply is always adapted to demand; if demand increases at a rate higher than the natural rate of increase of labour supply, then new workers immigrate; workers emigrate in the opposite case.

16. FIRMS' INTERACTIONS

Interactions between firms can occur both through the market and through their interdependent strategies. The evolution of demand for the product of a firm may be the result of changes in price (and therefore the effect of decisions taken by the firm) or of changes in consumers' income (resulting from the working of the entire economy), or of firms' activity (sales promotion). This is the way interaction between firms' decisions is registered by the market.

To the extent that interactions between the decisions of one firm and those of other specific firms may be directly perceived, we can say that the strategies of the firms are interconnected. The theory of games deals with them whereas the *monopolistic-competition* scheme allows us to deal only with market interactions.

The diverse possible interactions between the firms' strategies make the possible scenarios too numerous and vague. That is the reason why we shall adopt the monopolistic competition scheme: each firm tries to enlarge its market at the expense of *all* other firms. We shall avoid the difficulties entailed by the division of the economy in markets, by assuming that all products are competing with one another.

17. THE AGENTS IN THE MODEL

We shall assume that final production consists of consumer products competing with each other. There are as many markets (for consumer products) as there are firms. Final products are bought by workers-consumers. Intermediate commodities (capital goods) are produced inside the firms making use of them.

Money is internal money: normally, firms are indebted; their liabilities represent the consumers' monetary assets. We shall talk of money: that of consumers being positive whereas firms' money is negative.

Labour supply, as we have already remarked, is automatically adjusted to demand through immigration and emigration. Since we shall assume that labour plays the role of numeraire, wage rate is equal to 1.

I Firms (entrepreneurs)

Each firm carries on four activities:

- *the production of the final product bought by consumers-workers,*
- *the production of capital goods* required to increase the firm's potential capacity (*accumulation*),
- *sales promotion activity,*
- *research and technological innovation.*

The level of the first activity is measured by the quantity of final product, that of *accumulation activity* by the number of workers employed in the production of capital goods, the level of *sales promotion activity* and of *research and technological innovation* by the number of workers employed in these activities.

To produce the final commodity, labour and capital must be employed. Capital goods can be obtained through the employment of labour only. Labour is used also to implement R&D activities.

For the reasons already pointed out, development depends, to a large extent, on certain psychological and cultural features of the entrepreneur. They enter into the model as *entrepreneur's coefficients*:

mark-up μ_i,
research activity coefficients $\zeta_{r1,i}, \zeta_{r2,i}$,
sales promotion coefficients $\zeta_{s1,i}, \zeta_{s2,i}$
propensity to grow $\xi_{a,i}$ which relates the level of accumulation to the entrepreneur's growth objective (that is assumed to be proportional to the level of employment in production of the final product, an index of the size of the firm).

Our approach is akin to Joan Robinson's. She notes (1963, p. 87):

> the inducement to invest is conceived in terms of a desired rate of growth rather than a desired stock of capital. The natural rate of growth permits but does not cause actual growth. The actual trend of growth is generated from within by the propensity to accumulate inherent in the system.

Such propensity reflects, in Joan Robinson words, entrepreneurs' *animal spirits*. I think that we can give a different interpretation to the propensity to grow (propensity may then result not to be the proper name). We can assume that entreprenuer has a *strategy* that depends, to a large extent, on the size of the firm. For the sake of simplicity, we assume a rather rigid, linear strategy: this is a weak point of our model. A more realistic concept of the entrepreneur's strategy would have made the model too complex. Perhaps other more fruitful simplifications can be explored.

Mark-up reflects, at least *ab initio*, the entrepreneur's aggressiveness and confidence (the latter being based also on his expectations); processes of learning make it better reflect market conditions.

These coefficients are initially randomly drawn, expressing the entrepreneur's aggressiveness, his propensity to risk, his inclination to optimism. They will change in accordance with the experience that the entrepreneur will have developed through the knowledge of some reactions of the market and of the firm's conditions (changes in stocks, rentability).

Some initial conditions, too – money, namely the value of capital, stocks etc. – are initially drawn randomly.

Our approach is closer to principles of maximizing behaviour than to behaviourism. Taking the entrepreneur's socio-cultural peculiarities into account does not mean to abandon rationalistic criteria for behaviour. Such criteria are revealed by processes of learning and adjusting actions and reactions.

A firm has three labels: its number, the time of its birth, the time in which it operates: i, τ, t. It has a capital $K_{i,\tau,t}$ and a value $V_{i,\tau,t}$ which is the sum of the value of the accumulated fixed capital and of stocks $s_{i,\tau,t}$. The value of the fixed capital of the firm $V^f_{i,\tau,t}$ is assumed to increase in proportion to the amount of wages spent both for research and accumulation and to a quota of the expenditure for sales promotion. The firm's rentability $r_{i,\tau,t}$ is the ratio of the excess of the value of production over the wages paid for it to the value of the firm.

Research and innovation activity affects:

the labour and capital coefficients for final product $\lambda^p_{i,\tau,t}$, $\kappa_{i,\tau,t}$,

the labour coefficient for capital good $\lambda^k_{i,\tau,t}$.

Sales promotion activity affects:

the competition coefficient $a_{i,\tau,t}$; the ratio of such a coefficient to the sum of all competition coefficients expresses the effect of sales promotion on the consumers' demand for the firm's product: is an index of the firm's competitiveness.

The efficacy of the firm's R&D activities is expressed by the research *coefficients* α.

The target of sales promotion activities (advertising, in particular) is persuading consumers to spend more of their real income on the firm's product, as compared with other products.

The difference between the firm's revenue and its expenditures represents its financial flow which normally is negative (representing liabilities to banks), since expenditures also includes investments for accumulation and in R&D. Firms' money is negative and is equal to consumers' deposits.

A firm cannot be indebted to banks by more than its own value. Should such liabilities exceed this level, the firm will go bankrupt. Failures entail a decrease in consumers' monetary assets since banks cannot recover all their credits. A portion of the firm's capital goods - corresponding to the credit recovered by the banks - is taken over by the new firm.

II Consumers-workers. Money

The firms' final products are bought by consumers (workers). Consumers' income is made up by wages and interest on their (positive) money, corresponding, as has been noted, to the (negative) firms' financial assets (liabilities).

Optimizing behaviour by consumers has little sense when product changes are allowed for. In fact their demand for the different products is affected by the firms' sales promotion activities. It depends, of course, on their income and on the product prices.

We shall assume that consumers' savings is not a residual variable as it is assumed to be in Keynesian theory. Both Schumpeter and Keynes do not think that the rate of interest has a remarkable effect on investment. Their belief was differently grounded. For Keynes savings is a residual variable: the consumer's objective is consumption. However, we shall assume that workers, in deciding their consumption, take into account the excess of their money on a level deemed convenient.

Workers are all held to be alike.

In Schumpeterian theory money is a continuous flow of purchasing power that is created by the banking system, through loans granted to firms. By our assumption - of money being internal money - we shall try to isolate entrepreneurial activity and Darwinian selection from monetary policies.

III Firms and markets

Let us introduce some definitions to explain firm's choices. A firm starts out with a given capital and given stocks. Then we can determine:

- the *potential production* $q^p_{i,\tau,t}$, namely the quantity that, given the capital coefficient, we can get from the capital available,
- the *maximum supply* $q^m_{i,\tau,t}$, given by the production increased by the level of the stocks.

The firm plans its production. The *planned production* $q_{i,\tau,t}$ can be:

- *rentability-constrained* when rentability is negative, planned production is less than production potential,
- *stocks-constrained* when stocks are greater than the maximum level, capital is not fully utilized; some supply comes out of stocks,
- *constrained* when it is both rentability and stocks-constrained,
- *unconstrained*: then production equals the production potential.

The market can be *rationed for consumers*. That happens when demand is greater than maximum supply. Then the quantity effectively bought by consumers is equal to maximum supply. The market can never be rationed for the firms, since production plans are assumed to be carried on even if demand is less than planned production: in this case stocks will increase.

If markets are rationed for some products, then firms cannot fully exploit their commercial advantages. In most cases, this means that prices are too high. In fact price is sensitive to changes in stocks. More income is then available for the purchase of other commodities. We shall solve the problem of finding the structure of the economy that allows consumers to spend as much as they can (and will), given their income and their wealth objectives, by a sequence-of-decisions-process as the one visualized by Benassy-Malinvaud. After a rationed market is visualized and the quantity purchased determined, the residual income is computed upon which the demand for other products depends. Another rationed market is then found. If such a sequence leads to visualize a certain number of non-rationed markets, then consumers will be able to spend as much as they want, and the *equilibrium structure of the economy* resulting from consumers' demand is determined. If not, part of the purchasing power is not spent, and an *unintended increase of wealth* is produced.

An alternative way of dealing with the problem of rationed markets is to assume that the money that consumers cannot spend increases savings. This means that in future periods consumption can be enhanced. This will be our approach.

IV The Selection mechanism

We shall assume a given number of firms. As we have already said, the entrepreneurial coefficients as well as the initial money, stocks, capital, input and the research coefficients are chosen randomly *ab initio*.

The probability distributions are rectangular (uniform) distribution with minimum and maximum values.

When a firm goes bankrupt, a new firm takes over part of its capital, its liabilities being reduced. The structural features of the new firm result from *imitation* of the features of the most successful firms. The firms that are more likely to be imitated are those that have highest rentability and largest size. The distributions from which the structural coefficients of the new firms are randomly drawn are not the initial ones, but new distributions that reflect the evolution according to the two criteria just mentioned. The new distributions are obtained from the values of the relevant parameters of the operating firms, weighted by the product of the potential production and rentability.

18. THE STRUCTURE OF THE SYSTEM

Entrepreneurs play the role of engine of the economy. Consumers are substantially governed by the market that is affected by firms' activities and assesses their competitiveness. The neoclassical stand-point is reversed. Consumers' tastes concern essentially the saving objective.

Figure 6.1 offers a block representation of the system.

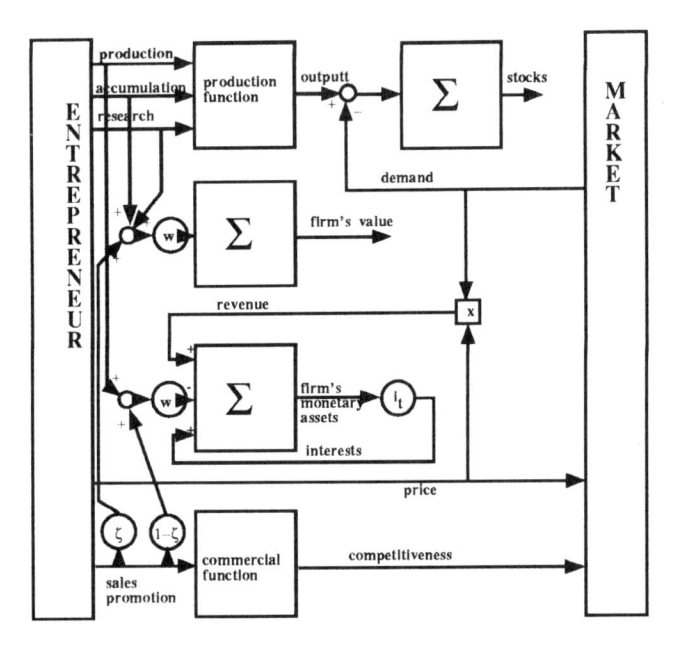

Figure 6.1

19. THE MODEL

I Price

We shall distinguish the *normal price* - which is established when demand is equal to production, production is not rentability-constrained and stocks are at the normal level - from the *actual price*. The first is given by the following equation:

$$p^n_{i,\tau,t} = \mu_{i,\tau,t}[w_t(\lambda^p_{i,\tau,t} + \zeta_{c,i}l^c_{i,\tau,t}/q_{i,\tau,t}) + i_t O_{i,\tau,t}/q_{i,\tau,t}] \quad (6.1)$$

where: $O_{i,\tau,t}$ are the financial costs that are incurred when the firm is indebted to banks. Thus:

$$O_{i,\tau,t} = -i_t M_{i,\tau,t} \quad \text{if} \quad M_{i,\tau,t} < 0$$

$$O_{i,\tau,t} = 0 \quad \text{if} \quad M_{i,\tau,t} > 0 \quad (6.2)$$

Costs also include part of the expenditures sustained for the sales-promotion activity which are considered as current costs.

As we have noted, rational behaviour does not result from the solution of an optimization problem. It entails a *learning process* that produces adjustments. The *initial* mark-up is an *entrepreneur index* reflecting some features of his personality. During the firm's life the entrepreneur will adjusts the mark-up to improve the firm's profitability.

In case of a sluggish market, namely if stocks are reaching the maximum level (see equation 6.17), rentability being positive (see equation 6.19), the entrepreneur deems that price is too high. He will accordingly decrease his mark-up. Therefore:

$$\text{if} \quad s_{i,\tau,t} > \bar{s}_{i,\tau,t}$$

$$\text{then} \quad \mu_{i,\tau,t} = \mu_{i,\tau,(t-1)} + \zeta_{\mu 1,i} \quad \zeta_{\mu 1,i} < 0 \quad (6.3)$$

The adjustment coefficient reflects entrepreneur's prudence. The time for adjustment depends from its level.

Should rentability be negative, market growth keeping stocks under the maximum level, the entrepreneur deems that price could be profitably increased; therefore:

$$\text{if} \quad r_{i,\tau,t} < 0$$

$$\text{then} \quad \mu_{i,\tau,t} = \mu_{i,\tau,(t-1)} + \zeta_{\mu 2,i} \quad \zeta_{\mu 2,i} > 0 \quad (6.4)$$

Should rentability be negative in case of a sluggish market, then the entrepreneur will deem it convenient to decrease the mark-up in order to increase sales:

$$\text{if} \quad r_{i,\tau,t} < 0 \quad \wedge \quad s_{i,\tau,t} > \overline{s}_{i,\tau,t}$$

$$\text{then} \quad \mu_{i,\tau,t} = \mu_{i,\tau,(t-1)} + \zeta_{\mu 3,i} \qquad \zeta_{\mu 3,i} < 0 \qquad (6.5)$$

To get the equation of the actual price we shall introduce a *disequilibrium index* $\eta_{i,\tau,t}$:

$$\eta_{i,\tau,t} = \xi_{1,i} \frac{q^d_{i,\tau,t} - q_{i,\tau,t}}{q_{i,\tau,t}} + \xi_{2,i} \frac{T_o q_{i,\tau,t} - s_{i,t}}{T_o q_{i,\tau,t}} \qquad (6.6)$$

where $T_o q_{i,\tau,t}$ is the normal level of stocks:

$$T_o q_{i,\tau,t} = s^n_{i,\tau,t} \qquad (6.7)$$

The disequilibrium index affects the difference between normal and actual price. The actual price is the normal price partially adjusted in relation to the disequilibrium index:

$$p_{i,\tau,t} = p^n_{i,\tau,t} \{\xi_{3i} + (1 - \xi_{3i}) \; \zeta_{i,\tau,t}\} \qquad (6.8)$$

$\zeta_{i,\tau,t}$ is the *adjustment index*: it decreases at a decreasing rate as the disequilibrium index increases when it is negative; it increases at decreasing rate, when the positive disequilibrium index increases.

We shall assume that:

$$\text{if} \quad \eta_{i,\tau,t} \leq 0, \quad \text{then} \quad \zeta_{i,\tau,t} = e^{\eta_{i,\tau,t}}$$

$$\text{if} \quad \eta_{i,\tau,t} \geq 0, \quad \text{then} \quad \zeta_{i,\tau,t} = 1 + \eta^o_{i,\tau,t}\left(1 - e^{-\eta_{i,\tau,t}}\right) \qquad (6.9)$$

The *adjustment index* is represented in Figure 6.2:

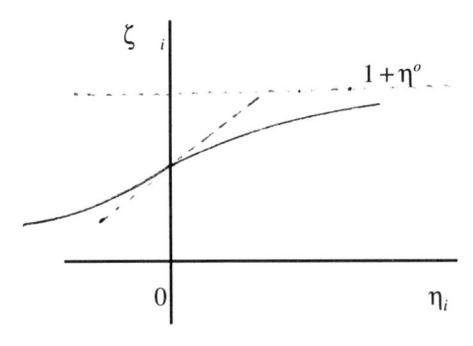

Figure 6.2

II Consumer's Demand and Income

The quantity of the firm's (i, τ, t) product demanded by each consumer is given by:

$$q_{i,\tau,t}^d = \frac{a_{i,\tau,t}}{\sum_j a_{j,\tau,t}} \left\{ \frac{w_t + i_t M_t^c / l_t}{p_{i,\tau,t}} \right\} \zeta_{d,i} \left\{ \frac{M_t^c / l_t}{p_{i,\tau,t}} \right\}^{\gamma_i} \quad (6.10)$$

whereas the parameter $a_{i,\tau,t}$ represents the effect of the firm's sales promotion activity on individual preferences for the product, as related to the same activity carried on by other firms. Thus $a_{i,\tau,t} / \sum_j a_{j,\tau,t}$ represents the effects of the *monopolistic competition* on the demand of the product of firm (i, τ, t).

A market is rationed if:

$$l_t q_{i,\tau,t}^d > q_{i,\tau,t}^m \quad (6.11)$$

If the market is not rationed, the quantity of product purchased is equal to the quantity demanded.

$$q_{i,\tau,t}^b = l_t q_{i,\tau,t}^d \quad (6.12)$$

If the market is rationed, then the quantity bought is equal to maximum supply (see equation 6.27):

$$q_{i,\tau,t}^b = q_{i,\tau,t}^m \quad (6.13)$$

Supposing that in the mentioned sequence-decisions process, all firms up to the j have found their markets rationed for consumers, the demand for the product of the following firm is given by:

$$q_{(j+1),\tau,t}^d = \frac{a_{(j+1),\tau,t}}{\sum_{(h=1)}^j a_{h,\tau,t}} \cdot$$

$$\frac{\{w_t + i_t M_t^c / l_t + \sum_{h=1}^j p_{h,\tau,t}(q_{h,\tau,t}^d - q_{h,\tau,t}^b / l_t)\}}{p_{(j+1),\tau,t}} \zeta_{d,i} \left\{ \frac{M_t^c / l_t}{p_{(j+1),\tau,t}} \right\}^{\gamma_i} \quad (6.14)$$

If all markets are rationed for consumers, there is an unintended increase in consumers' wealth given by:

$$\Delta M_t^c = \sum_h p_{h,\tau,t}(l_t q_{h,\tau,t}^d - q_{h,\tau,t}^b) \quad (6.15)$$

such an occurrence being unlikely.

An alternative approach to the problem of markets being rationed is to assume that firms cannot take advantage of income consumers were willing to spend for other products but were enable to because their markets were rationed. Then unintended increase in consumers' savings occurs: consumption in successive periods will increase.

III Stocks, Firm's Rentability

Stocks are given by equation:

$$\Delta s_{i,\tau,t} = q_{i,\tau,t} - q^b_{i,\tau,t} \tag{6.16}$$

We have a maximum value for stocks:

$$\overline{s}_{i,\tau,t} = \frac{TK_{i,\tau,t}}{\kappa_{i,\tau,t}} \tag{6.17}$$

When stocks tend to exceed such a value, the entrepreneur will reduce stocks both by increasing price and by reducing production.

There is also a normal value:

$$s^n_{i,\tau,t} = T_o \frac{K_{i,\tau,t}}{\kappa_{i,\tau,t}} \tag{6.18}$$

Part of the sales promotion expenditures are considered as current expenses; they are an element of costs. The rest is considered *commercial investments*. All expenditures for (technological) research are considered as *technological investments*. The wages spent to produce capital goods are *accumulation investments*. The firm's value is increased by the investments made.

The firm's rentability is defined by:

$$r_{i,\tau,t} = \frac{p_{i,\tau,t} q_{i,\tau,t} - w_t(l^p_{i,\tau,t} + \zeta l^c_{i,\tau,t})}{V_{i,\tau,t}} \tag{6.19}$$

where

$$V_{i,\tau,t} = V^f_{i,\tau,t} + p_{i,\tau,t} s_{i,\tau,t} \tag{6.20}$$

being:

$$\Delta V^f_{i,\tau,t} = w_t \{l^k_{i,\tau,t} + l^t_{i,\tau,t} + (1-\zeta)l^c_{i,\tau,t}\} \tag{6.21}$$

IV Production and supply

The production potential is given by:

$$q^p_{i,\tau,t} = \frac{K_{i,\tau,t}}{\kappa} \tag{6.22}$$

Let us now define the planned production. Four cases have to be distinguished:

1st case: Production is neither rentability nor stocks constrained. Then planned production is equal to production potential:

$$q_{i,\tau,t} = q^p_{i,\tau,t} \tag{6.23}$$

2nd case: Production is rentability constrained, namely $r_{i,\tau,t} < 0$. Then planned production is determined by leaving some production potential unutilized:

$$q_{i,\tau,t} = q^p_{i,\tau,t}(1 + r_{i,\tau,t})^{\varepsilon_{i,t}} \tag{6.24}$$

3rd case: Production is stocks constrained, namely $s_{i,\tau,t} > \bar{s}_{i,\tau,t}$. Then part of the expected demand that is supposed to be equal to production potential is satisfied out of stocks:

$$q_{i,\tau,t} = q^p_{i,\tau,t} - (s_{i,\tau,t} - \bar{s}_{i,\tau,t}) \tag{6.25}$$

4th case: Production is both rentability and stocks constrained. Then:

$$q_{i,\tau,t} = q^p_{i,\tau,t}(1 + r_{i,\tau,t})^{\varepsilon_{i,\tau}} - (s_{i,\tau,t} - \bar{s}_{i,\tau,t}) \tag{6.26}$$

The maximum supply is:

$$q^m_{i,\tau,t} = q_{i,\tau,t} + s_{i,\tau,t} \tag{6.27}$$

V Accumulation

Accumulation is not induced by population growth, but by the entrepreneurs' expectations and by their greed for power (propensity to grow). The financial conditions may enhance or lessen the accumulation process.

The financial conditions are expressed by a *health index* ($\omega_{i,\tau,t}$): the ratio of the excess of the firm's value over its indebtedness to the same firm's value. If we assume that the value of the firm corresponds to its risk capital, we can establish a relation between the health index and the *gearing ratio*, expressing the ratio of the firm's value to its indebtedness ($g_{i,\tau,t}$):

$$\omega_{i,\tau,t} = \frac{(V_{i,\tau,t} + M_{i,\tau,t})}{V_{i,\tau,t}} = 1 - \frac{1}{g_{i,\tau,t}} \tag{6.28}$$

We can assume that there is a value of the health index which is considered normal: $\bar{\omega}_{i,\tau}$.

If rentability is not negative $r_{i,\tau,t} \geq 0$, then the entrepreneur invests towards enlarging the firm's size. The rate of growth as related to the level of employment required for producing the final product reflects the entrepreneur's expectations and his animal spirits (his greed for power). The normal growth objective can be enhanced or hampered by the assessed financial conditions of the firm, namely on the basis of the ratio of its health index to its normal value.

$$l^k_{i,\tau,t} = \xi_{a,i} l^p_{i,\tau,t} \left(\frac{\omega_{i,\tau,t}}{\overline{\omega}_{i,\tau}} \right)^{\beta_i} \quad (6.29)$$

If rentability is negative $r_{i,\tau,t} < 0$, then:

$$l^k_{i,\tau,t} = 0 \quad (6.30)$$

The firm's capital increases by the amount invested:

$$\Delta K_{i,\tau,t} = \frac{l^k_{i,\tau,t}}{\lambda^k_{i,\tau,t}} \quad (6.31)$$

VI Sales Promotion Activity

The level of sales promotion activities is measured by the number of workers employed in them. The larger is the firm, the larger the sales promotion activities that will be enhanced when market is sluggish, rentability being positive, and lessened when rentability is negative.

$$l^c_{i,\tau,t} = \zeta_{s1,i,t} l^k_{i,\tau,t} + \zeta_{s2,i,t} \left(2 \frac{q^p_{i,\tau,t}}{\lambda^p_{i,\tau,t}} - l^p_{i,\tau,t} \right) \quad (6.32)$$

the coefficients $\zeta_{s1,i}; \zeta_{a2,i}$ being adjusted to arrive at an optimal (stable) sales promotion policy.

If rentability is negative, the entrepreneur deems it convenient to reduce costs; the sales promotion activity is lessened:

$$\zeta_{s1,i,t} = \zeta_{s1,i,\tau,(t-1)} \chi_{1,i} \quad \zeta_{s2,it} = \zeta_{s2,i(t-1)} \chi_{2,i} \quad \chi_{1,i}; \chi_{2,i} < 1 \quad (6.33)$$

If market is sluggish, rentability being positive, increase in sales promotion is deemed convenient to better the market situation of the firm. Then:

$$\zeta_{s1,i,t} = \zeta_{s2,i,(t-1)} \chi_{3,i} \quad \zeta_{s2,it} = \zeta_{s2,i,(t-1)} \chi_{4,i} \quad \chi_{3,i}; \chi_{4,i} > 1 \quad (6.34)$$

The amount of labour employed in sales promotion cannot be less than a minimum level and greater than a maximum one, minimum and maximum depending on the level of labour employed in final production:

$$l^c_m \leq l^c_{i,\tau,t} \leq l^c_M \quad (6.35)$$

being:

$$l_m^c = \omega_i, c, m l_{i,\tau,t}^p, \quad l_M^c = \omega_i, c, M l_{i,\tau,t}^p \qquad (6.36)$$

VII Research Activity

Research activity is the larger, the larger the size of the firm and the greater the growth objective. We can write:

$$l_{i,\tau,t}^t = \zeta_{r1,i,t} l_{i,\tau,t}^p + \zeta_{r2,i,t} l_{i,\tau,t}^k \qquad (6.37)$$

If the health index is below a critical value $\omega_{i,\tau}^m < \overline{\omega}_{i,\tau}$, namely if the financial conditions are deemed to be very bad, then costs for research have to be reduced. Then:

$$\zeta_{r1,i,t} = \zeta_{r1,i,(t-1)} \phi_{1,i}$$

$$\zeta_{r2,i,t} = \zeta_{r2,i,(t-1)} \phi_{2,i} \qquad \phi_{1,i}; \; \phi_{2,i} < 1 \qquad (6.38)$$

If financial conditions are good, namely if $\omega_{i,\tau,t} > \overline{\omega}_{i,\tau}$, research activity is enhanced:

$$\zeta_{r1,i,t} = \zeta_{r1,i,(t-1)} \phi_{3,i}$$

$$\zeta_{r2,i,t} = \zeta_{r2,i,(t-1)} \phi_{4,i} \qquad \phi_{3,i}; \; \phi_{4,i} > 1 \qquad (6.39)$$

If market is sluggish, namely if stocks are greater than the maximum level, the entrepreneur will deem it convenient to intensify his research activity so as to be able to lower his price and enlarge his market.

$$\zeta_{r1,i,t} = \zeta_{r1,i,(t-1)} \phi_{5,i}$$

$$\zeta_{r2,i,t} = \zeta_{r2,i,(t-1)} \phi_{6,i} \qquad \phi_{5,i}; \; \phi_{6,i} > 1 \qquad (6.40)$$

The amount of labour employed in research cannot be less than a minimum level and greater than a maximum one, minimum and maximum levels being defined in a way similar to that of equation (6.36).

$$l_m^t \leq l_{i,\tau,t}^t \leq l_M^t \qquad (6.41)$$

VIII The Effects of Sales Promotion and Research Activity

The firm's input coefficients vary after the effects of *research activity* according to the following laws:

$$\lambda_{i,\tau,t}^{p} = \lambda_{i,\tau,(t-1)}^{p} \exp\left\{\alpha_{i,\tau}^{1p}\frac{l_{i,\tau,t}^{t}}{l_{t}^{t}} + \alpha_{i,\tau}^{2p}\frac{\Delta l_{i,\tau,t}^{t}}{l_{i,\tau,t}^{t}}\right\}(1+\sigma_{p}u_{p}) \qquad (6.42)$$

$$\lambda_{i,\tau,t}^{k} = \lambda_{i,\tau,(t-1)}^{k} \exp\left\{\alpha_{i,\tau}^{1s}\frac{l_{i,\tau,t}^{t}}{l_{t}^{t}} + \alpha_{i,\tau}^{2s}\frac{\Delta l_{i,\tau,t}^{t}}{l_{i,\tau,t}^{t}}\right\}(1+\sigma_{r}u_{r}) \qquad (6.43)$$

$$\kappa_{i,\tau,t} = \kappa_{i,\tau,(t-1)} \exp\left\{\alpha_{i,\tau}^{1k}\frac{l_{i,\tau,t}^{t}}{l_{t}^{t}} + \alpha_{i,\tau}^{2k}\frac{\Delta l_{i,\tau,t}^{t}}{l_{i,\tau,t}^{t}}\right\}(1+\sigma_{k}u_{k}) \qquad (6.44)$$

where u_p, u_r, u_k are non-correlated random variables normally distributed with means 0 and standard deviations equal to 1.

The competition coefficient changes according to the law:

$$a_{i,\tau,t} = \alpha_{i}^{a} l_{i,\tau,t}^{c}(1+\sigma_{a}u_{a}) \qquad (6.45)$$

where the stochastic variable is defined as stated above.

IX Labour

The labour employed by the firm (i,τ,t) for production of the final commodity is

$$l_{i,\tau,t}^{p} = \lambda_{i,\tau,t}^{p} q_{i,\tau,t} \qquad (6.46)$$

The total labour employed by the firm (i,τ,t) is

$$l_{i,\tau,t} = l_{i,\tau,t}^{p} + l_{i,\tau,t}^{k} + l_{i,\tau,t}^{r} \qquad (6.47)$$

Total labour employed is:

$$l_{t} = \sum_{i,\tau} l_{i,\tau,t} \qquad (6.48)$$

As for wages we can make two assumptions:

1. wages are given: labour plays the role of numeraire;
2. wages increase as commercial activity is intensified mostly because entrepreneurs are less hostile to wage increases in view of the expected income effect on demand (remember Ford's attitude):

$$\frac{\Delta w_{t}}{w_{t}} = \xi_{w}\frac{\Delta\sum_{i,\tau}l_{i,\tau,t}^{r}}{\sum_{i,\tau}l_{i,\tau,t}^{r}} \qquad (6.49)$$

We have worked out the first hypothesis.

X Money

The increase in workers' money (wealth) is given by the absolute value of the increase in firms' indebtedness:

$$M_t^c - M_{t-1}^c = \Delta M_t^i \tag{6.50}$$

At time t the firms j for which:

$$V_{j,\tau,t} \geq -M_{j,\tau,t} \tag{6.51}$$

fail.

Part of the banks' credit claims from them are lost (m_t^f). This loss falls on consumers.[20] Part of the capital of these firms goes to those that will replace them in the market.

For all surviving firms, the financial flow of any firm is given by its sales minus the interest on outstanding bank loans and labour costs (both for production and for accumulation and research). Normally it is negative: which means that its debt towards banks increases:

$$M_{i,\tau,t}^i - M_{i,\tau,(t-1)}^i = p_{i,\tau,t} q_{i,\tau,t} - w_t l_{i,\tau,t} + i_t M_{i,\tau,t}^i \tag{6.52}$$

For all firms i that survive and for the new firms replacing the failed ones j, indebtedness corresponding to the financial assets of consumers is:

$$M_t^i = \sum_i M_{i,\tau,t}^i + \sum_j (1 - m_{j,t}^f) M_{j,\tau,t}^i \tag{6.53}$$

The absolute value of the increase in firms' indebtedness is equal to the increase in consumers' wealth (monetary assets):

$$|\Delta M_t^i| = \Delta M_t^c \tag{6.54}$$

The rate of interest has no direct impact on investments. Its increase causes an increase in costs and, thereby, in normal price. If R&D activity is not sufficiently efficient, failure prospects are more likely.

20. TRANSITION AND LONG-RUN PATH. FIVE SCENARIOS

A first set of simulations has been implemented so as to derive a few generalizations that look meaningful.

In evolution we can observe a *transition phase*. The structure of the economy is adjusted to initial conditions (particularly with regard to capital and money endowment). Failures cause fluctuations that are the smoother the larger the number of firms and the smaller the size of failing firms. Fluctuations can be noted also in the evolution of stocks. As time goes by, the economy settles on the long-run evolutionary path. After transition a phase of *moderate evolution* can be detected.

Five scenarios are considered:

1. *mere selection*. To analyse this scenario we shall assume that no research – and thus no innovation – is implemented. Decreases in input coefficients are due to the shift of the probabilistic distribution from which the initial values are drawn;
2. *final innovations* (affecting only labour productivity in consumer industries);
3. *intermediate innovations* (affecting either labour productivity in production of capital goods or productivity of the same goods): the two cases are labelled *a*) and *b*);
4. *global innovations* (affecting all input coefficients).

21. EMPLOYMENT AND PRODUCTION DYNAMICS IN THE FIVE SCENARIOS. RECESSION, STAGNATION AND GROWTH

Evolution can be described in terms of: a) employment dynamics (let us remember that if the economy is progressive population grows, any necessary labour coming from outside); b) production dynamics; c) production per capita. Employment and production are global variables, whereas production per capita is an average. Three different evolutions are obtained:

– *long-run recession*
– *stagnation*
– *long-run growth*.

The first kind of evolution is characterized by recession. It occurs in the first scenario when the reduction of employment entailed by the increase in labour productivity (reduction of labour input coefficients due to selection) is not compensated for by an increase in the quantity of labour employed for accumulation (to produce capital goods). This occurs when entrepreneurs' propensity to grow is not sufficiently high. Then, after transition, despite an increase in production (and income) per capita, both employment and production decline. This kind of evolution is reminiscent of the Rosa Luxemburg theory concerning the crash that technological improvement can produce; in

Selection, Innovation and Economic Development   195

our case improvement being obtained through selection. The dynamics of labour, total production and production per capita are represented in Figures 6.3-6.5.

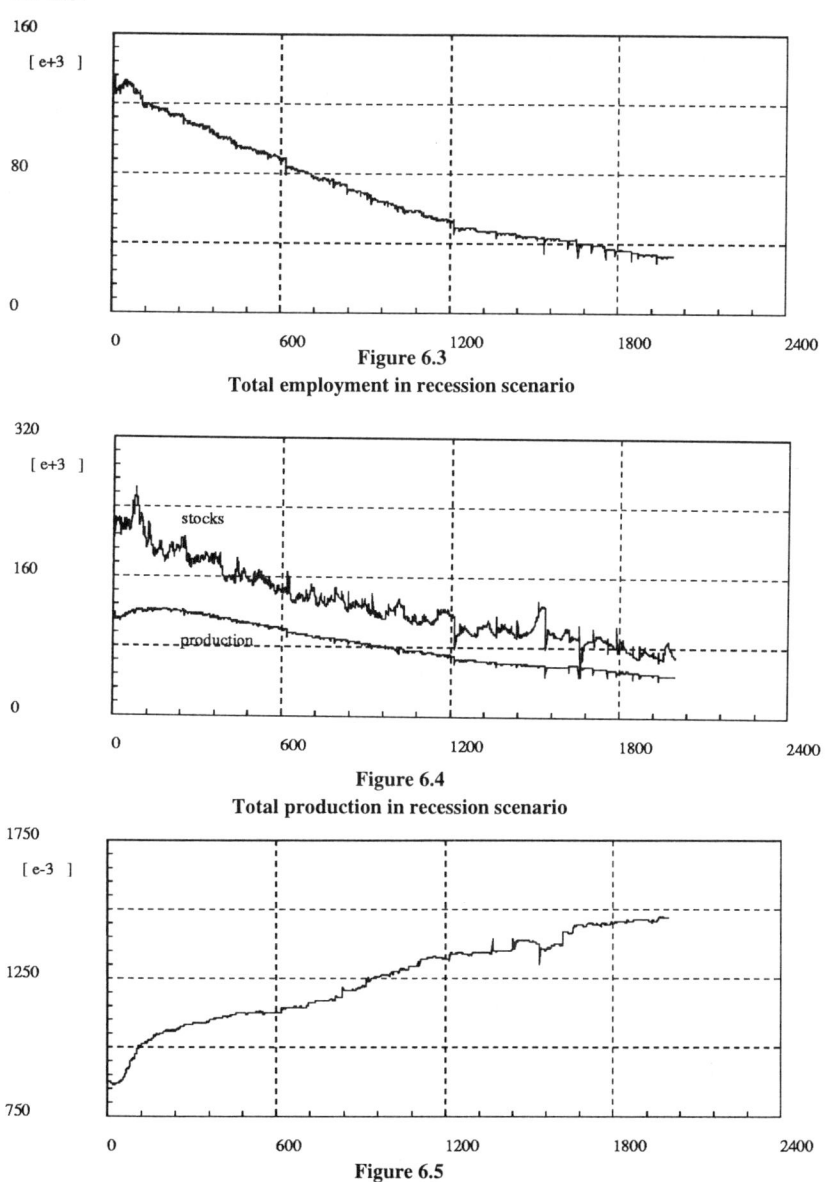

Figure 6.3
Total employment in recession scenario

Figure 6.4
Total production in recession scenario

Figure 6.5
Production per capita in recession scenario

196   *Growth and Economic Development*

The second type of evolution occurs when we have only final innovation. The main differences emerging from a comparison between such an evolution and that of the first type, consist in the increase in per capita income which in the first type occurs at an almost constant velocity, whereas in the second type it shows an accelerating movement and reaches much higher levels, and in the dynamics of stocks, showing ample fluctuations. Employment decreases in both types; in the second the level of production remains practically constant: that justifies the label of *stagnation*. The dynamics of labour, total production and per capita production are represented in Figures 6.6-6.8.

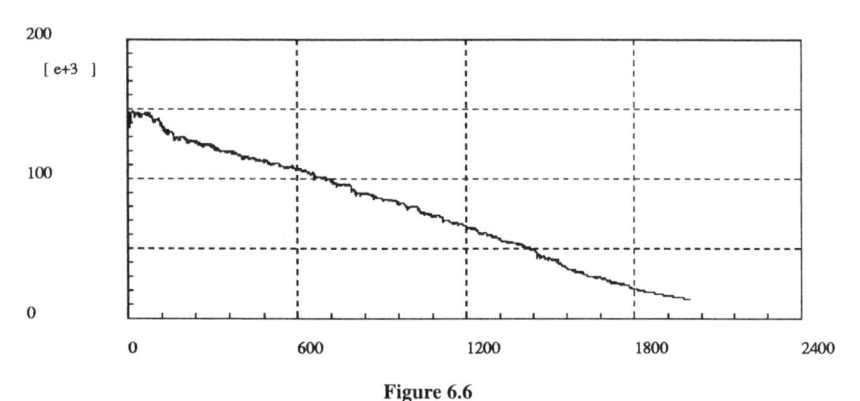

Figure 6.6
Total employment in stagnation scenario

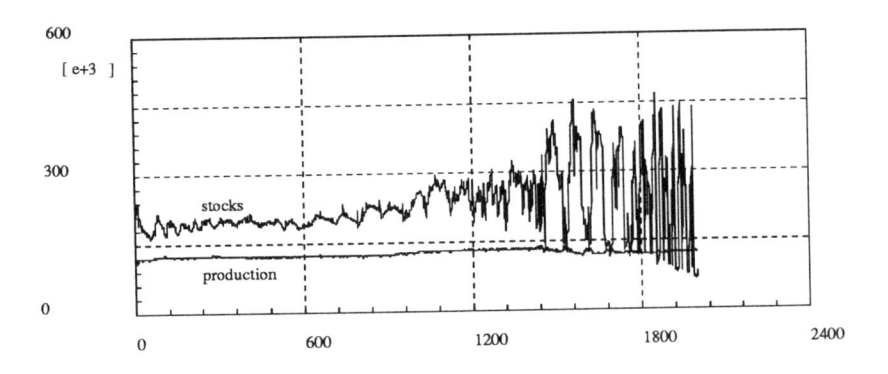

Figure 6.7
Total production in stagnation scenario

Selection, Innovation and Economic Development 197

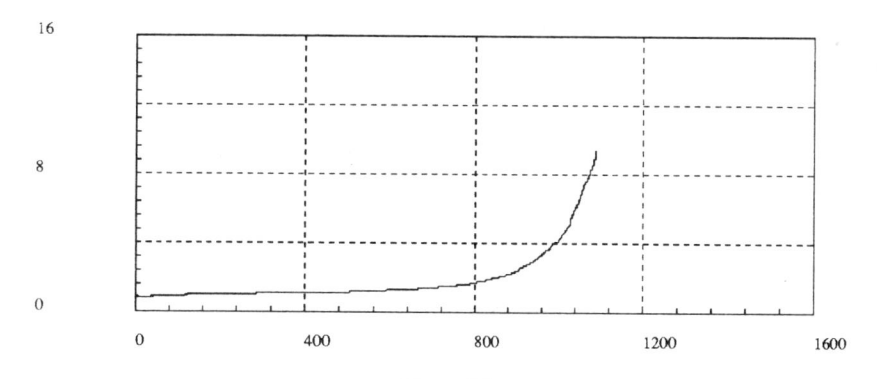

Figure 6.8
Per capita production in stagnation scenario

The third kind of evolution occurs: a) in a mere selection process, provided entrepreneurs' animal spirits are sufficiently high (their propensity to grow being greater than a critical level), b) in global innovations and c) in intermediate innovation cases.

In the first scenario (mere selection), if entrepreneurs' animal spirits are sufficiently high, employment and production increase. The level of per capita income is below that obtained in a recession. Production of final goods has to assure employment of a larger number of workers, those employed for accumulation being more numerous than in a recession. Total employment, total production and per capita income are represented in Figures 6.9-6.11

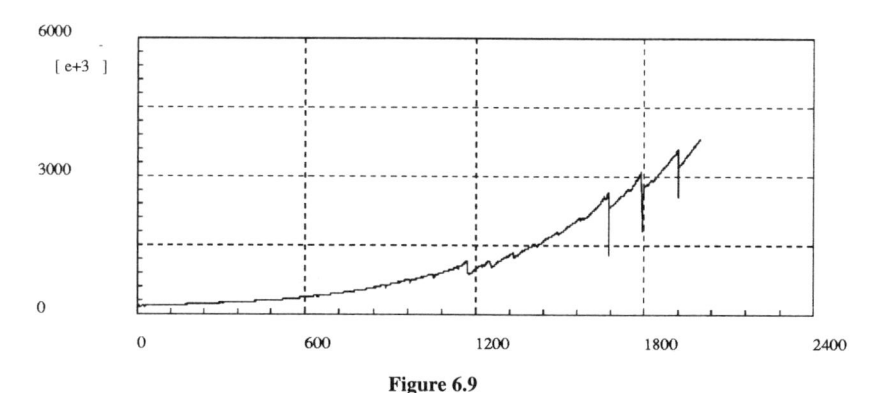

Figure 6.9
Total employment in growth produced by high animal spirits

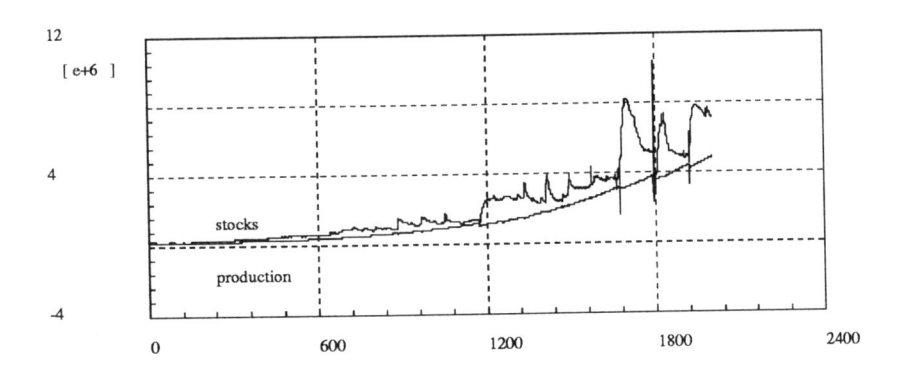

Figure 6.10
Total production in growth produced by high animal spirits

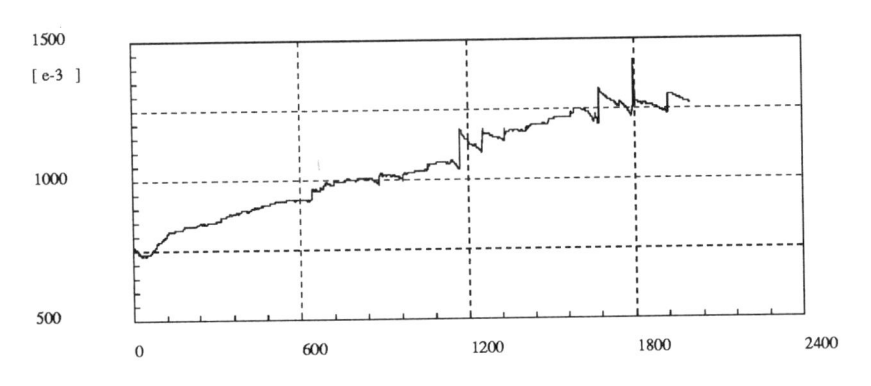

Figure 6.11
Per capita income in growth produced by high animal spirits

In growth (global innovation scenario), employment and production, after a phase of moderate increase, following the transition phase, will grow at accelerated rates *independently from the entrepreneurs' propensity to grow*. A similar trend is observed for the per capita income (acceleration being smaller). Total employment, total production and per capita income are represented in Figures 6.12-6.14. Per capita income reaches a level which is several times higher that that attained in other scenarios.

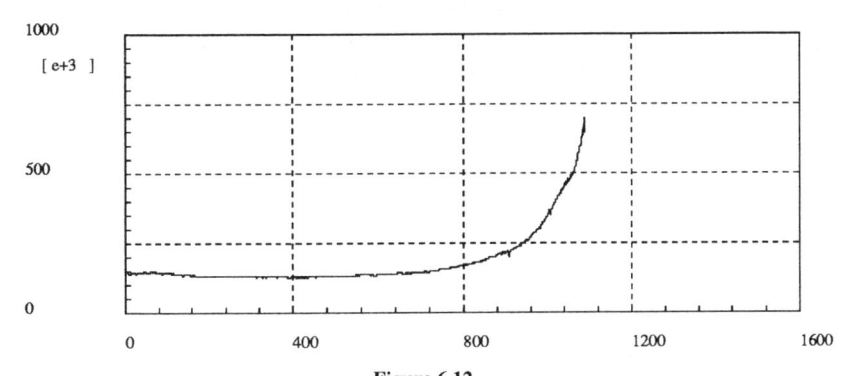

Selection, Innovation and Economic Development 199

Figure 6.12
Total employment in growth scenario (global innovation)

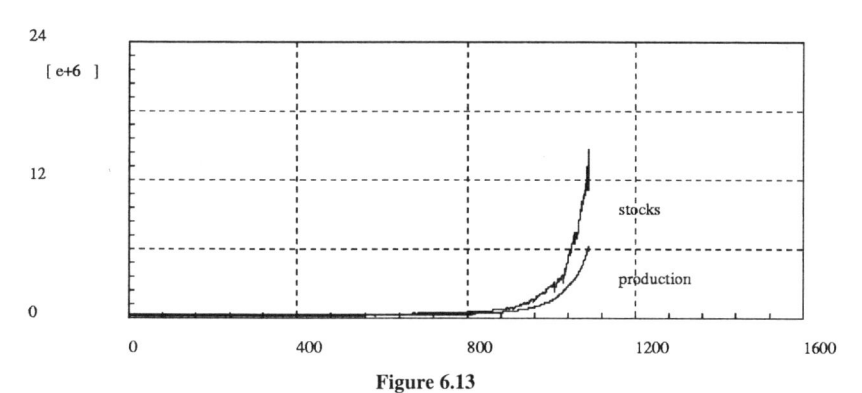

Figure 6.13
Total production in a growth scenario (global innovation)

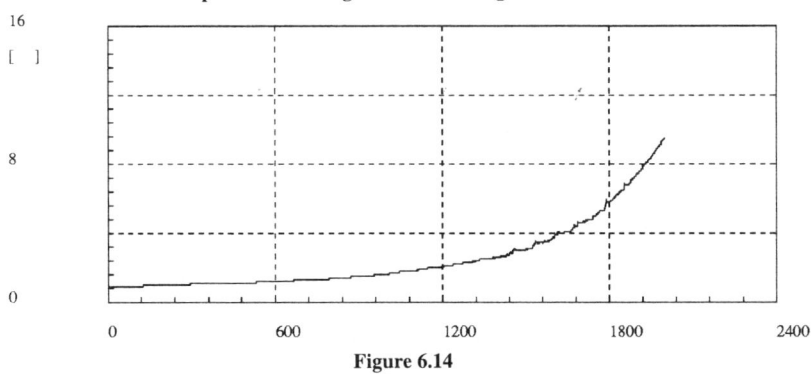

Figure 6.14
Per capita production in growth scenario (global innovation)

200   *Growth and Economic Development*

Total employment, total production and per capita income are represented in Figures 6.15–6.17 for the intermediate innovation, case *a* scenario; in Figures 6.18–6.20 those for the intermediate innovation, case *b* scenario are represented. Total employment in intermediate innovation cases reaches a much higher level, which is in fact particularly high when innovation decreases the capital coefficient (case *b*). This is due to the peculiarities of the technology and to the fact that, given the propensity to grow, the effect of accumulation on growth will increase sharply because of such innovations, causing a general increase in employment. The increase in employment is particularly rapid in accumulation (as we shall see later on), especially in case *b*). That implies both a moderate increase in production of final commodities and in per capita income.

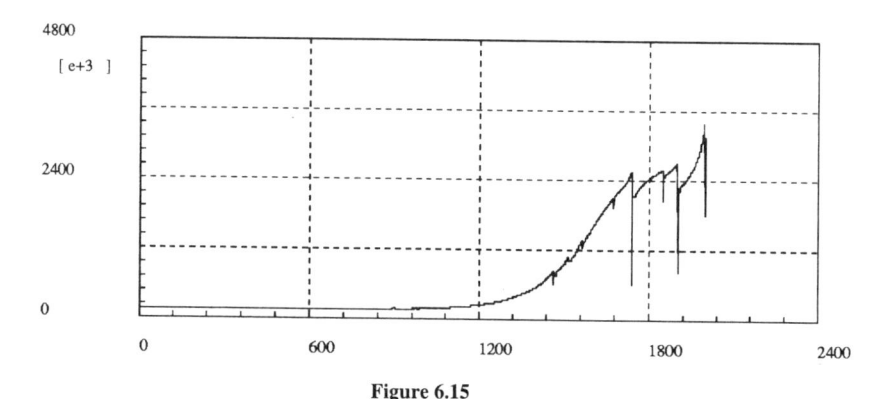

Figure 6.15
Total employment in a growth scenario (intermediate innovation: a)

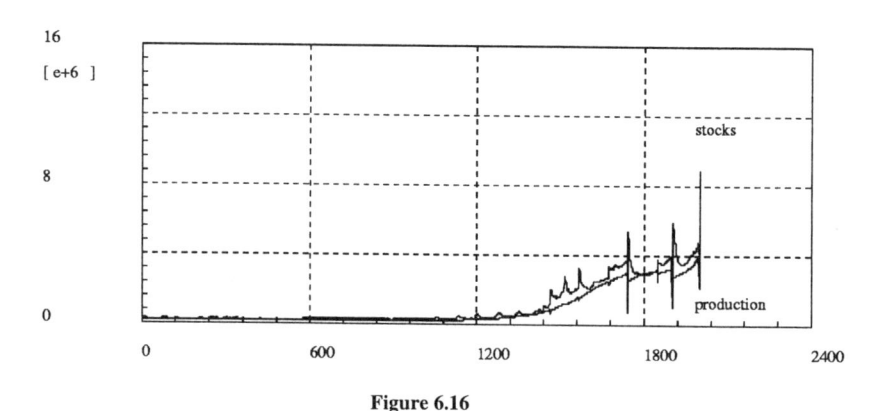

Figure 6.16
Total production in a growth scenario (intermediate innovation: a)

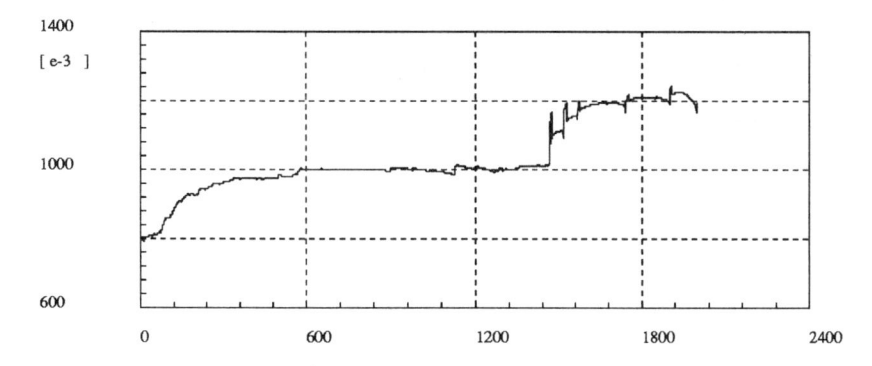

Selection, Innovation and Economic Development   201

Figure 6.17
Per capita production in a growth scenario (intermediate innovation: a)

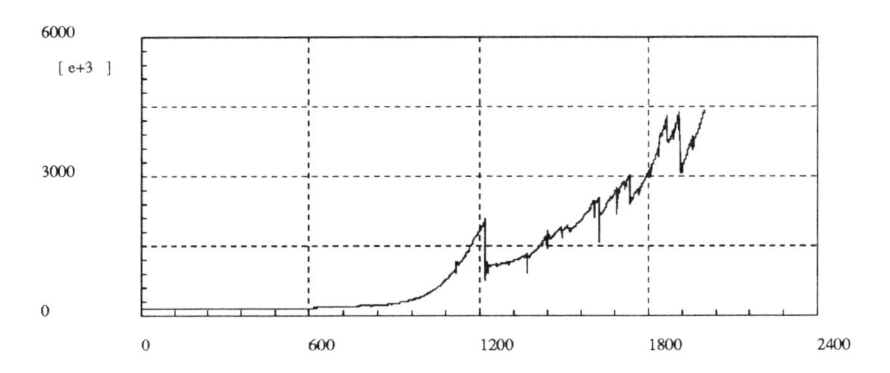

Figure 6.18
Total employment in a growth scenario (intermediate innovation: b)

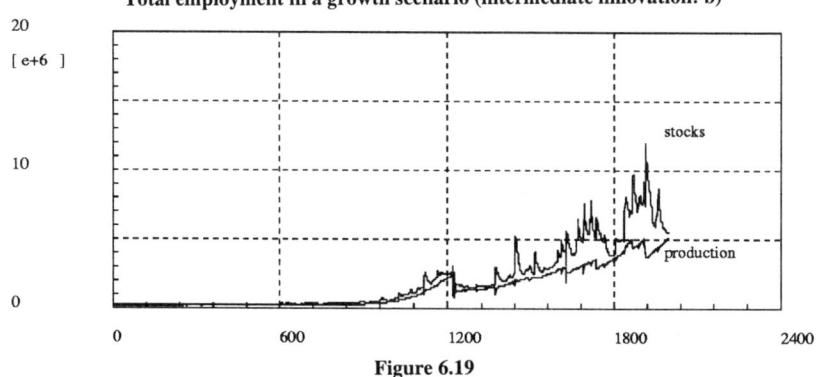

Figure 6.19
Total production in growth scenario (intermediate innovation: b)

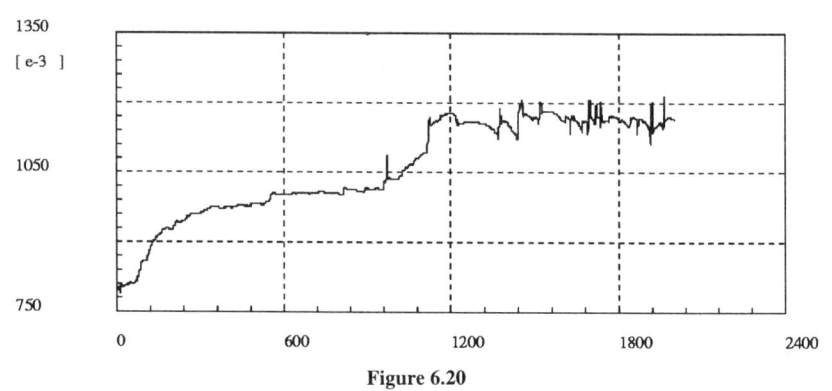

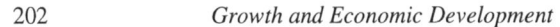

Figure 6.20
Per capita production in a growth scenario (intermediate innovation: b)

22. RESEARCH AND SALES PROMOTION IN THE FIVE SCENARIOS

In the first type of evolution (recession), labour employed for sales promotion and for accumulation, after adjustment during the transition phase, showes a decrease (see Figure 6.21). Let us remember that there is no research activity.

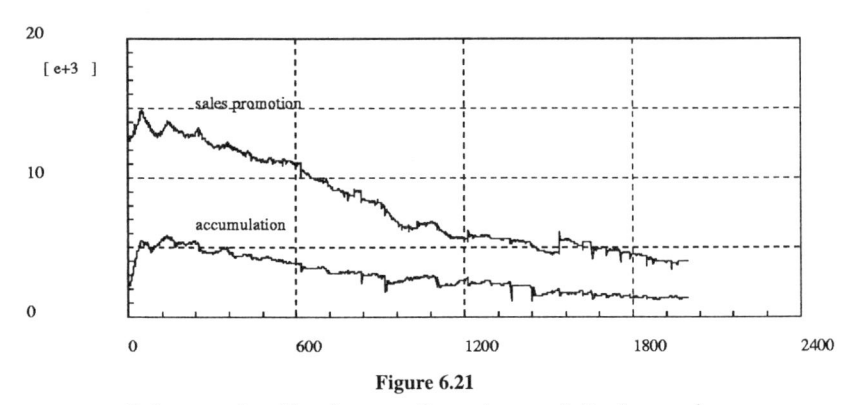

Figure 6.21
Labour employed in sales promotion and accumulation in recession

A similar dynamic appears in the stagnation scenario (dynamic of labour employed in research being similar to that of labour employed in sales activities, see Figure 6.22).

Selection, Innovation and Economic Development 203

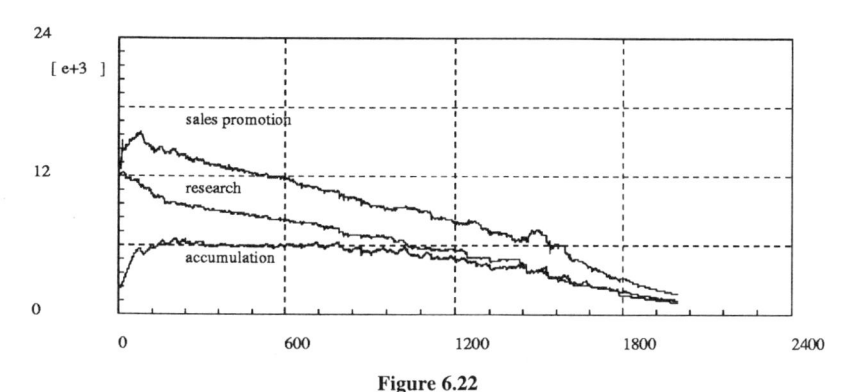

Figure 6.22
Labour employed in R&D and accumulation in stagnation

In all other scenarios, after transition and a phase of moderate growth, labour employed in development activities increases rapidly (especially in the global innovation scenario). In the intermediate innovation case, fluctuations are relevant (see Figures 6.23–6.25).

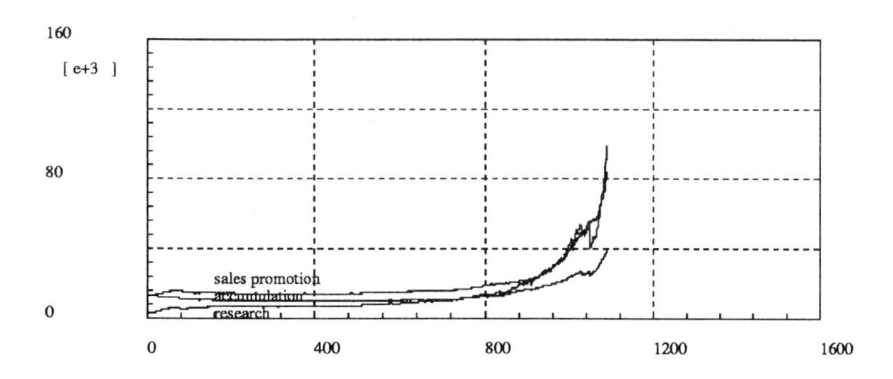

Figure 6.23
Labour employed in sales promotion, research and accumulation in growth scenario (global innovations)

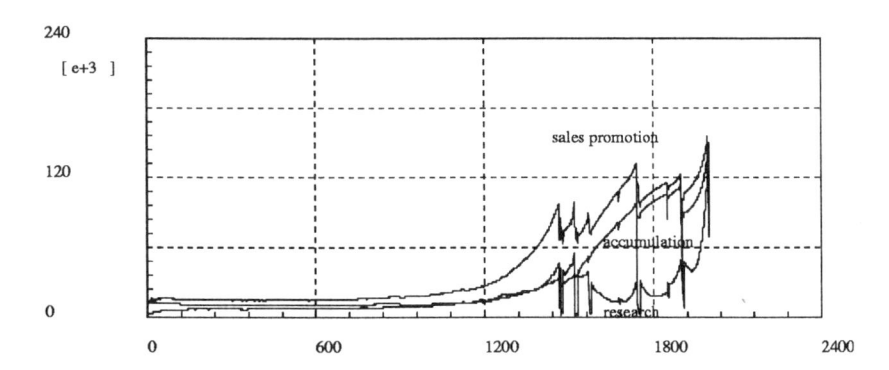

Figure 6.24

Labour employed in sales promotion, research and accumulation in growth scenario (intermediate innovations: a)

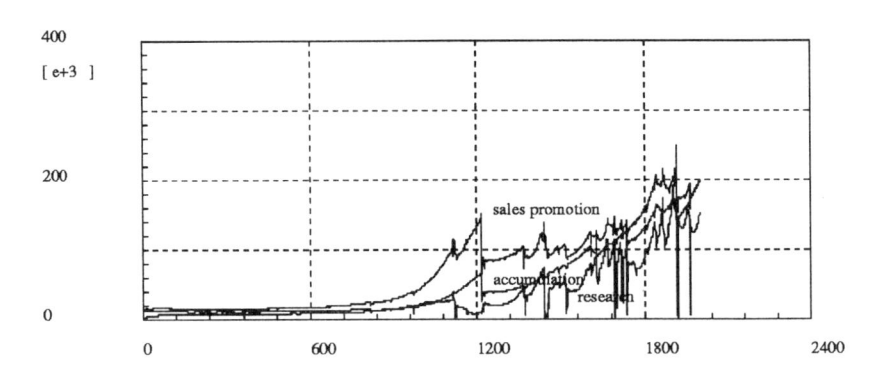

Figure 6.25

Labour employed in sales promotion, research and accumulation in growth scenario (intermediate innovations: b)

23. PRODUCTIVITY DYNAMICS

Labour Coefficients in Final Production

Let us now considered the labour coefficient in final production, as being an average of the values it has for the various firms. After transition it decreases, except in the intermediate innovation scenarios where it tends to stabilize thorough fluctuations. The decrease accelerates in the growth scenario (global innovations) shown in Figure 6.26. We shall represent the dynamic of the labour input coefficient in the recession scenario in Figure 6.27 (the dynamic in the mere selection process with a high propensity to grow and in the stagnation process are similar). In the growth scenario (intermediate innovation), the labour-input coefficient tends to stabilize through fluctuations, as is shown in Figure 6.28 for case *a* (the dynamic for case *b* is similar).

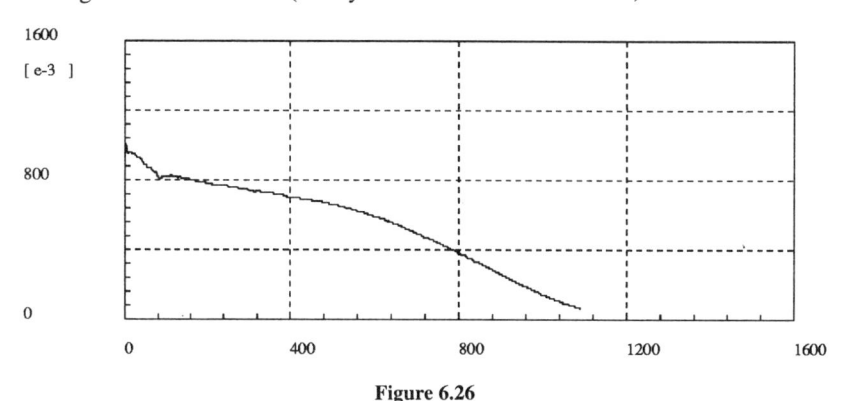

Figure 6.26
Labour input coefficient in final production in growth scenario (global innovation)

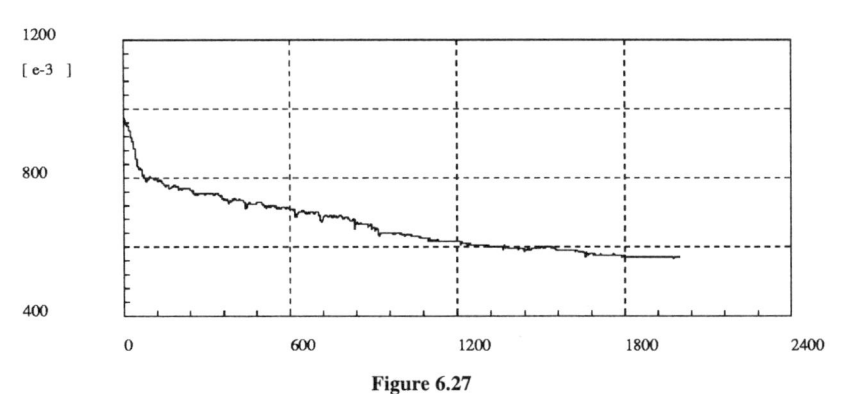

Figure 6.27
Labour input coefficient in final production in recession scenario

206 *Growth and Economic Development*

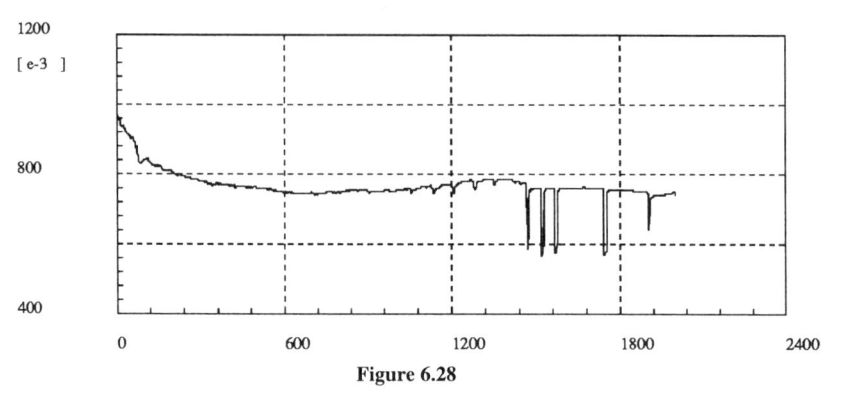

Figure 6.28
Labour input coefficient in final production in growth scenario (intermediate innovation)

Capital Coefficients

A greater variety is detected in the dynamic of the capital coefficient (this being, like the labour input coefficient, an average). In growth scenario (global innovation), after the phase of moderate reduction it declines rapidly (Figure 6.29). In recession, it shows a big fluctuation (Figure 6.30). In stagnation, after a phase of decline, it tends to stabilize (Figure 6.31). The same occurs in the growth scenario (intermediate innovations). The tendency to stabilization occurs through large fluctuations. The decline is very rapid in case *b*, as shown in Figure 6.32.

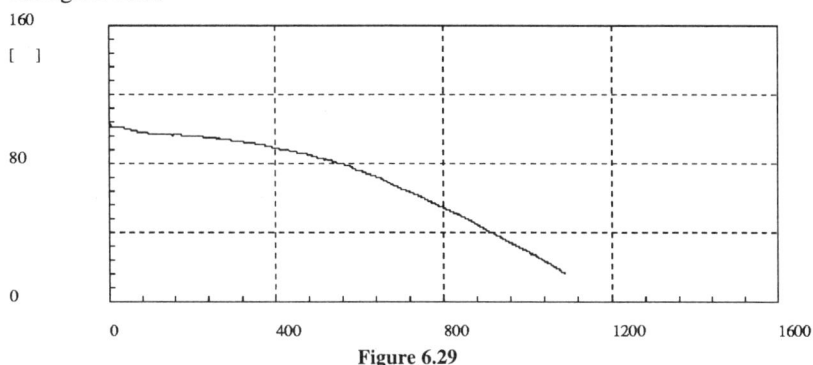

Figure 6.29
Capital coefficient in growth scenario (global innovation)

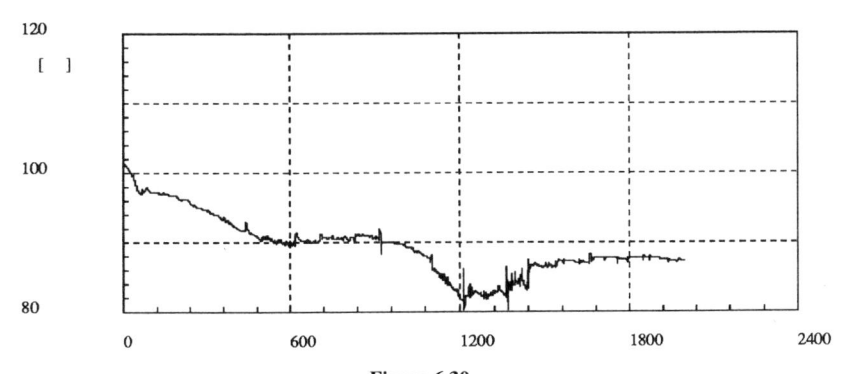

Selection, Innovation and Economic Development 207

Figure 6.30
Capital coefficient in recession scenario

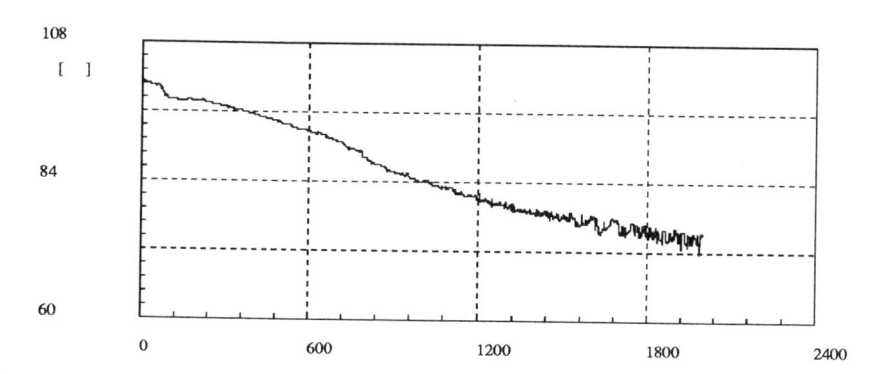

Figure 6.31
Capital coefficient in stagnation scenario

Figure 6.32

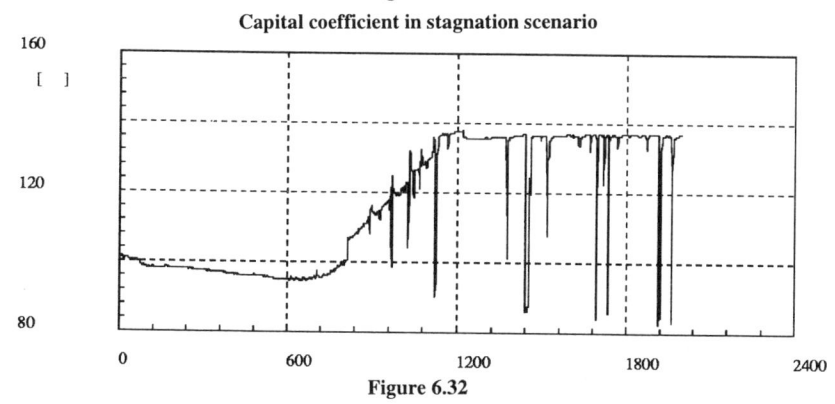

Capital coefficient in final production in growth scenario (intermediate innovation: b)

208   *Growth and Economic Development*

Labour Coefficients in Production of Capital Goods

The labour coefficient in the production of capital goods declines in all scenarios, except in that of intermediate innovations (case *b*) represented in Figure 6.35: after a sharp increase, it tends to stabilize through fluctuations. In recession scenario it tends to stabilize through fluctuations (Figure 6.33). In growth produced by entrepreneurs' aggressiveness it shows downward leaps (Figure 6.34).

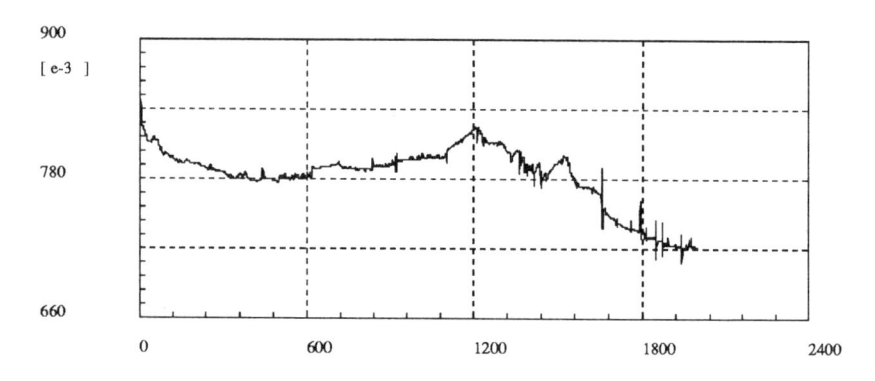

Figure 6.33

Labour coefficient in the production of capital goods in recession

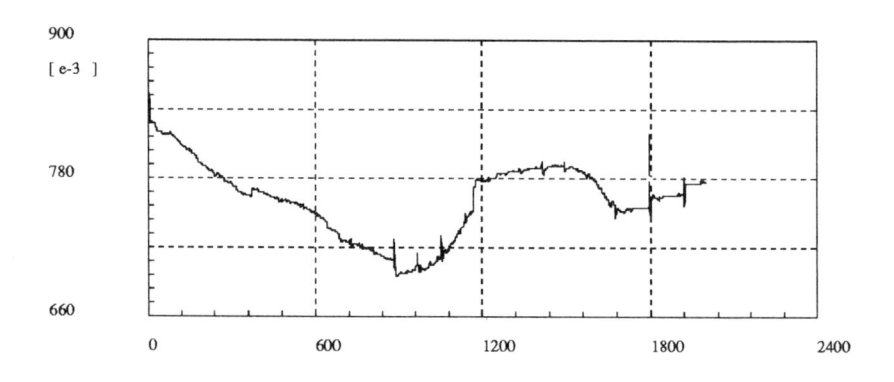

Figure 6.34

Labour coefficient in the production of capital goods in growth (produced by entrepreneurs animal spirits) scenario

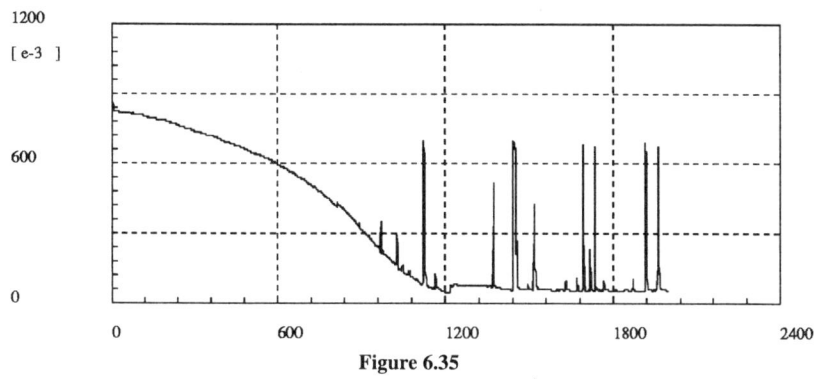

Figure 6.35
Labour coefficient in the production of capital goods in growth scenario (intermediate innovation: b)

24. RENTABILITY AND MARK-UP

In our analysis, let us now turn to the evolution of mark-up and of rentability as averages of the values of the two coefficients for the various firms. The mark-up dynamic reflects evolution of market power. By comparing the various scenarios we can see that only innovations increasing labour productivity cause a long run increase in mark-up. The two cases are represented in Figure 6.36 and Figure 6.37. In Figure 6.38 the evolution of mark-up in recession is depicted. The mark-up in the growth produced by entrepreneurs' high animal spirits is presented in Figure 6.39. The mark-up tends to stabilize through different kinds of fluctuations in the intermediate innovation cases which are presented in Figures 6.40–6.41. The result appears to support Marx's view of the link existing between 'labour exploitation' and surplus.

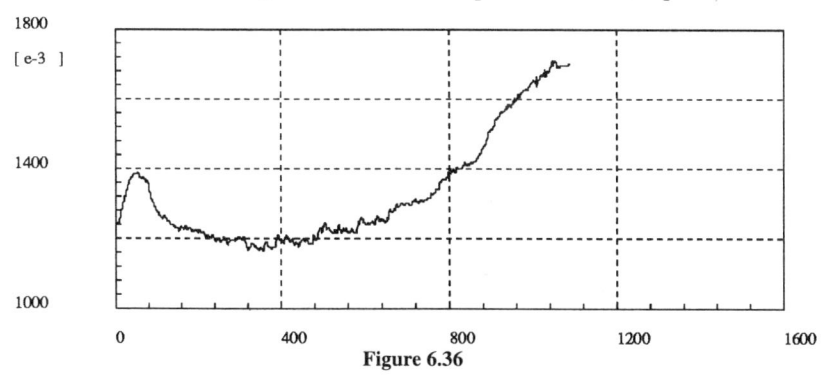

Figure 6.36
Average mark-up in growth scenario (global innovation)

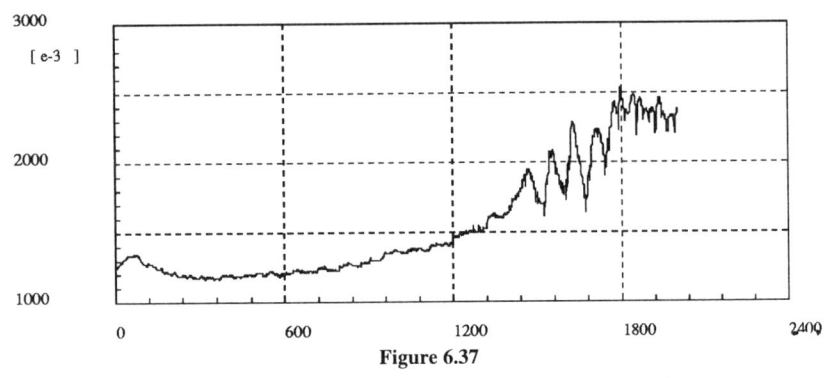

Figure 6.37
Average mark-up in growth scenario (final innovation)

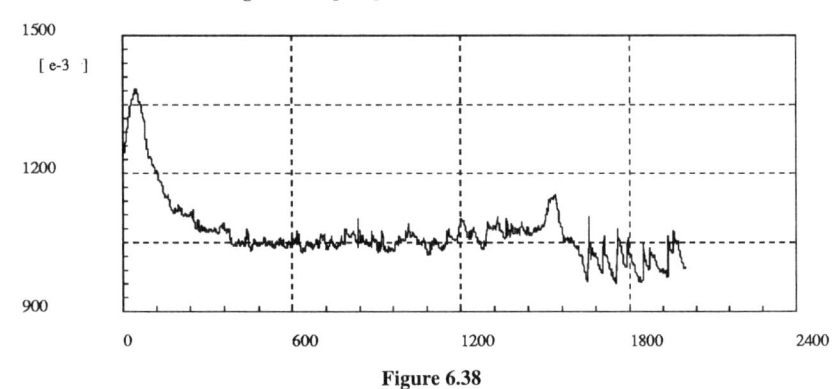

Figure 6.38
Average mark-up in recession scenario

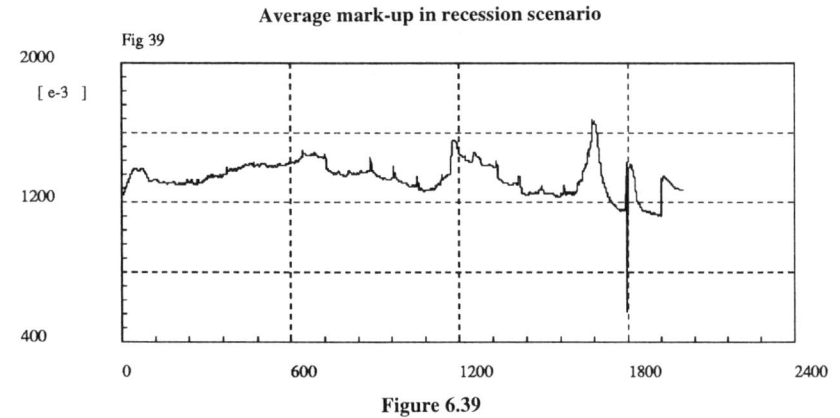

Figure 6.39
Average mark-up in growth (entrepreneurs' animal spirits) scenario

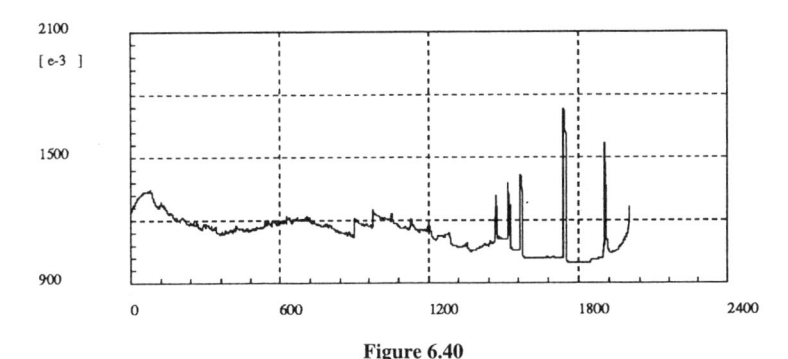

Selection, Innovation and Economic Development 211

Figure 6.40
Average mark-up in growth scenario (intermediate innovation: a)

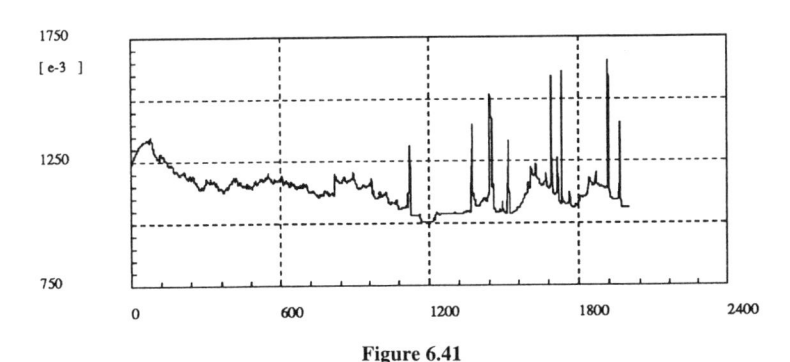

Figure 6.41
Average mark-up in growth scenario (intermediate innovation: b)

Average rentability tends to increase in the long run only in the growth intermediate innovation case *a* scenario (Figure 6.43). In all other scenarios it tends to stabilize. In Figure 6.42 the dynamic of rentability in the growth scenario (global innovation) is shown.

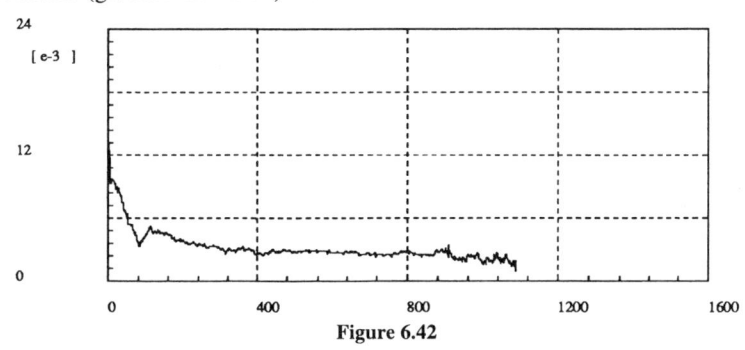

Figure 6.42
Average rentability in the growth scenario (global innovation)

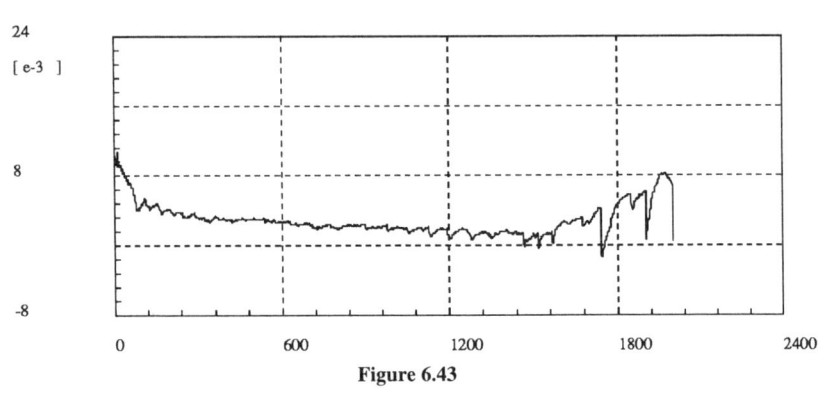

Figure 6.43
Average rentability in the growth scenario (intermediate innovation: a)

25. FINANCIAL RELATIONS AND THE VALUE OF THE FIRM

We have assumed that consumers' wealth (in financial assets) is represented by the firms' liabilities to banks. The dynamic of consumers' wealth, specular to that of firms' debts, is twofold: consumers' wealth will either increase *or* decrease over time. The first occurrence is recorded when growth is induced by entrepreneurs' aggressiveness (Figure 6.44) or by intermediate innovations (as shown in Figure 6.45 for case *a*). In both cases, the firm's value increases over time since growth is produced by entrepreneurs' accumulation activity either because of their propensity to grow or as a result of their innovations increasing the productivity of capital or that of labour employed in the production of capital goods.

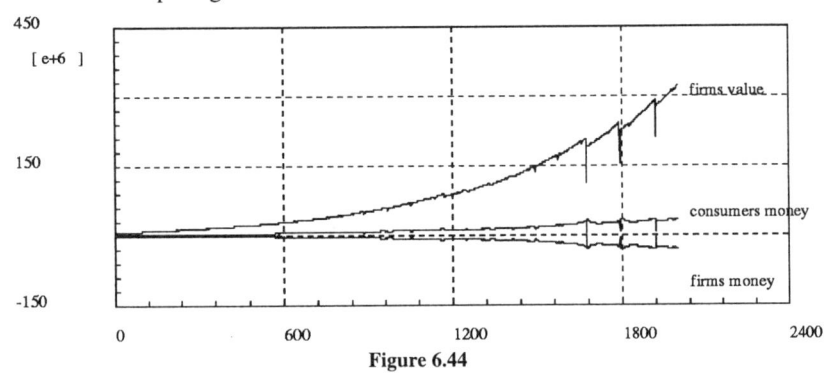

Figure 6.44
Money and firm's value in the growth scenario (entrepreneurs' aggressiveness)

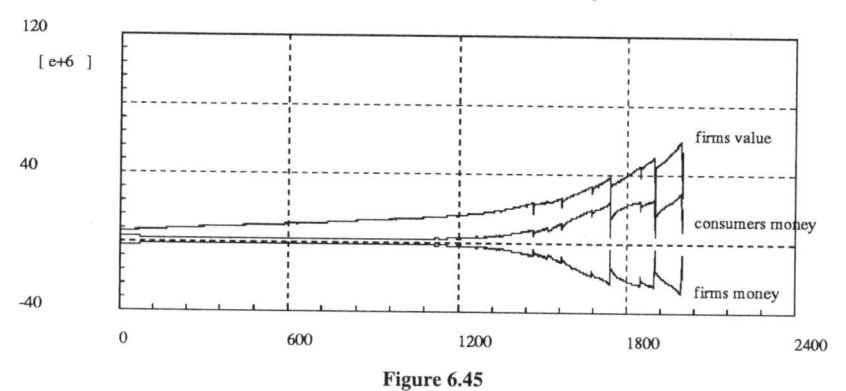

Selection, Innovation and Economic Development   213

Figure 6.45
Money and firm's value in the growth scenario (intermediate innovation: a)

In all other scenarios, consumers' wealth decreases over time. In recession and in stagnation, the value of firms will decrease in the long run.

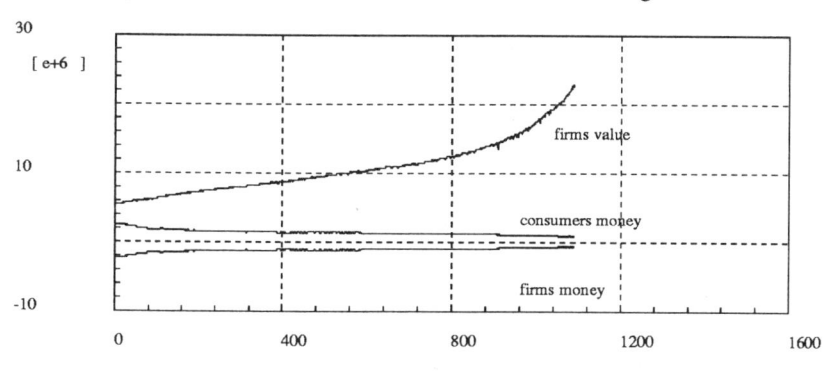

Figure 6.46
Money and firm's value in the growth scenario (global innovation)

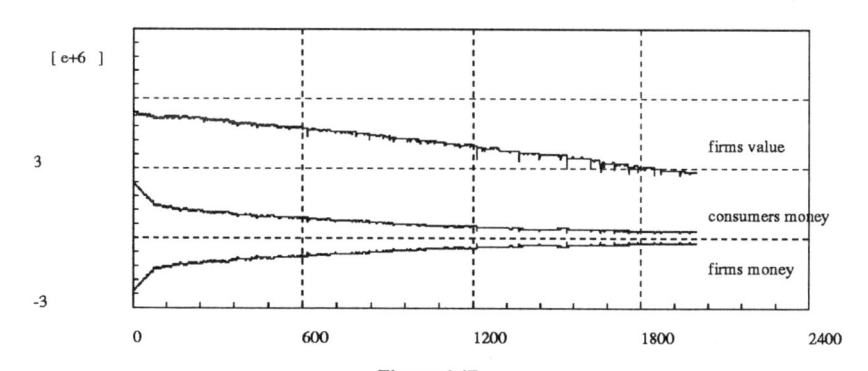

Figure 6.47
Money and firm's value in the recession scenario

214 Growth and Economic Development

26. THE PROPENSITY TO GROW

In mere selection, the propensity to grow (being the average of the propensities to grow of the various entrepreneurs) tends to decrease, even in the case of aggressive entrepreneurs (Figure 6.48). Innovation is associated with an increasing propensity to grow (in Figure 6.49 the evolution of propensity to grow in stagnation case is represented); in intermediate innovations it tends to stabilize through fluctuations (in Figure 6.50, the evolution for case *b* is represented).

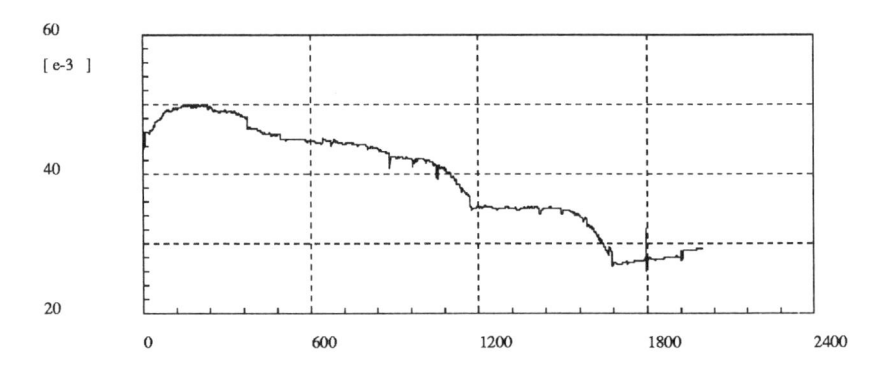

Figure 6.48
Propensity to grow in growth scenario (aggressive entrepreneurs)

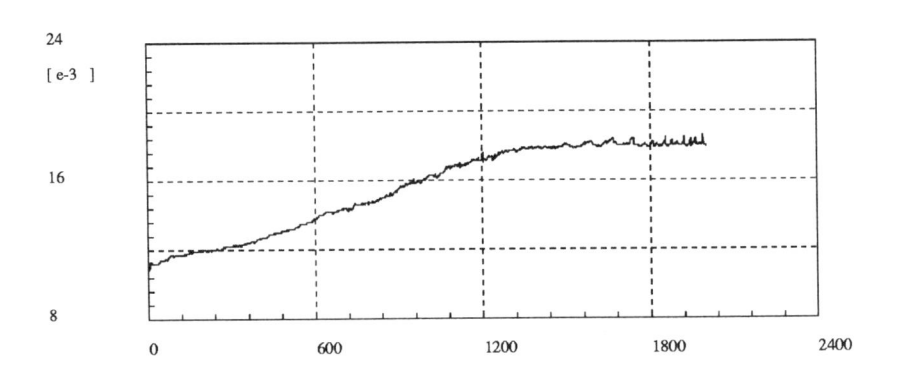

Figure 6.49
Propensity to grow in stagnation scenario

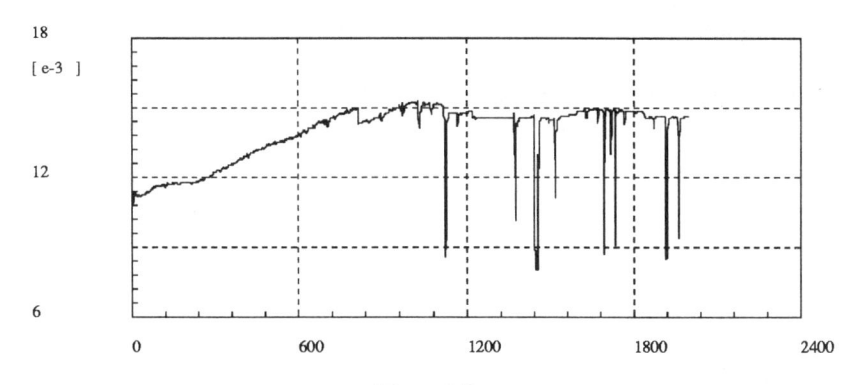

Figure 6.50
Propensity to grow in intermediate innovations (case b)

27. MONETARY POLICY

We have ignored monetary policy, which may contribute to further growth or, in certain conditions, curb it. When considering an open economy, the checking role of monetary policy needs to be analysed. In our model, fluctuations are induced both by stock adjustments and by certain discontinuities in failures of firms. Should we have considered the two possible roles of monetary policy, business fluctuations would have become more important. The Wicksellian theory could have been revisited.

Monetary policy may also have a relevant effect on selection. It can spur the 'natural' process, as well as restrain it. Many firms (especially the larger ones) can survive thanks to the financial support that the 'spontaneous' working of the credit system may provide. The same system may allow potential entrepreneurs to enter the arena of Schumpeterian competition.

In fact, social selection processes differ from the natural ones because they are affected by institutions and socio-political reactions.

28. BRAKES TO GROWTH

In our model, if the economy is brought to a growth path, growth will accelerate for two reasons: the increase in per capita income and the growth of population. This however, is due to the fact that, in order to isolate the effects of innovations and selection, we have chosen to disregard the existence of the braking mechanisms which play a remarkable role. There are three braking mechanisms that should be noted.

1. *scarcity of labour*. In order to isolate the effects of innovations and selection on growth, we have assumed that the labour market does not impose any constraint to growth. Should we have assumed equilibrium in the labour market, demand for labour being always equal to supply as determined by the rate of growth of population λ, the equilibrium path would have been determined essentially by λ and by a coefficient expressing the effect of technical progress in *golden age*. The endogenous growth models differ in explaining how this coefficient results from the optimizing behaviour of agents (thus reflecting also the coefficients characterizing the utility function: discount rates, intertemporal elasticity of substitution). In the historical evolution of an economy, population is a relevant factor. Immigration and emigration cannot always occur at the rate required to satisfy the labour demand induced by internal factors for growth. Thus, the evolution of population may induce changes in wage rates and may affect the innovation strategies of the firm. The global effect may be a curb on growth.
2. *scarcity of natural resources*. The Ricardian theory of rent is well known. Schumpeterian theory may in some respect be regarded as specular to the Ricardian one. The latter analyzes the brakes to growth represented by scarcity of lands which are considered of different quality; the former the accelerator represented by the increase in productivity produced by innovations. The way that the brake represented by the scarcity of natural resources operates depends on institutions and market reactions (as the oil crisis has made clear to everybody). As Ricardo himself has pointed out, the effect of the scarcity of land can be overcome by technical progress. Should limited availability of land resources be taken into account, deceleration may eventually occur, or the economy may settle down on a steady growth path.
3. *ecological constraints*. Among the natural resources, the most important have become *energy* and *environment*. The two are connected. The use of energy spoils and depletes the environment (pollution). The environment can also be impaired as a result of waste mismanagement. This problem is the more serious, given present standards of consumption, the higher is the increase in population (that may thus represent a brake also via *ecological effects*). People do not seem to be sufficiently aware of ecological constraints. In order to make then more effectively perceived, institutional changes and proper fiscal policies are required. In the neoclassical context the effect of these changes and interventions is essentially represented by the different choices the agents are induced to make among the alternatives available (as are essentially represented by utility and production functions). The Schumpeterian lesson should help in visualizing other effects: changes can be induced in consumers' preferences and in technologies (production functions). That may be brought about in various ways (by

orienting education and other social services,[21] by promoting changes in orientation of technological research); even prohibitions concerning the use of certain commodities in consumption and in production activities if announced a certain time in advance of their implementation, may be of help in re-orienting firms' development strategies.

29. CONCLUSIONS

By means of our model, with the method of computational economics, we have been able to analyse the interaction between selection and innovation. Let us summarize the main results of our analysis.

1. Selection is sufficient to produce growth, provided accumulation, at a rate higher than that at which per capita income increases, is assured by a sufficiently high entrepreneurs' propensity to grow. More generally, we can say that selective competition cannot induce growth in the absence of an adequate cultural system. Then workers achieve a per capita production lower than in recession or stagnation; their number increases whereas, in opposite conditions, it eventually decreases. Such a fact is associated with another one, which is beneficial to workers: they will control a larger amount of wealth represented by the value of new capitals. We can therefore say that entrepreneurs, by their aggressiveness, impose a higher rate of savings on the economy.
2. When innovation occurs (and for that, the condition just mentioned must be met), growth is assured. A process of adjustment of the economy is required.
3. In the growth path a relationship is established between consumption coefficients and technical coefficients. However, such a relationship is not the one that is required for the growth path to be an equilibrium path - as it is assumed in Pasinetti[22] - but rather the one resulting from: a) the strategies of the firm which aim both at enlarging their market shares, and at adjusting their mark-ups and prices in order to regulate the stocks' dynamic (that implies a tendency to equilibrium in commodities markets) and b) the birth and death of firms. Equilibrium is a partial equilibrium akin to Marshall biological concept (equilibrium entailing a certain balance between births and deaths).[23]
4. The mark-up which reflects the market power, depending initially upon entrepreneurs' personalities, is largely affected by innovation activities. Mark-up tends to increase only when labour productivity in final production increases because of innovation. Such a result seems to reconcile Schumpeter with Marx.

5. In the long run the main factor for growth appears to be accumulation. The model has thus a classical flavour.

30. VARIABLES AND PARAMETERS OF THE MODEL

Simulations have been carried on by assuming 100 firms. Initial values of the firms' coefficients are written in square brackets: when they are randomly distributed, the smallest and the largest values of the rectangular distribution are indicated. For some parameters or magnitudes initial values differ in the different scenarios: 1a: mere selection with low propensity to grow; 1b: mere selection with high propensity to grow; 2: final innovations; 3a) intermediate innovations affecting labour productivity in production of capital goods; 3b) intermediate innovations affecting capital coefficient; 4) global innovation.

I Entrepreneur's coefficients _ Adjustment coefficient

$\mu_{i,\tau,t}$, mark-up; [1,1-1,3]

$\zeta_{\mu,1,i}, \zeta_{\mu,2,i}, \zeta_{\mu,3,i}$, the mark-up adjustment coefficient; $\zeta_{\mu,1,i}$ [-0.005]; $\zeta_{\mu,2,i}$ [0,005]; $\zeta_{\mu,3,i}$ [-0,01]

$\xi_{a,i}$, entrepreneur propensity to grow; *1a* scenario: [0-0,08]; *other* scenarios [0-0,02]

β_i, effect of financial conditions on accumulation index; [=2]

$\zeta_{r,1,i}, \zeta_{r,2,i}$, research coefficients; [0-02]

$\phi_{h,i}$ ($h = 1,...,6$), research adjustment coefficients; $\phi_{h,i}$ ($h = 1,2$) [0,975]; $\phi_{h,i}$ ($h = 3,...,6$) [1,01]

$\zeta_{s,1,i}, \zeta_{s,2,i}$, sales promotion coefficients; $\zeta_{s,1,i}$ [0-0,4]; $\zeta_{s,2,i}$ [0-02]

$\chi_{h,i}, \chi_{h,i}$ ($h = 1,...,4$), sales promotion adjustment coefficients; $\chi_{h,i}, \chi_{h,i}$ ($h = 1,2$) [0,975]; $\chi_{h,i}, \chi_{h,i}$ ($h = 3,4$) [1,025]

II Price, wages and rate of interest

$p^n_{i,\tau,t}$, normal price

$p_{i,\tau,t}$, current price

w_t, current wages; $w = 1$ (numeraire)

i_t, rate of interest; $i = 0,015$

III Production, costs, demand and stocks

$\zeta_{c,i}$, quota of sales promotion expenditure representing current costs; [=1]

$O_{i,\tau,t}$, financial costs,

$q^p_{i,\tau,t}$, firm's potential production,

$q^m_{i,\tau,t}$, firm's maximum supply,

$q_{i,\tau,t}$, firm's planned production,

$q^d_{i,\tau,t}$, consumers' demand for the firm's final product,

$q^b_{i,\tau,t}$, quantity effectively bought,

$s_{i,\tau,t}$, firm's stocks,

$s^n_{i,\tau,t}$, normal firm's stocks,

$\overline{s}_{i,\tau,t}$, maximum level of firm's stocks,

IV Price adjustment and demand function

$\eta_{i\tau}$, disequilibrium index

ξ_1, ξ_2, imbalance coefficients; ξ_1 [0.05-0,15]; ξ_2 [0,15-0,45]

ξ_3, price adjustment coefficient; [=0,4]

$\zeta_{i,ta,t}$, price adjustment index

T_o, time coefficient of normal stocks; [=1]

T, time coefficient of maximum level of stocks; [=5]

$\zeta_{d,i}$ wealth-on-demand-effect scalar coefficient; [=0,33]

γ_i wealth-on-demand-effect exponential coefficient; [=2]

$\eta^o_{i\tau}$, disequilibrium adjustment coefficient; [=1]

V Capital and financial assets, firm's value

$K_{i,\tau,t}$ firm's capital; initial capital $K^o_{i,\tau,t}$ [500-1500]

$\omega_{i,\tau,t}$ firm's health index

$\overline{\omega}_{i,\tau,t}$ normal value of firm's health index; [=0,4]

$g_{i,\tau,t}$ firm's gearing ratio

$V_{i,\tau,t}$, the firm's value; [25.000-75.000]

$V^f_{i,\tau,t}$, the value of the firm's fixed capital

$r_{i,\tau,t}$, the firm's rentability

VI Production

$\varepsilon_{i,t}$, capacity utilization coefficient; [=2]
$l^p_{i,\tau,t}$, labour employed in production of final product

VII Accumulation, research and sales promotion

$l^k_{i,\tau,t}$, labour employed in accumulation
$l^I_{i,\tau,t}$, labour employed in research activity
$l^c_{i,\tau,t}$, labour employed in sales promotion activity
$l_{i,\tau,t}$, total labour employed by the firm,
l_t, total labour employed by the economy

VIII Financial assets

M^c_t, consumers money (bank deposits); M^c_o equal to absolute value of initial firms' debts
$M^i_{i,\tau,t}$, firm's financial flow (change in its debt towards bank)
M^i_t, firm's money (indebtedness)
m^f_t, debt cancellation for firms that fail [=0,5]

IX Technological and commercial coefficients

$\lambda^p_{i,\tau,t}$, labour coefficient in the production of final product, $\lambda^p_{i,\tau,o}$ [0,5-1.5]
$\kappa_{i,\tau,t}$, capital coefficient in the production of final product; $\kappa_{i,\tau,o}$ [0,5-1,5]
$\lambda^k_{i,\tau,t}$, labour coefficient in the production of capital good; $\lambda^k_{i,\tau,o}$ [50-150]
$a_{i,\tau,t}$, competition coefficient,
$\alpha^{1p}_i, \alpha^{2p}_i$, effect of research on labour coefficients for final production; α^{1p}_i 2 and 4 scenarios [-0.01], *other* [0]
$\alpha^{1s}_i, \alpha^{2s}_i$, effects of research on labour coefficients for production of capital good; α^{1s}_i *3a* and *4* scenarios [-0,001], *other* [0]

$\alpha_i^{1k}, \alpha_i^{2k}$, effects of research on capital coefficients; $\alpha_i^{1k}, \alpha_i^{2k}$ *3b* and *4* scenarios –[0,005–0,015], *other* [0]

α_i^a, effect-of-sales-promotion-on-inputs coefficient [1]

NOTES

1. Smith, too, has analysed the interaction between accumulation and innovation, resulting from division of labour. Contrary to Schumpeter, he assumes that savings is a prerequisite, innovation being induced by accumulation. According to Schumpeter, accumulation is the result of innovation increasing the productivity of labour.
2. According to Bessel the values of a stochastic variable can be assimilated to errors being the result of a several causes, each producing an imperceptible perturbation. The most likely error, being the sum of such a large number of perturbations, is zero; the larger the error the lower its probability.
3. It is with reference to such a possibility that Schumpeter's thought diverges from Knight's. In Knight's individuals can improve their capability of understanding and thus forecasting the external world (environment) including also technology. In Schumpeter's entrepreneurs tend to adapt environment in order to make their activity more successful.
4. By saying so, we do not mean to oppose Laplace's mechanistic view of a purely stochastic concept of changes. Essentially, for two reasons: a) even systems interpreted by mechanistic models can entail unpredictable changes (as the chaos theory has proved); b) all models are always partial models (either in the sense that they interpret pieces of the world or inasmuch they entail pre-analytical concepts of the system).
5. As Sober (1993, p. 69) notes: 'Who survives? Those who are the fittest. And who are the fittest? Those who survive.'
6. As Boulding (1992, p. 249) states
    'In the human race ... both learning and evaluation are dominant, though within still certain limits set by biogenetic structure of the genes ... there is no doubt that any biogenetically produced nervous system has a potential for learning, which may or may not be realized, depending on the life experience of organisms, and in human beings there is no doubt that this potential is enormous'.
7. We shall say that a new firm has been born both when a firm which is new as an institution has been established and when an old firm has been completely re-organized.
8. Boulding has noticed 'As we move into biological and social systems, information and its derivatives, such as the know-how that the fertilized egg has and the know-what that humans have, become increasingly important and parametric change occurs all the time. A genetic mutation, for instance, is a parametric change in ecosystem, and social mutations – new ideas, new organizations, new fashions, new patterns of behaviour – are dominant in social systems, except perhaps in the most primitive of human society, which may reach some kind of mutational equilibrium, though even this is very dubious' (1992 p. 305).
9. Similar remarks can be made on Prigogine's dissipative structures versus optimal structures. Town development, being more akin to dissipative structures, is usually different from the town organization that can be obtained by urban planning.
10. However, some entrepreneurs, having being successful in creating a firm, project new ones that, as the first, are then transferred to other agents. When such a process occurs, the analogy between natural selection and selection in economics become closer.

11. Such a possibility has been considered in the models of endogenous growth analysed in Chapters 3 and 4.
12. 'The life of man in society, just as the life of other species, is a struggle for existence, and therefore it is a process of selective adaptation. The evolution of social structure has been a process of natural selection of institutions. The progress which has been and is being made in human institutions and in human character may be set down, broadly, to a natural selection of the fittest habits of thought and to a process of enforced adaptation of individuals to an environment which has progressively changed with the growth of community and with the changing institutions under which men have lived. Institutions are not only themselves the result of a selective and adaptive process which shapes the prevailing or dominant types of spiritual attitude and aptitudes; they are at the same time special methods of life human relations, and are therefore in their turn efficient factors of selection. So that the changing institutions in their turn make for a further selection of individuals endowed with the fittest temperament, and a further adaptation of individual temperament and habits to the changing environment through the formation of new institutions' (Veblen, 1899, p. 188).
13. As L. Soete and R. Turner (1984, p. 612) note 'if the diffusion process is slow and the occurrence of new innovations is more or less continuous, then "equilibrium" will rarely occur'.
14. 'Like other animals, human beings engage in a cost-benefit analysis in the pursuit of their goals, including the economic ones. In so doing sometimes they are "rational" in Pareto's sense of "logical". Very often they are not. What appears to be certain is that they, too, are creatures of natural selection. Hence, in the last analysis the point is not whether they are "rational" or not; the point is that they have evolved to prefer benefits over costs - to act *as if* they were logical' (Lopreato, 1993, p. 83). The difference remains since for non human beings what are the benefits seen to be uniquely determined for the species, whereas benefits and costs are not uniquely perceived by human beings. Ecological costs, to make an instance, are in general not adequately perceived.
15. The exomatic evolution can interfere with biological evolution. Men will be able to produce, in a few decades, mutations equivalent to those that have been obtained naturally in million of years. The perspectives of such an exomatic evolution may be dramatic.
16. However the discovery obtained by what we have called the Darwinian approach can help us in formulating and in working out hypotheses in biology.
17. In large firms the entrepreneurial functions are carried on by the management. In some cases a person plays in the managerial structure the role of the Schumpeterian entrepreneur, in some others the staff of researchers contribute substantially to the orientation and implementation of research activity. The most favourable conditions occur when a Schumpeterian entrepreneur, that can be the President or the general manager, supports a cooperative staff of researchers well organized and is supported by them. Neil Kay (1988, pp. 287-90) has analysed the implications of Williamson organizational scheme comparing the U-form (unique firm) with the M-form (multi-divisional firm) on research activity.
18. The limitation re-emerges when the model is used to assess facts. Being a stochastic model, the probability that it has to be confirmed by facts may make empirical evidence scarcely relevant.
19. This is in line with Schumpeter's thought:
'Only a few people have these qualities of leadership and only a few in such a situation, that is a situation which is not itself already a boom, can succeed in this direction. However, if one or a few have advanced with success many of the difficulties disappear. Others can then follow these pioneers, as they will clearly do under the stimulus of

the success now available. Their success again makes it easier ... for more people to follow suit, until finally the innovation becomes familiar and the acceptance of it a matter of free choice' (Schumpeter 1934a, p. 228).
20. How that can happen can better be understood if we assume that banks play mainly an intermediary role in selling firms' bonds to consumers, the firms bonds being the monetary assets.
21. In Chapter 2, page , I have pointed out the dependence of individuals' utility function on social choices.
22. To maintain the economy moving along an equilibrium path is assumed to be a goal of economic policy. As we have remarked, in agreement with Schumpeter, the equilibrium path is not the optimal path (in assessing evolution the notion of optimality is rather ambiguous). Economic policy has a twofold objective: to foster growth and to stabilize the economy.
23. Solow has rightly stressed the need of 'a theory of deviations from the equilibrium growth path'. He notes that 'Growth theory was invented to provide a systematic way to talk about and to compare equilibrium paths for the economy. In that task it succeeded reasonably well. In doing so, however, it failed to come to grips adequately with an equally important and interesting problem: the right way to deal with deviations from equilibrium growth. One possibile solution strikes me as wrongheaded: that is to deny the existence of an analytical problem by claiming that "economic fluctuations" are not deviations from equilibrium growth at all, but examples of equilibrium growth.' (1988, p. 311). The analysis of deviations may rise the problem of the possible feedbacks of deviations on the long-run equilibrium path.

7. Concluding Remarks

1. GROWTH FACTORS AND DEVELOPMENT

The oldest factor accounting for economic growth is the expansion of population, provided there is enough accumulation and a proper structure of the economy. Then growth can be characterized by constant prices and constant rate of interest and by all commodities increasing at the same rate (the warranted rate of growth equal to the natural rate). Even in such a simple case the essentially static Walrasian-Paretian paradigm may be inadequate because of the intertemporal relations which may characterize technological processes, as has been shown by von Neumann's contribution.

Strictly associated with the population factor is the cultural factor. The pre-capitalistic economic expansion can hardly be qualified growth in the modern sense of the term. Surplus was produced also in pre-capitalistic economies; however, it has been utilized to build cathedrals and to increase luxuries of the ruling class. For growth to occur we had to wait for the historical emergence of the entrepreneur. Some of his features were anticipated by the merchant (greed for profits and power). His essential features on which potential surplus depends are propensities to accumulate and to innovate (in Smith's terms intensification of division of labour). Different are the cultural contexts that can breed entrepreneurs (think of England, the United States, Japan and Germany). Entrepreneur may be a single, autonomous individual, an organized team of individuals, an individual or a team operating in larger organizations (the larger being, in Japan in particular, the State).

Other factors may foster or curb growth. In Chapter 2 (section 19), we have mentioned the market power. Labour market flexibility is - at least to a certain extent - a prerequisite for growth. Various institutions can help economic growth. Economic policy may be growth oriented or may be the result of pressure groups aiming essentially at preserving their socio-political power. The horizon of the State action is decisive. To offset certain negative effects of the Darwinian process of development, a sufficiently large horizon is required to build adequate infrastructures, spur research and qualification along proper lines, adapt institutions to the needs of the society and the economy.

The relations between financial institutions and firms are of paramount importance.

In the models presented in this book, attention has been concentrated on the role of human capital accumulation and technological accumulation. Technological accumulation, as well as human capital accumulation, may be considered as the result of agents' optimizing choices. Then, starting from Solow's and Lucas' models we can build a model of endogenous growth that allows us to state the conditions for an equilibrium path of growth. The effects of human capital accumulation and technological accumulation can be assessed: that has been done in Chapter 4. Technological accumulation may be related to innovations by entrepreneurs. Product changes are involved. The effects of innovations cannot be foreseen to such an extent as to make optimal choices possible. However, rationality, of the procedural type rather than substantial, can materialize thorough adjustments (to changes in stocks for instance). Consumers are no longer autonomous agents maximizing their utility function independent of firms' choices. However, we can express their choices by means of demand functions. By the quasi-Schumpeterian models of Chapters 5 and 6 I have tried to explore - in co-operation with Donati - the working of an economy where Schumpeterian innovations occur engendering a social selection process.

2. THE BRAKES

We have analysed only the effect of factors accounting for growth. In the endogenous growth models, growth occurs along an equilibrium path. In the Schumpeterian models steady-growth paths are eventually attained along which accelerated growth occurs. Should we have considered a population increasing at a given rate, the limited quantity of labour available would eventually slacken growth, acting as a brake.

Other brakes ought to be considered. They have not been introduced for the sake of singling out the effects of the fundamental growth factors. We shall mention limited availability of natural resources and environment, possibly rigidities associated with consumers' tastes, some institutional constraints as those regulating working hours in many countries. For consumers to be able to take advantage of the new consumptions made possible by the informatic revolution, a reduction of the wage hours is required (the increased productivity being utilized more to increase leisure than to increase real wages).

The working of the growth engine and of brakes looks more complex if we consider the world economy, the economic system being an open economy. Lagging economies can eventually become a brake in the process of global development; different institutional set-ups in the various countries may jeopardize freedom of commerce in the world economy with negative effects on growth.

3. MECHANISM OF GROWTH AND CONSUMER'S AND STATE'S OPTIMIZATION

In most models of endogenous growth, evolution of the economy is the result of consumers' optimal choices (maximization of discounted aggregate utility). The inverse problem has also been stated and analysed: 'Given a descriptive growth equation and a behavioural (observable) consumption function, find a utility function and a discount rate so that the given consumption function is indeed a solution to the associated optimal growth model.' (Chang 1988, p. 147). Then, firms are subsidiary agents, whose decisions are assumed to produce such a spatial and time allocation of resources as to implement the optimal growth of consumption.

Assumption of everlasting consumers, all alike, is a very heroic assumption. Overlapping generation models do not get rid of such a theoretical cage: they may only help better understanding of the role of discount rate and of certain institutions. However, envisaging evolution as it can be obtained through a consumption optimal policy may be of some use since it allows us to compare different optimal paths arrived at starting from different concepts of utility function. That can be done in the direct formulation of the problem (as we have done in Chapter 4) as well as in the analysis of the inverse problem. A link can be established between behavioural models and models for rational choices (see the Chang's set of theoretical assumptions that make the Keynesian consumption function with a constant saving rate compatible with consumer optimization: 1988, pp. 162-3). In the model presented in Chapter 4 a special case of the endogenous growth process has some essential properties of the Sraffa system. In fact one advantage that exploration by means of different models can offer is to single properties out that are valid under a large set of structural assumptions and, possibly, independently from the method chosen among those of a predetermined set.

These theoretical insights may help critical reasoning when interactions between cultural and economic systems are debated. In its turn, critical reasoning may help understanding the limitation of the theoretical assumptions which have been made. Explanation of real processes is not a mechanical result of building and applying some specific model. Behind certain theoretical parameters (as, for instance, the consumers' discount rate) we can visualize properties of the socio-cultural system and of the personality of the consumers. Thus, the consequences of different sets of such qualitative features, which are deemed relevant to envisage possible evolutions of the economy, can be investigated. The tools of economic analyses can only be adequately utilized by people who have also those insights of the social system which are provided by other social sciences.

There is no socio-economic system where evolution is the result of the mere choices made by autonomous and independent consumers. No doubt that the final assessment of an economy has to be referred to individual needs. However individual needs depend both on other agents' decisions and on the State policy. Apart from the complications entailed by the concept of market power, the firms cannot be mere subsidiary agents, as is assumed substantially to be the case in models of endogenous growth, just because of the State policy affecting the context in which the firm has to frame its optimization policy.

The effect that firms' decisions have on consumers preferences cannot be ignored. I think that such effects cannot be analysed by any kind of optimization model. Even on a theoretical plan we cannot conceive of a model explaining the interactions between consumers maximizing their utility for a given set of commodities and firms trying to increase their profits through product innovation and sales promotion (not even by resorting to differential games). That does not mean that there is no cybernetic relation between firms' decisions and consumers' behaviour. One of the issues that I face in Chapters 4 and 5 (together with Donati) is just the visualization of some of these relations.

In all models analysed we have ignored the learning processes which are relevant also for consumption choices, as well as the interdependences between individual consumption. The effects of sales promotion activities depend, to a large extent, on these interdependences. It might be sufficient to convince some consumers of the utility of certain commodities to attain a relevant effect on sales because of imitation. Sales promotion may contribute to freeze consumers' tastes. It is for this reason that the effect of current sales promotion activities may depend on the same activity carried on in the past. For the sake of simplicity we have ignored these temporal interdependences. However, I think that the substantial effects of product innovation and sales promotion on economic evolution can be envisaged by stylized models as the ones presented in Chapters 5 and 6.

4. FIRMS' STRATEGIES AND OPTIMIZATION

The Schumpeterian approach makes it clear why we cannot attribute a mere role of subsidiary agent to the firm. In fact, the firms are primary agents as Smith has already recognized. The main role of entrepreneurs is to change the contexts in which choices are made. Most of the changes considered exogenous in the Walras-Pareto models look endogenous (produced from inside the economy) if the economic system is not considered a mere adaptive system, but a propulsive one. A step in this direction has been made by endogenous growth models, namely by considering human capital accumulation together with physical capital accumulation. A further step is the one I have suggested: to consider also technological accumulation. Then, it becomes difficult to single out the classical capital accumulation. As Scott (1989) has emphasized, even investments entail technical changes. The theoretical device of conceiving capital goods which remain constant in quantity but change in quality (and in efficiency) allows us to distinguish the three kind of accumulation and to analyse the relations among them. It is through technological accumulation depending substantially on firms' strategies that firms change the context in which choices are made.

Interdependences exist also among the technological strategies of the firms. The models presented could not account for them. Technological accumulation entails time interdependences. However, I think that the models of Chapters 4, 5 and 6 allow us to single out the main impact of technological accumulation on economic evolution.

More relevant perhaps with reference to the issues faced is the neglect of the role that the State can play in fostering technological progress. In part, such a role can be assumed to be linked with the decisions producing human capital accumulation having the external effect which has been considered. However, the State plays a role (particularly in Japan, but also in the USA) in fostering technological accumulation mostly in certain industries and of certain types.

The inadequate attention I play to the State's choices is perhaps justified by the objective of clarifying the role of the entrepreneur. Bringing the entrepreneur from the rear to the front of the scene implies changing the meaning and the role of profits. Profits are no longer subsidiary to consumption. That is the case in neoclassical models, in spite of the relation between profits and rate of growth, profits being required for accumulation, both as a necessary stimulus and as the required fuel to finance investments, in part, at least, through firms' internal savings. However, the final result of the whole process is increased consumption. This is the objective of all consumers, included shareholders and managers both striving for higher profits. For the Schumpeterian entrepreneurs, profit means, first of all, power. The money road is inadequate to measure power. Certain speculative activities may produce higher profits than the implementation of a strategy of innovation and development; however, the latter may allow the entrepreneurs to gain more power in society. It is mainly for this reason that, with reference to a Schumpeter entrepreneur, it is difficult to define a function to be maximized. That does not mean that the 'system' does not strive for profits. Even the entrepreneur seeking for power is a rational agent, ready to utilize signals (coming from the market or from inside the firm, as are changes in stocks) to improve his decisions. However, the drive of the economy is primarily assured by the growth propensities of the entrepreneurs. Economic development will certainly be favourably affected by the adjustments made by 'rational' entrepreneurs and by the exit of less efficient firms, as well as by the entry of new more efficient ones.

Therefore, when referring to entrepreneurs, it would be better to talk of *strategy* rather than *optimizing behaviour*. Strategy reflects both the propensity to grow and the capability of efficiently adjusting behaviour (a kind of Simon's procedural rationality).

5. THE ROLE OF THE FINANCIAL SYSTEM

The main shortcoming of the analysis of the Schumpeterian process of development is the inadequate attention to the role of the financial system. To single out the pure role of technological innovation, I deemed convenient to consider internal money only. In fact, two are the agents of the process of development in Schumpeterian analysis: the entrepreneur and the banker. The banker can foster innovations as well as suddenly impose brakes to economic development. The result are cyclical fluctuations of the economy. Expansions occur both because of the increased propensity of the banker to finance firms and of the fact that innovations comes in clusters. Depressions stimulate adjustment improving the efficiency of the economy. It is for this reason that Schumpeter was rather sceptical towards stabilization policies.

Money plays the role of financial assets. Finance is granted to firms by consumers through banks. That is the reason why the normal situation is that in which firms are indebted towards banks.

A proper assessment of the role of external money requires considering the State. Then the strategy of the State has to be considered. We want to emphasize the effect of public expenditure on growth: it depends not only on the level but also on the structure of expenditure, namely on the strategy of economic policy. An important link between firms' strategies and the State's one is established through expectations. If the expansion of public expenditure is perceived as merely due to welfare reasons, agents reactions may be unfavourable to growth; they may eventually lead to monetary policies curbing expansion. If public expenditure increases because of a development strategy adopted by the state, improving the perspectives for growth of some industries, the expansion of the economy can be fostered.

6. ENTRY AND EXIT OF FIRM. THE SELECTION PROCESS

In models of perfect competitions ‑ as are the endogenous growth models ‑ entry of firms is regulated by the market mechanism. The firms entering into the market, all alike to the old firms, are in such a number as to make prices equal to average costs. The entrepreneur's role is played, to a very limited extent, at the beginning, when he is assumed to make the choice of the most convenient combinations of inputs and outputs, among those technologically possible. Then he disappears. New firms are mere copies of the old ones. The best combination of factors of production is replicated. Expansion is obtained through the increase of firms: the relations between the quantities employed (and, therefore, prices) remain unchanged. Competition is merely a reflection of the market mechanism capable of assuring the best allocation of resources given consumers' preferences and technology. The quantity of each factor employed in each industry is such as to make the value of its productivity equal to its price.

Similar results have been generalized by the models of endogenous growth we have presented in Chapters 4 and 5. A step towards a more meaningful approach to the problem of births and deaths of firms has been carried on by Aghion and Hovitt (1992). Innovations affect growth also because of the death and birth of firms causing certain external effects. However, the stationary equilibrium context does not allow to elicit the positive effects of the selection process on long-run development. Similar consideration can be made with reference to Hoppenhayn's contribution (1992).

In the model presented in Chapter 6, births and deaths of firms is strictly related to a selection process engendered by firms' Schumpeterian strategies.

7. EFFICIENCY IN STATICS AND IN DYNAMICS

To a Pareto optimum we can associate a competitive market equilibrium, provided some properties of the system are granted. Pareto optimum is an ideal economy, whereas with the model of competitive equilibrium we want to describe a concrete market situation to which the current one is supposed to converge. The association of competitive equilibria to Pareto optima does not entail only certain synchronic properties of the economy; it raises also the problem of the mechanism by which competitive equilibrium is attained. The problem has been solved either by assuming some kind of *Deus ex machina* (the Walras auctioneer) or by dropping the assumption of perfect competition (Hahn). A completely different approach was Samuelson's: the optimal behaviour approach is abandoned and a dynamic model built on the assumption of adaptive expectations is associated to the static model. Equilibrium is the asymptote of the adjustment process.

When the system is not merely an adaptive system but a propulsive one, a specific problem arises: by what mechanisms are propensities and expectations made congruent with the other diachronic features of the economy? The answer is: there are no mechanisms of this kind.

The Schumpeterian growth mechanism, as has been interpreted in the models in Chapter 5 and 6, entails adjustment processes that will eventually produce a coherent diachronic structure of the economy. In the static approach it is sufficient that competitive equilibrium be possible descriptions of real situations to be able to assess their efficiency, by applying the Paretian criterion of optimality. When we turn to an evolving economy, assessment of efficiency becomes an intricate matter as it appears from the considerations of section 15 of Chapter 1.

8. DEVELOPMENT AND INCOME DISTRIBUTION. EFFICIENCY ASSESSMENT

Income distribution has always been considered a central issue of economic analysis. It is relevant since both the rate of growth and, eventually, the adjustment processes are not independent of the share of income accruing to workers, entrepreneurs, rentiers and landowners. Income distribution is a central topic also in welfare economics. Therefore, we need to justify our scarce attention to this facet of the economic system.

When we turn to the Schumpeterian approach income distribution becomes an intricate issue. First of all because the distribution is likely to change in the evolution of the economy, the changes being functional to the process of development. Secondly because it loses much of the appeal it has with reference to welfare-economics issues. The rod for measuring efficiency is the consumers' tastes. We want a system that makes it possible for each consumer to satisfy his tastes in best possible way, a similar possibility being offered to all other consumers. In the Schumpeterian process of evolution product changes entail changes in utility functions. In fact, with reference to the Schumpeterian process the main welfare-economics issues are:

1. how to eliminate the inefficiency represented by the persistent unemployment that could be a result of the Darwinian process of selection associated to innovation, without renouncing the advantages of the Schumpeterian evolution,
2. how to help cultural development sufficiently independent of the firms' sales promotion activities.

References

Aghion, P. and Howitt, P. (1992), 'A model of Growth through Creative Destruction', *Econometrica*, vol. 60, 323-51.
Aghion, P. and Howitt, P. (1994), 'Endogenous Technical Change: The Schumpeterian Perspective', in L.L. Pasinetti and R.M. Solow (eds), *Economic Growth and the Structure of Long-Term development*, London: Macmillan.
Antonelli, G.B. (1886), *Sulla teoria matematica dell'economia politica*, Pisa, reprinted in *Giornale degli Economisti*, May-June 1951.
Arrow, K.J. (1962), 'The Economic Implications of Learning by Doing', *Review of Economic Studies*, 29 (80), June, 155-73.
Arrow, K.J. (1971), 'The Firm in General Equilibrium Theory', in R. Marris and A. Wood (eds), *The Corporate Economy: Growth, Competition and Innovative Potential*, London: Macmillan.
Arrow, K.J. and Hahn, F.H. (1971), *General Competitive Analysis*, San Francisco: Holden Day Inc.
Arthur, W.B. (1989), 'The Economy and Complexity', in *Lectures in the Science of Complexity*, D. Stein, Addison-Wesley Longman.
Axelrod, R. (1984), *The Evolution of Theories and Models of Growth Cooperation*, New York: Basic Books.
Bachelard, G. (1983, 1st ed. 1940), *La philosophie du non*, Paris: Quadrige/Presses Universitaires de France.
Barkley Rosser, J. Jr. (1992), 'The Dialogue Between the Economic and the Ecologic Theories of Evolution', *Journal of Economic Behavior and Organization*, 17, 195-215.
Basalla, G. (1988), *The Evolution of Technology*, Cambridge: Cambridge University Press.
Baumol, W.J. (1952), *Welfare Economics and the Theory of the State*, London, New York, Toronto: Longmans, Green and Co.
Becattini, G. (1989), 'Small Firms and/or Districts: Some Remarks on the Conceptual Foundations of Industrial Economics', in E. Goodman and J. Bamford (eds), *Small Firms and Industrial Districts in Italy*, London: Routledge.
Benassy, J.P. (1976), 'Théorie du déséquilibre et fondaments microéconomiques de la macroéconomie', *Reviw of Economic Studies*, October
Bergson, A. (1938), 'A Reformulation of Certain Aspects of Welfare Economics', *Quarterly Journal of Economics*, n. 52
Bernheim, D. (1984), 'Rationalizable Strategic Behavior', *Econometrica*, 52, 1007-1028.
Binmore, K. (1987), 'Modeling Rational Players', Part 1, *Economics and Philosophy*, 3, 179-214.
Binmore, K. (1988), 'Modeling Rational Players', Part 2, *Economics and Philosophy*, 4, 9-35.
Binmore, K. and Dasgupta, P. (eds) (1987), *Economic Organization as Games*, Oxford: Basil Blackwell.
Boulding, K.E. (1992), *Evolutionary Economics*, London: Sage Publications.
Bridgman, P.W. (1927), *The Logic of Modern Physics*, New York: The Macmillan Company.

Buican, D. (1989), *La révolution de l'évolution*, Paris: Presses Universitaires de France.
Chang, F.R. (1988), 'The Inverse Optimal Problem: A Dynamic Programming Approach', *Econometrica*, 56, 147-72.
Chiaromonte, G. and Dosi, G. (1993), 'Heterogeneity, Competition, and Macroeconomic Dynamics', *Structural Change and Economic Dynamics*, vol. 4, n. 1.
Chipman, J.S. (1970), 'External Economies of Scale and Competitive Equilibrium', *Quarterly Journal of Economics*, August, 347-85.
Cozzi, T. (1966), *Movimenti in equilibrio nell'analisi macroeconomica*, Torino: Edizioni Giappichelli.
Cozzi, T. (1982), 'Marco Fanno e la teoria moderna del ciclo', *Rivista Internazionale di Scienze Economiche e Commerciali*, XXIX, n. 1-2, January-February.
Darwin, C. (1859), *On the Origin of Species*, Cambridge Mass.: Harvard University Press (1964).
Dasgupta, P. and Stiglitz, J. (1980), 'Industrial Structure and the Nature of Innovative Activity', *Economic Journal*, 90.
Day, R.H. (1975), 'Adaptive Processes and Economic Theory', in Day R.H. and Groves T. (eds), *Adaptive Economic Models*, New York: Academic Press.
Day, R.H. (1983), 'The Emergence of Chaos from Classical Economic Growth', *Quarterly Journal of Economics*, 98, 201-13.
Day, R.H. and Walter, J.L. (1989), 'Economic Growth in the Very Long Run. On the Multiple Interaction of Population, Technology and Social Infrastructure', in W. Barnett, J. Geweke and K. Shell (eds), *Economic Complexity: Chaos, Sunpots, Bubbles and non Linearity*, Cambridge: Cambridge University Press, 253-89.
Domar, E.V. (1957), *Essays on the Theory of Economic Growth*, Oxford: Oxford University Press.
Dosi, G. (1982), 'Technological Paradigms and Technological Trajectories', *Research Policy*, vol. 11, 147-62.
Dosi, G. (1984), *Technological Change and Industrial Transformation*, London: Macmillan.
Dosi, G. (1988), 'The Nature of Innovative Process', in G. Dosi, C. Freeman, R. Nelson, G. Silverberg, L. Soete (eds), *Technical Change and Economic Theory*, London-New York: Pinter Publishers.
Dosi, G. and Orsenigo, L. (1988), 'Coordination and Transformation: an Overview of Structures, Behaviours, and Changes in Evolutionary Environments', in G. Dosi, C. Freeman, R. Nelson, G. Silverberg and L. Soete (eds), *Technical Change and Economic Theory*, London-New York: Pinter Publishers.
Dosi, G., Freeman, C., Nelson, R., Silverberg, G., and Soete, L. (eds) (1988), *Technical change and economic theory*, London-New York: Pinter Publishers.
Duesenberry, J.S. (1949), *Income, Saving, and the Theory of Consumer Behavior*, Harvard: Harvard University Press.
Elster, J. (1989), *Nuts and Bolts for the Social Sciences*, Cambridge: Cambridge University Press.
Fisher, F.M. and Temin, P. (1979), 'The Schumpeterian Hypothesis: Reply', *Journal of Political Economy*, 87, 386-9.
Friedman, M. (1953), The 'Methodology of Positive Economics', in *Essays in Positive Economics*, Chicago: The Chicago University Press.
Freeman, C. (1982), *The Economics of Industrial Innovation*, 2nd edn, London: Frances Pinter (1st edn by Penguin, 1974).
Freeman, C. and Perez, C. (1988), 'Structural Crises of Adjustment', in G. Dosi, C. Freeman, R. Nelson, G. Silverberg and L. Soete, (eds), *Technical Change and Economic Theory*, London-New York: Pinter Publishers.
Frish, R. (1933), 'Monopole, polypole: la notion de force dans l'économie', *Nationalekonomist Tidsskrift*.
Futia, C. (1977), 'The Complexity of Economic Decision Rules', *Journal of Mathematical Economics*, vol. 4, 289-99.

Futia, C.A. (1980), 'Schumpeterian competition', *Quarterly Journal of Economics*, 94, 675-95.
Georgescu-Roegen, N. (1986), 'Man and Production', in *Foundations of Economics*, M. Baranzini and R. Scazzieri (eds), Oxford: Oxford Basil Blackwell.
Gibbard, A. and Harper, W. L. (1978), 'Counterfactuals and Two Kinds of Expected Utility', in C.A. Hooker, J.J. Leach and E.F. McClennen (eds), *Foundations and Applications of Decision Theory*, vol. 1, Boston: Reidel.
Godley, W. (1990), 'Tempo, rendimenti crescenti e istituzioni in macroeconomia', in *Istituzioni e mercato nello sviluppo economico*, Saggi in onore di Paolo Sylos Labini, Bari: Laterza.
Goodwin, R. (1990), *Chaotic Economic Dynamics*, Oxford: Clarendon Press.
Goodwin, R. and Pacini P.M. (1992), 'Nonlinear Economic Dynamics and Chaos', in A. Vercelli and N. Dimitri (eds), *Macro-Economics A Survey of Research and Strategies*, Oxford: Oxford University Press.
Gould, S.J. and Eldredge (1993), 'Punctuated equilibrium comes of ages', *Nature*, vol. 366, 18 Nov.
Graziani, A. (1989), 'The Theory of Monetary Circuit', *Thames Paper in Political Economy*, London.
Grossman, G.M. and Helpman, E. (1991), *Innovation and Growth in the Global Economy*, Cambridge Mass.: MIT Press.
Hahn, F. (1966), 'Equilibrium Dynamics with Heterogeneous Capital Goods', *Quarterly Journal of Economics*, vol. 80, 633-46.
Hahn, F. (1977), 'Exercises in Conjectural Equilibria', *Scandinavian Journal of Economics*, 79.
Hahn, F. and Matthews, R.G.O. (1965), 'The Theory of Economic Growth: A Survey', *Surveys of Economic Theory*, American Economic Association, Royal Economic Society, vol. II, Growth Development.
Harrod, R.F.(1948), *Towards a Dynamic Economics*, London: Macmillan.
Hayek, F.A. (1962), *The Pure Theory of Capital* (1 ed. 1941), London: Routledge & Kegan Paul Ltd.
Hayek, F.A. (1983), *Knowledge, Evolution and Society*, London: Adam Smith Institute.
Hayek, F.A. (1985), 'Order Without Orders', *Reason*, May.
Hicks, J.R. (1950), *A Contribution to the Theory of Trade Cycle*, Oxford: Clarendon.
Hicks, J. (1959), *A Contribution to the Theory of the Trade Cycle*, Oxford: Clarendon Press.
Hirshleifer, J. (1978), 'Competition, Cooperation and Conflict in Economics and Biology', *American Economic Review*, 68 (May).
Hodgson, G. (1993), *Economics and Evolution: Bringing Back Life into Economics*, New York: Oxford University Press.
Holland, J.H. (1975), *Adaptation in Natural and Artificial Systems*, Ann Arbor, Michigan: University of Michigan Press.
Hoppenhayn, H.U. (1992), 'Entry, Exit, and Firm Dynamics in Long Run Equilibrium', *Econometrica*, 40, 1127-50.
Iwai, K. (1984a), 'Schumpeterian Dynamics, Part I: An Evolutionary Model of Innovation and Imitation', *Journal of Economic Behaviour and Organization*, 5, 159-90.
Iwai, K. (1984b), 'Schumpeterian Dynamics, Part II: Technological Progress, Firm Growth and "Economic Selection"', *Journal of Economic Behaviour and Organization*, 5, 321-51.
Kaldor, N. and Mirrlees, J.A. (1962), 'A New Model of Economic Growth', *Review of Economic Studies*, 29.
Kay, N. (1988), 'The R. and D. Function: Corporate Strategy and Structure', in G. Dosi, C. Freeman, R. Nelson, G. Silverberg and L. Soete (eds), *Technical Change and Economic Theory*, London-New York: Pinter Publishers.

Khalil, E.L. (1992), 'Economics and Biology: Eight Areas of Research', *Methodus*, vol. 4, n. 2 (December).
Knight, F.H. (1921), *Risk, Uncertainty and Profit*, Chicago: University of Chicago Press.
Knight, F.H. (1925), 'On Decreasing Cost and Comparative Cost: A Rejoinder' *Quarterly Journal of Economics*, February, 331-33
Lamarck, J.B. (1809), *Zoological Philosophy*, Chicago: University of Chicago Press (1984).
Lombardini, S. (1953), *Il monopolio nella teoria economica*, Milano: Vita e Pensiero.
Lombardini, S. (1957), *L'analisi della domanda nella teoria economica*, Milano: Giuffrè.
Lombardini, S. (1971), *Concorrenza, monopolio e sviluppo*, Franco Angeli, Milano.
Lombardini, S. (1981), 'Economics Past and Future', in G. Szego (ed.), *New Quantitative Techniques for Economic Analysis*, New York: Academic Press, Inc.
Lombardini, S. (1992), 'A new approach to economic analysis: computational economics', in A. Vercelli and N. Dimitrov (eds), *Macroeconomics: a Survey of Research Strategies*, Oxford University Press, Oxford.
Lombardini, S. (1994), 'The Development of Monopolistic Firm', *Italian Economic Papers*, vol. II, Oxford: il Mulino, Oxford University Press.
Lombardini, S. and Nicola, P.C. (1974), 'Income Distribution and Economic Development in Ricardian and Walrasian Models', in *Proceeding of 11th Polish-Italian Conference on Applications of System Theory in Economic Management and Technology*, Pugnochiuso.
Lopreato, J. (1993), 'Theoretical Links between Economics and Evolutionary Biology', *Methodus*, vol. 5, n. 1 (June).
Lorenz, K. (1970), *Essay sur le comportement animal et humaine*, Paris: Ed. du Seuil.
Lotka, A.J. (1925), *Elements of Physical Biology*, Baltimore: Williams and Wilkins.
Loury, G.C. (1979), 'Market Structure and Innovation', *Quarterly Journal of Economics*, 93, 395-410.
Lucas, R.E. (1988), 'On the Mechanism of Economic Development', *Journal of Monetary Economics*, 22, 3-42.
Luce, R.D. and Raiffa, H. (1957), *Games and Decisions: Introduction and Critical Survey*, New York: John Wiley and Sons, Inc. Publ.
Malinvaud, E. (1953), 'Capital Accumulation and Efficient Allocation of Resources', *Econometrica*, 21, 233-68.
Malinvaud, E. (1975), *Une nouvelle formulation générale pour l'étude des fondements microéconomiques de la macroéconomie*, Paris: INSEE and CEPRE-MAP.
Malinvaud, E. (1977), *The Theory of Unemployment Reconsidered*, London: Basil Blackwell.
Malinvaud, E. (1980), *Profitability and Unemployment*, Cambridge: Cambridge University Press.
Malinvaud, E. (1982), 'Wages and Unemployment', *Economic Journal*, March.
Mansfield, E. (1968), *Industrial Research and Technological Innovation: An Econometric Analysis*, London, Longman.
Marschak, J. (1950), 'Rational Behavior, Uncertain Prospects and Measurable Utility', *Econometrica*, April.
Matthews, R.C.O. (1984), 'Darwinism and Economic Change', *Oxford Economic Papers, Supplement*, November.
Mayumi, K. (1993), 'The Exomatic Mode of Human Evolution, and a Clarification of Nicholas Georgescu-Rogen's Thought on Entropy, the Economic Process, Dialectics and Evolution', *Methodus*, vol. 5, n. 1 (June).
McKenzie, L.W. (1963), 'Turnpike Theory, Discounted Utility, and the von Neumann Facet', *Journal of Economic Theory*, 30 (2), August, 330-52.

Modigliani, F. and Brumberg, R. (1954), 'Utility Analysis and the Consumption Function: an Interpretation of Cross-Section Data', in K. Kurihara (ed.), *Post-Keynesian Economics*, New Brunswick, Rutgers: University Press.

Montesano, A. (1987), 'Utility and Uncertainty in Intertemporal Choice', in C. Carraro and D. Sartore (eds), *Developments of Control Theory for Economic Analysis*, Dordrecht: Kluwer.

Morishima, M. (1969), *Theory of Economic Growth*, Oxford: Clarendon Press.

Myrdal, G. (1957), *Economics Theory and Under-developed Regions*, London: Gerald Duckworth & Co.

Nasbeth, L. and Ray, G.F. (1974), *Diffusion of New Industrial Processes*, Cambridge: Cambridge University Press.

Nash, J.F. (1950),'Equilibrium Points in a n-Person Games, in *Proceeding pf the National Academy of Sciences*, 36

Negishi, T. (1960), 'Monopolistic Competition and General Equilibrium', *Review of Economic Studies*, 28, 196-201.

Nelson, R.R. (1982), *An Evolutionary Theory of Economic Change*, Cambridge Mass: The Belknap Press of Harvard University Press.

Nelson, R.R. (1988), 'Institutions Supporting Technical Changes in the United States,' in G. Dosi, C. Freeman, R. Nelson, G. Silverberg and L. Soete (eds), *Technical change and economic theory*, London-New York: Pinter Publishers.

Nelson, R.R. and Winter, S.G. (1974), 'Neoclassical vs. Evolutionary Theories of Economic Growth: Critique and Prospectus', *Economic Journal*, 84, 886-905.

Nelson, R.R., Winter, S.G. and Schuette, H.L. (1976), 'Technical Change in an Evolutionary Model', *Quarterly Journal of Economics*, vol. 90, 90-118.

Nelson, R.R. and Winter, S.G. (1982), *An Evolutionary Theory of Economic Change*, Cambridge Mass.: The Belknap Press of Harvard University Press.

Nicola, P.C. (1994), *Equilibrio generale imperfetto*, Bologna, il Mulino.

Nicolis, G. and Prigogine, I. (1977), *Self-Organization in Non-Equilibrium Systems*, New York: Wiley-Interscience.

Pareto, W. (1896), *Corso di Economia Politica*, 2 vol., Torino: Giulio Einaudi (1943).

Pareto, V. (1935), *The Mind and Society* (English translation by A. Livingston and A. Buongiorno of *Trattato di Sociologia Generale*) 4 vol., New York and London.

Pareto, V. (1964), *Trattato di Sociologia Generale*, 2 vol., Milano: Edizioni di Comunità.

Pasinetti, L. (1974), *Growth and Income Distribution - Essays in Economic Theory*, Cambridge, Cambrige University Press.

Pasinetti, L. (1993), *Structural Economic Dynamics*, Cambridge: Cambridge University Press.

Phelps, E.S. (1961), 'The Golden Rule of Accumulation: A Fable for Growthmen', *American Economic Review*, vol. 51, 638-643.

Phelps, E.S. (1987), 'Marchés speculatifs et anticipations rationelles', *Revue Francaise d'Économie*, vol. 2.

Phelps, E.S. (1992), 'Expectations in Macroeconomics and the Rational Expectatios Debate', in A. Vercelli and N. Dimitri (eds), *Macroeconomics - A Survey of Research Strategies*, Oxford: Oxford University Press.

Quirmbach, J. (1986), 'The Diffusion of New Technology and the Market for an Innovation', *Rand Journal of Economics*, 17 (1), 33-47.

Ramsey, F.P. (1928), 'A Mathematical theory of Savings', *The Economic Journal*, 38, 543-59.

Reichling, P. and Siconolfi, P. (1983), 'Aspettative razionali, mercato atomistico e principio del costo marginale', *Giornale degli Economisti e Annali di Economia*, Nov.-Dic.

Robinson, J. (1956), *The Accumulation of Capital*, London: Macmillan (1969).

Robinson, J. (1963), *Essays on the Theory of Economic Growth*, London: Macmillan.

Roger, J. (1985), *Note sul ruolo del «caso» nel sistema darwiniano*, in Various Authors, *L'anno di Darwin - Problemi di un centenario*, Parma: Pratiche Editrice.

Romer, P.M. (1986), 'Increasing Returns Endogenous and Long Run Growth', *Journal of Political Economy*, 94, 1002-37.

Romer, P.M. (1990), 'Endogenous Technological Change', *Journal of Political Economy*, 98, 71-102.

Samuelson, P.A. (1938), 'A Note on the Pure Theory of Consumers's Behavior' and 'An Addendum', *Economica*, February and August.

Samuelson, P.A. (1939), 'Interactions Between the Multiplier Analysis and the Principle of Acceleration', *The Review of Economic Studies*, XXI, n. 2, May, 75-8.

Samuelson, P.A. (1948), *Foundations of Economic Analysis*, Harvard: Harvard University Press.

Samuelson, P.A. (1958), 'An Exact Consumption-Loan Model of Interest with or without the Social Contrivance of Money', *Journal of Political Economy*, 66, 467-82.

Samuelson, P.A. (1967), 'Indeterminacy of Development in a Heterogeneous-Capital Model with Constant Saving Propensity', in K. Shell (ed.), *Essays on the Theory of Optimal Economic Growth*, The M.I.T. Press.

Schmookler, J. (1966), *Invention and Economic Growth*, Cambridge Mass.: Harvard University Press.

Schumpeter, J.A. (1934a), *The Theory of Economic Development*, Cambridge Mass.: Harvard University Press, (1964).

Schumpeter, J.A. (1934b), *Business Cycle, A Theoretical, Historical and Statistical Analysis of the Capitalist Process*, abridged with an introduction by Rendings Fels, New York: McGraw-Hill, (1964).

Schumpeter, J.A. (1942), *Capitalism, Socialism and Democracy*, New York, Harper.

Scott, M.FG. (1989), *A New View of Economic Growth*, Oxford: Clarendon Press.

Scott, M.FG. (1992), 'A New Theory of Endogenous Economic Growth', *Oxford Review of Economic Policy*, 8, No. 4.

Silverberg, G., Dosi, G. and Orsenigo, L. (1988), Innovation, Diversity and Diffusion: a Self-organisation Model', *Economic Journal*, vol. 98, forthcoming.

Silverberg, G. (1984), 'Embodied technical Progress in a Dynamic Economic Model: the Self-organization Paradigm', in R.M. Goodwin, M. Krüger and A. Vercelli (eds.), *Non Linear Models of Fluctuating Growth*, Berlin, Heidelberg, New York, Tokyo: Springer-Verlag.

Silverberg, G. (1987), 'Technical Progress, Capital Accumulation and Effective Demand: a Self-organization Model', paper presented at the Fifth International Conference on Mathematical Modelling, Berkeley, June 1985, in D. Batten, J. Casti and B. Johanson (eds.), *Economic Evolution and Structural Adjustment*, Berlin, Heidelberg, New York, Tokio: Springer-Verlag.

Silverberg, G. (1988), 'Modelling economic dynamics and technical change: mathematical approaches to self-organisation evolution', in G. Dosi, C. Freeman, R. Nelson, G. Silverberg and L. Soete (eds), *Technical change and economic theory*, London-New York: Pinter Publishers.

Silverberg, G. (1990), 'Adoption and Diffusion of Technology as a Collective Evolutionary Process', in C. Freeman and L. Soete (eds), *New Explorations in the Economics of Technical Change*, London and New York: Pinter Publishers.

Silverberg, G. and Lehnert, D. (1993), 'Long Waves and "Evolutionary Chaos" in a Simple Schumpeterian Model of Embodied Technical Change', in *Structural Change and Economic Dynamics*, vol. 4, n. 1.

Simon, H.A. (1951), 'Effects of technological change in a Leontief model', in T.C. Koopmans (ed.), *Activity Analysis of Production and Allocation*, New York: Wiley, 260-81.

Simon, H. (1969), 'The architecture of complexity', in *Science of the Artificial*, Cambridge: MIT Press.

Simon, H. (1976), 'From substantive to procedural rationality', in S. Latsis (ed.), *Method and Appraisal in Economics*, Cambridge: Cambridge University Press.
Sober, E. (1993), *Philosophy of Biology*, Oxford: Oxford University Press.
Soete, L. and Turner, R. (1984), 'Technology Diffusion and the Rate of Technical Change', *Economic Journal*, 94, 612-23.
Solow, R.M. (1956), 'A Contribution to the Theory of Economic Growth', *Quarterly Journal of Economics*, 70 (1), February, 65-94.
Solow, R.M. (1960), 'Investment and Technical Progress', in K.J. Arrow, S. Karlin and P. Suppes (eds.), *Mathematical Methods in the Social Sciences*, Stanford: Stanford University Press.
Solow, R.M. (1970), *Growth Theory: An Exposition*, New York: Oxford University Press.
Solow, R.M. (1988), 'Growth Theory and After', *The American Economic Review*, 78, 307-316.
Solow, R.M. (1992), *Siena Lectures on Edogenous Growth Theory*, edited by Serena Sordi, Siena.
Solow, R.M. and Temin, P. (1985), 'The Inputs for Growth', in J. Mokyr (ed.), *The Economics of the Industrial Revolution*, London: Allen & Unwin, Chapter 3.
Spence, M. (1984), 'Cost Reduction, Competition, and Industry Perfomance', *Econometrica*, 52, 101-21.
Sraffa, P. (1960), *Production of Commodities by Means of Commodities, Prelude to a Critique of Economic Theory*, Cambridge: Cambridge University Press.
Sylos Labini, P. (1962), *Oligopoly and Technical Progress*, Cambridge, Mass., Harvard University Press.
Tobin, J. (1955), 'A Dynamic Aggregative Model', *Journal of Political Economy*, LXIII, April.
Velupillai, K. (1994), 'Computable Economics: A Synopsis', *Ryde Lectures 1994*, UCLA Center for Computable Economics, Department of Economics, Los Angeles: University of California.
von Neumann, J. (1945-46) 'A Model of General Economic Equilibrium', *Review of Economic Studies*, 13, 1-9.
Waldrop, M.M. (1992), *Complexity - The Emerging Science at the Edge of Order and Chaos*, London: Simon & Schuster, New York.
Williamson, J.G. (1976), 'Technology, Growth and History', *Journal of Political Economy*, Part 1, 8, 809-20.
Williamson, O.E. (1965), 'A dynamic theory of interfirm behavior', *Quarterly Journal of Economics*, vol. 79, 579-607.
Winter, S.G. (1984), 'Schumpeterian Competition in Alternative Technological Regimes', *Journal of Economic Behaviour and Organisation*, 5, 287-320.
Wiskovatoff, A. (1993), 'Can Biology Inspire Economics?', *Methodus*, vol. 5, n. 1 (June).
Young, A.A. (1928), 'Increasing Returns and Economic Progress', *Economic Journal*, 528-42.

Authors Index

Aghion, P. 230, 232
Antonelli, G.B. 42, 232
Arrow, K.J. 18, 37, 53, 61, 169, 232, 238
Arthur, W.B. 9, 16, 25, 232
Axelroad, R. 168, 232
Bachelard, G. 232
Bamford, W.J. 232
Baranzini, M. 234
Barkley Rosser, J. Jr. 163, 232
Barnett, W. 233
Basalla, G. 67, 232
Batten, D. 236
Baumol, W.J. 44, 232
Becattini, G. 16, 232
Beltratti, A. viii
Benassy, J.P. 183, 232
Bergson, A. 53, 232
Bernheim, D. 10, 232
Bernoulli, J. 46
Bertola, G. viii
Binmore, K. 10-12, 167, 168, 232
Böhm-Bawerk, E. 6, 51
Boulding, K.E. 163, 232
Bresolin, F. viii
Bridgman, P.W. 43, 232
Brumberg, R. 42, 236
Buican, D. 233
Candoso, E. viii
Canuto, E. viii
Carraro, C. 235
Castellino, O. viii
Casti, J. 236
Chang, F.R. 226, 233
Chiaromonte, G. 71, 233
Chipman, J.S. 14, 94, 233
Cobb, C.W. 29, 78, 79, 101, 102
Condorcet, M.J. 2
Cournot, A. 161
Cozzi, T. viii, 19, 30, 109, 233
Darwin, C. 4, 155, 157, 159, 162, 233
Dasgupta, P. 168, 233
Day, R.H. 163, 233

Dimitri, N. 234, 236
Dimitrov, N. 235
Dobb, M. 236
Domar, E.V. 18, 29, 76, 151, 233
Donati, F. viii
Dosi, G. 62, 71, 173, 232-234, 237
Douglas, P.H. 29, 78, 79, 101, 102
Duesenberry, J.S. 42, 51, 233
Einstein, A. 43
Eldredge, N. 159, 160, 167, 234
Elster, J. 158, 164, 233
Fanno, M. 109
Fisher, F.M. 71, 233
Franceschi, C. viii
Freeman, C. 65, 68, 233, 234, 236, 237
Friedman, M. 70, 175, 233
Frish, R. 233
Futia, C. 71, 233, 234
Georgescu-Rogen, N. 166, 234
Geweke, J. 233
Gibbard, A. 234
Godley, W. 234
Goodman, E. 232
Goodwin, R. 27, 234, 237
Gould, S.J. 159, 160, 167, 234
Graziani, A. 234
Grossman, G.M. 77, 78, 234
Groves, T. 233
Hahn, F. 9, 20, 29, 31, 32, 230, 233-234
Harper, W.L. 234
Harrod, R.F. 18, 29, 51, 52, 76, 151, 178, 234
Hayek, F.A. 6, 23, 33, 34, 47, 165, 166, 171, 234
Hegel, G.W.F 4
Helpman, E. 77, 78, 234
Hicks, J. 13, 18, 19, 234
Hirshleifer, J. 165, 234
Hodgson, G. 162, 234
Holland, J.H. 234
Hooker, C.A. 234
Hoppenhayn, H.U. 230, 234

Howitt, P. 230, 232
Iwai, K. 33, 66, 71, 169, 234
Johanson, B. 236
Jung, C.G. 161, 176
Kaldor, N. 18, 151, 234
Karlin, S. 238
Kay, N. 37, 234
Keynes, J.M. 29, 33, 178, 182
Khalil, E.L. 157, 166, 172, 175, 235
Knight, F.H. 14, 17, 235
Koopmans, T.C. 236
Kopernik, N. 4
Krüger, M. 237
Kurihara, K. 235
Lamarck, J.B. 155, 235
Laplace, P.S. 155, 156
Leach, J.J. 234
Lehnert, D. 71, 169, 234, 237
Leontief, W.W. 8
Lombardini, S. 7, 8, 21, 25, 26, 37, 42, 44, 235
Lopreato, J. 235
Lorenz, K. 158, 235
Lotka, A.J. 157, 163, 235
Loury, G.C. 235
Lucas, R.E. 7, 17, 78, 84, 86, 87, 90, 94, 95, 96-100, 104, 105, 111-114, 117, 130-132, 235
Luce, R.D. 9, 10, 235
Luxemburg, R. 194
Malinvaud, E. viii, 20, 22, 28, 56, 83, 183, 235
Mansfield, E. 235
Marris, R. 232
Marschack, J. 46, 235
Marshall, A. 14, 53, 171
Marx, K. 4, 52, 209, 217
Matthews, R.C.O. 29, 165, 168, 234, 235
Mayumi, K. 166, 235
McClennen, E.F. 234
McKenzies, L.W. 19, 235
Mill, J.S. 145
Mirrlees, J.A. 18, 234
Modigliani, F. 42, 236
Mokyr, J. 237
Monod, V. 172
Montesano, A. 48, 236
Morgenstern, O. 46, 54
Morishima, M. 19, 236
Myrdal, G. 15, 236
Nasbeth, L. 236
Nash, J.F. 9, 10, 29, 167, 236
Negishi, T. 236
Nelson, R.R. 68, 165, 173, 233-236, 237
Newton, I. 1
Nicola, P.C. viii, 7, 8, 234, 236
Nicolis, G. 236
Nietzsche, F. 162, 172
Orsenigo, L. 62, 233, 233, 237
Pacini, P.M. 27, 234
Pareto, V. 5, 14, 19, 20, 28, 42, 45, 53-55, 76, 168, 170, 230, 236
Pasinetti, L. 13, 28, 71, 217, 232, 236
Perez, C. 65, 233
Phelps, E.S. 20, 24, 26, 236
Pigou, A.C. 14, 51, 53
Popper, K.R. 39, 71
Prigogine, I. 16, 236
Quirmbach, J. 236
Raiffa, H. 9, 10, 234
Ramsey, F.P. 47-49, 115, 117, 236
Ray, G.F. 236
Reichling, P. 25, 236
Ricardo, D. 2, 4, 38, 145, 216
Robinson, J. 21, 22, 24, 27, 39, 173, 180, 236
Roger, J. 155, 237
Romer, P.M. 17, 78, 96, 237
Samuelson, P.A. 5, 18, 20, 30, 31, 42, 52, 55, 230, 237
Sartore, D. 236
Scazzieri, R. 234
Schmookler, J. 17, 61, 65, 237
Schuette, H.L. 236
Schumpeter, J.A. vii, 4, 26, 32-36, 38, 41, 52, 68-70, 76, 95, 109, 141, 151, 152, 154, 155, 162, 168, 169, 171, 172, 178, 182, 217, 237
Scott, M.FG. viii, 64, 173, 228, 237
Shell, K. 233, 237
Siconolfi, P. 25, 236
Silverberg, G. 71, 169, 233, 234, 237
Simon, H. 166, 175, 178, 237, 238
Smith, A. 1-4, 14, 17, 28, 35, 38,

76, 154, 168, 178, 227
Sober, E. 238
Soete, L. 71, 233, 234, 237, 238
Solow, R.M. vii, viii, 7, 17, 30, 49, 78, 79, 83, 85-88, 94, 98, 99, 104, 117, 130-132, 232, 238
Sordi, S. 237
Spence, M. 238
Sraffa, P. 38, 117, 118, 226, 238
Stiglitz, J. 232
Suppes, P. 238
Sylos Labini, P. 16, 238
Temin, P. 71, 233, 238
Tobin, J. 30, 238
Turner, R. 71, 236
Veblen, T. 162, 163, 165, 166
Velupillai, K. viii, 43, 238
Vercelli, A. 234, 235, 236, 237
von Neumann, J. 6-8, 19, 20, 28, 38, 46, 76, 238
Waldrop, M.M. 238
Walras, L. 4, 5, 76, 230
Walter, J.L. 163, 233
Weber, W.E. 52
Weinrich, G. viii
Wicksell, K. 6, 33
Williamson, J.G. 37, 238
Williamson, O.E. 238
Winter, S.G. 165, 174, 236, 238
Wiskovatoff, A. 176, 238
Wood, A. 232
Young, A.A. 17, 238
Zamagni, S. viii

Subject Index

accelerator and multiplier 18
accumulation 2, 6, 18, 52, 53, 154, 188, 189
  and innovation 76
  and investments 188
  and long-run growth 218
  and power 161
  and technical progress 17
  many period model of 56
  of knowledge 78
  physical and human capital 78, 88
action 57
  and enjoyment 57
  and outcomes 47
actual price 185, 186
adaptation 156
  and changes in techniques 173
  and environment 155, 156, 159, 161
  and group utility 158
  and natural selection 156
  and optimization 158
  and rationality 157
  goal-oriented 157
  optimal and evolution 158
adaptive system 5, 8, 129
adjustments 5, 30
  and income distribution 38
  and neoclassical equilibrium 171
  coefficients 185
  gradual and externally constrained 158
  index 186
adjusting expectations processes 27
advertising 58

agents' expectations (in LC) 114
agents' plans 6
aggregation 78
altruism 157
antitrust policy 69
aspiration (level of) 44, 45
average embodied technical efficiency 63
balance of trade 1
banking system 182
bastard golden age 22
birth of firms and selection 170, 176
births and deaths of firms 161, 164
brakes to growth 215, 225
breaking monopolies 21
budget constraint 58
business cycle 18, 33
cameralism 1
capital 70, 182-184, 189, 190, 193
  accumulation and learning 64
  coefficients 206
  goods 134
  in Austrian school 6
  in Romer model 78
  in terms of efficiency units 63
  circular flow (Schumpeter's stationary state) 141
classical unemployment 22
commercial activity 135
  effects on savings 135
  in LD and first Schumpeter models 134
commercial investments 188
commodities markets equilibrium 135

Subject index

commodity market (in LC model) 103
commodity space 58, 61, 62
comparative statics 2, 5
competition 68
  and innovations 38
  and optimization 20
  and selection 36, 164
  and state action 2
  coefficients 192
  in Marx 4
  Schumpeter 36, 170
competitive firm's strategy (in LC model) 116
competitive market mechanism (in LC model) 114
competitive selection 165
computability 43, 71
computational economics 71, 167, 171, 217
conjectural functions and equilibrium 9
constant-rate-of-growth path 97
consumers (workers) 182
  allocation of time 101, 116
  budget equation 137
  expectations 100
  income 182
  optimization 82, 87, 115
  propensity to work 84
  savings and indebtedness 148
  wealth 99, 212
consumption 2
  and growth 178
  and technical coefficients 217
  externalities 44
  neoclassical theory 43, 44
  optimal evolution of 58
  private and social 43
contestable markets 35
cooperation 68
cosmos as entity 158
credit and development 33

credit (in Schumpeter) 133
creeping platinum age 21
cultural and economic system, 226
cultural and sociological system 164, 224
cultural evolution 165
cumulative causations 15
Darwinian evolution 70, 76
Darwinian natural selection 154, 155
death of firms 175, 176
decreasing and increasing returns 13
demand and labour product 143
demand driving growth 29
demand functions 133, 135
demand growth and innovation 17
depletion of resources 156
depression 70
descriptive and normative models 13
development 1-4, 12, 27, 28, 32-34, 39, 41
  and history 33
  in Marx 4
  Smith and Schumpeter 76
  strategies of firms 136
discount rate 50, 51, 54
  consumers 82, 89, 90, 105, 115, 120
  firms 109, 110
  in pseudo-Sraffian case 118
disequilibria 7
  and changing paths 28
  and history 23
  in Schumpeter 133
  index 186
dissipative models 16
division of labour 2
division of labour between firms 17
dynamics and historical 5
dynamics (in Ricardo) 5
dynamics of employment 194
ecological constraints 216
econometrics 73
economies and diseconomies of scale 13

education 69
efficiency (dynamics) 230
efficiency (statics) 230
emigration 156
employment dynamics in LD second Schumpeter model, 194 and ff.
endogenous growth 2, 17, 22, 26, 27, 32, 34, 39
  factors for firm's growth 15
  LC model 98
  models 77
energy minimization 157
enjoyment (maximum rate of) 48
entrepreneur 68
  animal spirits 180
  characteristics as genes 160
  coefficients 175, 180
  propensity to grow 177
  Schumpeterian 67
environment 156 - 159, 161, 162, 164 - 166, 174, 177, 216
  and economic evolution 168
  micro changes in 156
envy 44
equilibrium 4, 5
  and expectations 114
  in growth path 7
  in Hayek 6
  long and short-run 12, 33
  multiperiod 19
  one-point 19
  over time 19
  path 6, 19
  Walrasian 7
evolution 5, 156 - 160, 162, 166 - 172
  after Schumpeter 155
  and efficiency 28
  and history 159, 160, 167
  and optimizing behaviour 165
  as complex phenomenon 156
  biological 163, 166
    and social selection 163
  discontinuous 160
  economic 161, 162, 164, 171, 172, 176, 177, 184, 193, 194, 216
  effects on environment 162
  in Hayek 6
  in LD second Schumpeter model 194
  in prospect 166, 167
  macro and micro 159
  of population 216
  social economic 166
  versus foreseeable changes 156
evolutionary changes 159
evolutionary processes 167, 172
evolutionary struggle and game theory 168
ex ante variables 6
ex post variables 6
expectations 5, 6, 22, 24, 97
  adaptive 7
  adaptive and rational 27
  and collusive behaviour 25
  and decisions 177
  and Hayekian equilibrium 23
  and profits 17
  consumers' 42
  disconnected 27
  firms' 101, 102
  in equilibrium path 78
  on human-capital-growth-rate 115
  uniform and correct 31
expected rate of growth of finance 109
expected rate of growth of population 110
externalities 96
  external economies and income distribution 129
  external economies of innovation 34
  external effect of human capital accumulation 122
  external effects and income distribution 87

external effects of labour qualification 85, 90
external effects of R&D 77
external effects of technical progress 17, 87
external effect on accumulation (index of) 110
external effects on income distribution (index of) 99
external growth-factors 76
facts (empirical) 72
facts (theoretical) 71
feedbacks (negative and positive) 15
feedbacks produced by growth 176
financial flow 181, 193
financial market and equilibrium 15
financial market (in LC model) 103
financial system, 229
firms 59, 179
　and finance 169
　and political power 169
　as individuals of species 160
　debts 193, 212
　economic strategy 60
　entry and exit, 229
　failure 182, 184, 193
　financial flow 138
　propensity to accumulate 139
　random distribution of their coefficients 181
　rentability 138, 181, 183, 184, 185, 188
　strategies and optimization, 227
　value 181, 212
flexible and rigid prices 20
forecast (infinite and perfect in Solow) 83
forecast of technological progress 79
freedom of entry 155
frugality 52
gallopping platinum age 21
gearing ratio 189
generations welfare 54
generations (overlapping) 55, 226
goals and economic development 12
global orientation 162
golden-age equilibrium 20, 21
golden-age uniqueness 31
golden rule 7, 20
group survival 157
growth 1, 2, 5-8, 12-14, 17-22, 27, 33, 34, 38, 39
　and income distribution 38
　and investments 18
　and market forms 35
　and population expansion, 224
　and technical progress 18
　balanced 7, 31
　demand push 61
　history and theory 130
　in Keynes theory 33
　normal 18
　path stability 30
　with stationary population 95
health index of firms 189, 191
heterogeneous capital and uniqueness 31
hierarchical model of selection 159
holistic concepts and local explanations 158
human-capital accumulation 84, 96, 225
human-capital accumulation and wages 100
hypothetical empirical law, 72
imitations 44, 66, 67, 69, 155, 161, 163, 170, 173, 174, 176, 177, 184
　and changes in firms'population 177
　leading to equilibrium 169
income distribution 2, 3, 45, 53
　and development 231
　and tastes 59
　index 99
income share 86, 90, 91, 110
increasing return and equilibrium 14

individual mutations 156
individual values and social preferences 53
individuals and environment 155, 156
industrial districts 16
inequalities and social evolution 163
inflation 52
inflation in development 152
informations and predictions 25
innovations 2, 32, 41, 66, 67, 69, 161, 173, 225
  and changes in techniques 59
  and discontinuities 34
  and efficiency of the system 168
  and evolution 164
  and growth 133
  and market changes 169
  and natural selection 155
  and school system 174
  and selection process 177
  by large firms 168
  clusters of 174
  competition, evolution 168
  hard 61, 65
  in competition and monopoly 168
  incremental 65
  minor 66
  radical 65
  soft 61, 65
  space and time connections 175
  strategies 37
input coefficients (in Schumpeterian model) 134
instability of adaptive system 29
instability of capitalism 18
institutions 68
institutions as replicators and units of 163
interactions and adjustments 162
interdependences between consumers' taste 45
interest rates (monetary and real) 52

net interest rate for consumers 107
internal and external economies 14
intertemporal elasticity of substitution 49, 80, 82, 83, 87, 89 - 91, 100, 111, 116
inventions 65, 67
investments 5, 68, 138
  investment and technical progress 64
  investments (function of) 154
invisible hand 171
irreversible processes 16
Japan 68
Keynesian unemployment 22
Keynesian versus Schumpeterian models 151
kin selection 168
knowledge (operative) 60, 61
knowledge (technical) 60
labour 3, 57
  alienation 57
  allocation by consumers 114
  allocation by firms (in LC) 102, 108
  allocation in circular flow 142
  allocation in stationary state 120
  allocation in the first Schumpeter model 147
  allocation (research and accumulation) 135
  coefficients 208
  demand for 137
  employed in final production 192
  employed in research activity 191
  employed in sales promotion 190
  exploitation 4
  gratification 57
  in Lucas model 78
  in production (Lucas) 90
  market 135
  market disequilibria 22
  market equilibrium 114
  market flexibility, 224
  market (in LD first Schumpeterian

Subject index

model) 133
productivity 63, 112
productivity-growth rate 20
qualification 63, 84, 87, 89, 90
supply 135, 171, 178
large firms and innovations 36
law 3
leaden age 21
learning 41, 66, 175
  and beliefs 26
  and evolution 167
  and intuition 26
  by consuming 42, 58
  by doing 94
  internal and public 95
  process and adjustment 185
  process (in production) 60
limping golden age 21
macroeconomic production function 70
Malthusian mechanism 22
management and entrepreneurship 37
many-sectors economy 30
marginal productivity of capital (Solow) 81
marginal productivity of labour (in LC) 109
marginal utility 100
  of consumption (in LC) 104
  of consumption (Lucas) 87
  of consumption (Solow) 81
mark-up 139, 185, 209
  and aggressiveness 181
  and market power 217
  and price 135
  dynamics in LD second Schumpeterian model 209 and ff.
  evolution (LD first Schumpeterian) 148
market (roles of) 4, 179
market equilibrium path 84
  and optimal path 97

path (Lucas) 85 94
path (Solow) 83
market power 67, 224
market power and growth 139
market rationed 187
Marshallian theory of firm 171
maximum supply (in LD second Schumpeterian model) 182, 189
means and goals 157
mechanical rationality versus human 166
mechanization index (in LD fist Schumpeterian model) 138
mercantilism 1
mergers 169
Millian growth process 145
minimax principle 11
money 56, 229, 135, 193, 215
monetary flow 138
monopolistic competition 20, 94, 134, 179, 187
monopoly in Schumpeterian theory 35
monopoly power 138
monopoly power and entrepreneur's aggressiveness 169
moral expectation 46
movements (virtual and actual) 5
mutations
mutations and structural stability 159
Nash criterion 9
natural prices 1, 3
natural resources and environment, 225
natural selection 156, 162
natural selection and need to survive 157
neoclassical versus Schumpeterian models 151
New Classical Macroeconomics 9, 56
Newtonian approach 71
numeraire 97, 137

obstacles to entry 15
oligopolies 15, 34, 35, 134
operationalism 43
ophelimity 45
optimal growth 19, 35, 96
  and market equilibrium 122, 128
  von Neumann 76
optimal path of growth 6, 7
  and fiscal adjustments 97
  and market equilibrium 93
  Lucas 84, 85
  Solow 83
optimal per-capita consumption (Solow) 83
optimization over time 77
optimization through adjustments 165
order 1, 2, 3, 4, 34
order after Hayek 165
organizations and structures 172
Pareto and optimality criterion 12, 28
patents 66
philanthropy 44
phyletic gradualism 159
physiocracy 1
planned production 182, 189
planning and evolution 161
point equilibria and equilibrium paths 8
population rate of growth 2, 5, 7, 15, 18, 20, 21, 30, 53, 178
power 164
  different strategies for 169
  the entrepreneur's goal 172
preferences (ordered field) 42
preferences (revealed) 42
price changes and changes in technology 174
price system in equilibrium path 8
price (normal) 185
probability 46, 155, 172
probability distribution of firms 183
product (new) 58

product and technological innovation 20
product demand 187
product differentiation 58, 61
productct differentiation and new products 133
product innovation and competition 170
product innovations 77
production (externalities) 44
production function 41, 59, 60
  and technical change 174
  in Solow 79
  LC model 97
  Lucas 85
  neoclassical 61
production (in neoclassical analysis) 59
production dynamics in LD second Schumpeter model, 194 and ff.
production potential 188
production rentability constrained 189
production stocks constrained 189
productivity dynamics in LD second Schumpeterian model 205 and ff.
productivity of capital (in LC) 109
productivity of labour qualification 126
products (differentiated and different) 59
profits 3
  and power 32
  in LC 102
progress 1, 2
propensity to grow 214 and ff.
propensity to innovate 95
propensity to save (Solow) 83
pseudo-Sraffian case (in LC model) 117
public goods 53
punctuated equilibrium 163
quasi equilibrium growth path (LC

Subject index

first Schumpeter model) 147
quasi-stationary state (in LC model) 119
R&D activities 181
R&D and growth 147
R&D effects on the coefficients 137
R&D (in LD first Schumpeterian model) 134
Ramsey bliss 142
rate of growth 4, 6-8, 19-21, 24, 28, 29, 36, 38, 190
  rate of growth and accumulation 38
  rate of growth (natural) 29
  rate of growth of consumption (in LC) 112, 113
  rate of growth of consumption (Solow) 80
  rate of growth of labour qualification 110
  rate of growth of population 82
  rate of growth of production (in LC) 110
  rate of growth (warranted) 18, 29
rate of human capital accumulation 86
rate of increase of consumption (Lucas) 86
rate of interest 52
  and investments 182, 193
  effect on consumption 115
  effects in Schumpeterian models) 139
  in LC model 112
rate of population-growth 85, 89, 103
rate of technical progress (Lucas) 86
rational allocation 12
rational behaviour and equilibrium 8
rational expectations 23, 24
rational expectations in LC model 115
rationality and equilibrium 12
rationality (procedural) 171, 175

rationed markets 183
recession 194
recursive models 7
refutability 71
rent 3
rentability 190, 209
  and investments 189, 190
  average 211
  dynamics 211
  in LD second Schumpeterian model 209 and ff.
repressed inflation 22
reproduction of individual characteristics 156
research 191, 202
  activity and general efficiency 34
  and accumulation 181
  and development (R&D) 68
  and innovation 96, 181, 188
  dynamics in LD second Schumpeterian model 200 and ff.
restrained golden age 21
Ricardo's theory of evolution 2
Ricardo's theory of value 4
risk and research activity 36
risk aversion 49, 100
sales promotion 21, 58, 100, 178, 181, 182, 187, 188, 190, 191, 202, 227
  sales promotion and propensity to work 133
  sales-promotion costs 185
  sales promotion in LD second Schumpeterian model 200 and ff.
savings 5, 52, 183
  and consumers' tastes 184
  and investments 30
  in Schumpeter and in Keynes 151
  in Smith, Schumpeter and Keynes 178
scarcity of labour 216
scarcity of natural resources 2, 216

scenarios in LD second Schumpeterian model 194
Schumpeterian innovations 23
Schumpeterian process of development 20, 34
Schumpeterian process of innovation 133
selection 156, 177, 229
  and growth 217
  and innovation 154
  environment 174
self-organization 166
self-sustainable growth 15, 21
sexual activities 156
shadow price for labour qualification 105
sluggish market 185, 190, 191
small firms 35, 69
  and innovations 38
  and research activity 36
Smith labour theory of value 3
Smithian invisible hand 4
snobbish attitude 44
social and economic systems 73
social-cultural system 44, 68
social darwinism 28
social decisions and individual choices 53
social environment 10
social evolution 165, 170
social services 44, 53
social welfare function 53
socio-economic evolution 163 - 165
solidarity and competition 157
species and environment 156
species evolution 166
speculation and expectations 33
stability of Harrodian paths 29
stagnation 194, 196
stases in evolution 159
state and the theory of games 11
state (role of) 41, 224, 228
stationary state 3

optimal path and market 125
process leading to 144
steady growth 7, 8, 27, 28, 30, 97
steady growth and optimality 28
stochastic processes 155
stocks 185, 186, 188, 191, 194, 196, 217
stocks normal value 188
structural changes and equilibrium 13
structure (stable) 3
subinvention 65
surplus, 224
  in agriculture 1
  in Marx 4
technical progress 2, 6, 173
  and capital 62
  disembodied 62
  embodied 63
technology 41
  and organizations 160
  in von Neumann and Sraffa 118
  system 65
technological accumulation 78, 96, 100, 225
technological competition 169
technological innovations and product change 178
technological investments 188
technological paradigm 173
technological revolution 65
technological trajectories 173
telescopic faculty 51
temporary equilibrium 47
theory of games (normative value) 9
theory of games (rationality in) 9
theory of games (rules and expectations) 10
thriftiness and growth 90
time optimal allocation by consumers 105
time preference 52
transition phase 152, 193

Subject index

transmission by creation of new forms 161
transmission of improvements 155
transmission through imitation 161, 164
transmission through institutions 163
Turing machine 11
turnpike level (Samuelson) 142
turnpike theorem 19
uncertain prospect 46
undereactions and overreactions 25
United States 69
units of evolutionary selection 163
urban plans 16
utility 4, 42, 44, 79
  and new commodities 59
  community's 53
  expected 46
  measurable 46
  moral 45
  neoclassical theory 56
  over time 47
utility function 41, 45, 99
  independence of 43
  long run 46
  short run 46
value of the firm's in LD second Schumpeterian model 212 and ff.
variety of individual goals 157
von Neumann model 19
wages 3, 192
wages and rate of growth 38
Walrasian auctioneer 9
workers' qualification 85